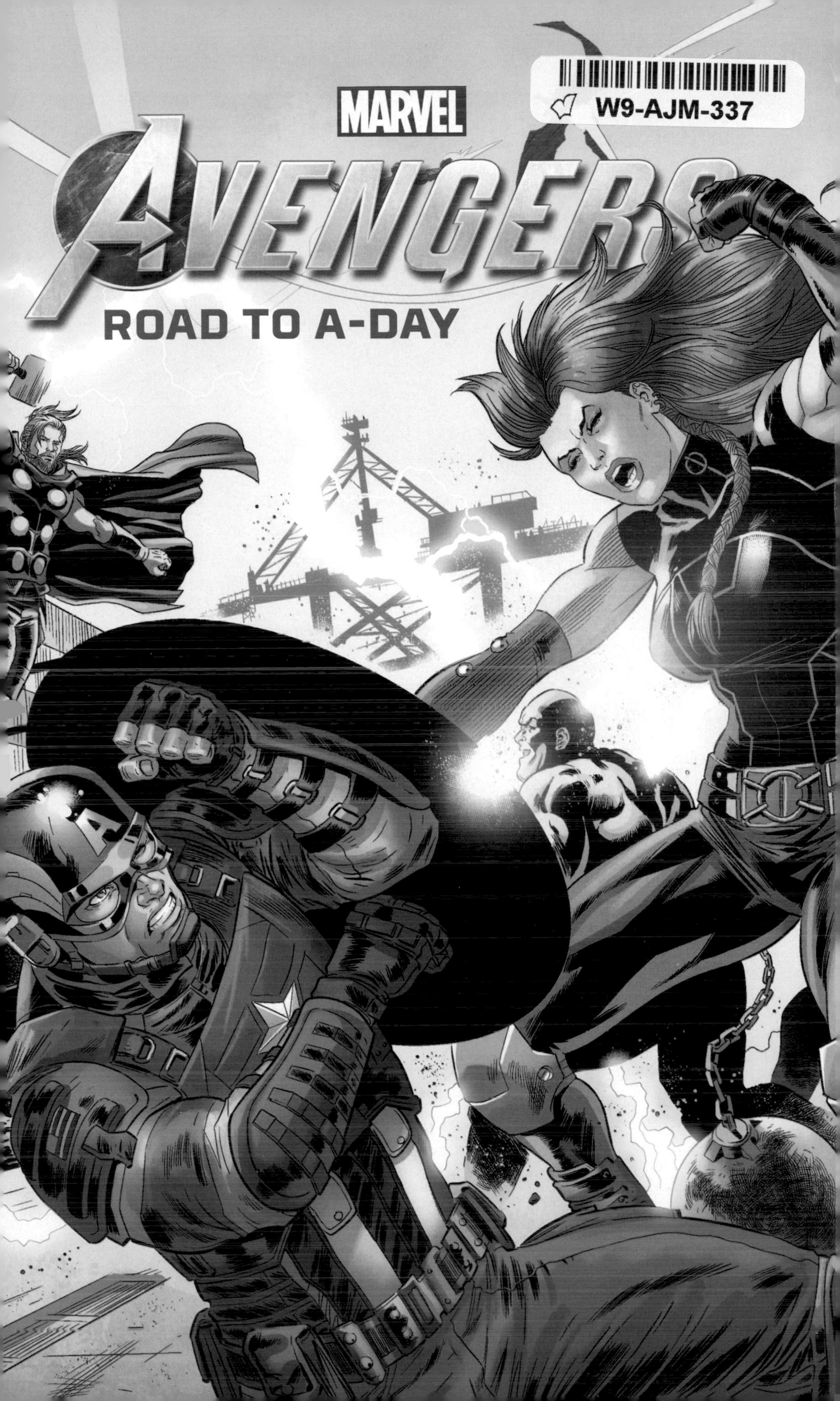
MARVEL
AVENGERS
ROAD TO A-DAY
W9-AJM-337

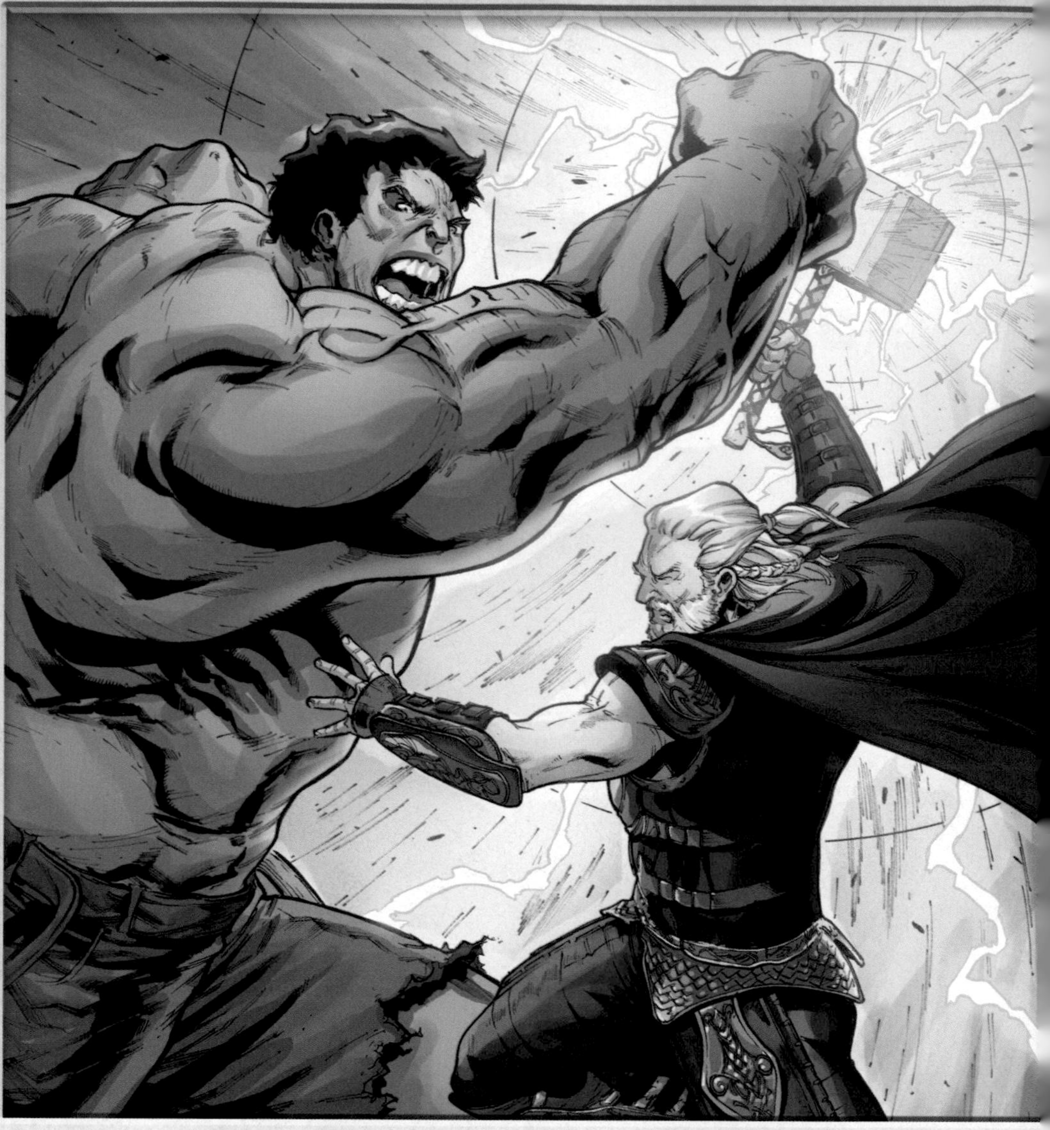

COLLECTION EDITOR: **Mark D. Beazley**
ASSISTANT MANAGING EDITOR: **Maia Loy**
ASSISTANT MANAGING EDITOR: **Lisa Montalbano**
ASSOCIATE MANAGER, DIGITAL ASSETS: **Joe Hochstein**
SENIOR EDITOR, SPECIAL PROJECTS: **Jennifer Grünwald**
VP PRODUCTION & SPECIAL PROJECTS: **Jeff Youngquist**
BOOK DESIGNER: **Adam Del Re**
SVP PRINT, SALES & MARKETING: **David Gabriel**
EDITOR IN CHIEF: **C.B. Cebulski**

FOR MARVEL GAMES
CREATIVE ASSISTANT: **Dakota Maysonet**
DIRECTOR OF GAME PRODUCTION: **Eric Monacelli**
VP & CREATIVE DIRECTOR: **Bill Rosemann**

AVENGERS CREATED BY **Stan Lee** & **Jack Kirby**

MARVEL'S AVENGERS: ROAD TO A-DAY. Contains material originally published in magazine form as MARVEL'S AVENGERS: IRON MAN (2019) #1, MARVEL'S AVENGERS: THOR (2020) #1, MARVEL'S AVENGERS: CAPTAIN AMERICA (2020) #1, MARVEL'S AVENGERS: HULK (2020) #1 and MARVEL'S AVENGERS: BLACK WIDOW (2020) #1. First printing 2020. ISBN 978-0-7851-9465-1. Published by MARVEL WORLDWIDE, INC. a subsidiary of MARVEL ENTERTAINMENT, LLC. OFFICE OF PUBLICATION: 1290 Avenue of the Americas, New York, NY 10104.

Printed in Canada. KEVIN FEIGE, Chief Creative Officer; DAN BUCKLEY, President, Marvel Entertainment; JOHN NEE, Publisher; JOE QUESADA, EVP & Creative Director; TOM BREVOORT, SVP of Publishing; DAVID BOGART, Associate Publisher & SVP of Talent Affairs, Publishing & Partnership; DAVID GABRIEL, VP of Print & Digital Publishing; JEFF YOUNGQUIST, VP of Production & Special Projects; DAN CARR, Executive Director of Publishing Technology; ALEX MORALES, Director of Publishing Operations; DAN EDINGTON, Managing Editor; SUSAN CRESPI, Production Manager; STAN LEE, Chairman Emeritus. For information regarding advertising in Marvel Comics or on Marvel.com, please contact Vit DeBellis, Custom Solutions & Integrated Advertising Manager, at vdebellis@marvel.com. For Marvel subscription inquiries, please call 888-511-5480. **Manufactured between 2/28/2020 and 3/31/2020 by SOLISCO PRINTERS, SCOTT, QC, CANADA.**

10 9 8 7 6 5 4 3 2 1

MARVEL
AVENGERS
ROAD TO A-DAY

NOTE: THE EVENTS OF THIS STORY TAKE PLACE BEFORE THE EVENTS OF THE MARVEL'S AVENGERS GAME.

IRON MAN

WRITER: **Jim Zub**
ARTIST: **Paco Diaz**
COLORISTS: **Rachelle Rosenberg** & **Andy Troy**

THOR

WRITER: **Jim Zub**
ARTIST: **Robert Gill**
COLORIST: **Andy Troy**

HULK

WRITER: **Jim Zub**
ARTIST: **Ariel Olivetti**
COLORISTS: **Andy Troy**

CAPTAIN AMERICA

WRITER: **Paul Allor**
PENCILER: **Georges Jeanty**
INKERS: **Marc Deering** WITH **Scott Hanna**
COLORISTS: **Andy Troy** WITH **Chris Sotomayor**

BLACK WIDOW

WRITER: **Christos Gage**
ARTIST: **Michele Bandini**
COLORISTS: **Rachelle Rosenberg**

LETTERER: **VC's Joe Caramagna**   COVER ARTIST: **Stonehouse**

ASSISTANT EDITORS: **Martin Biro** & **Shannon Andrews Ballesteros**
EDITOR: **Mark Basso**

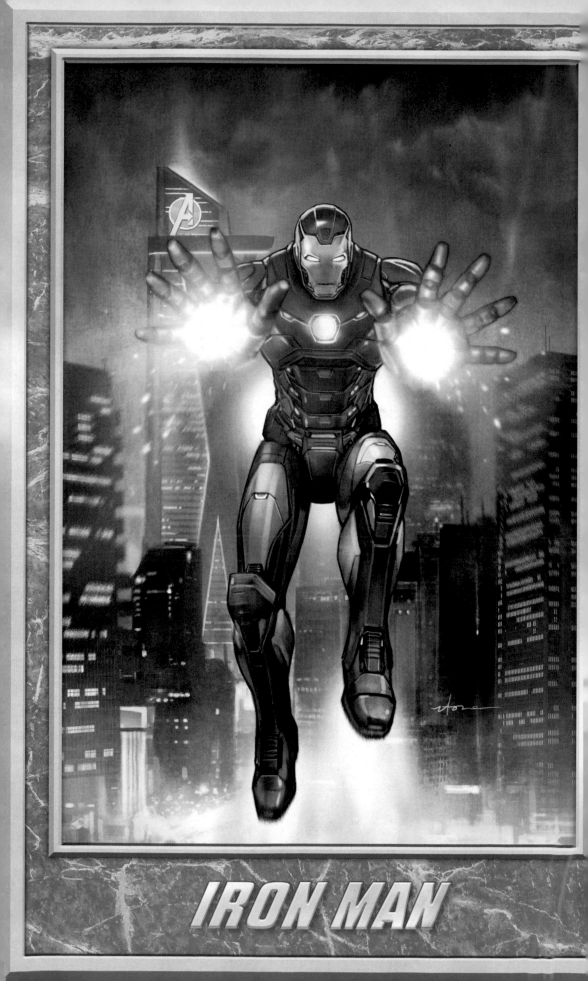

IRON MAN

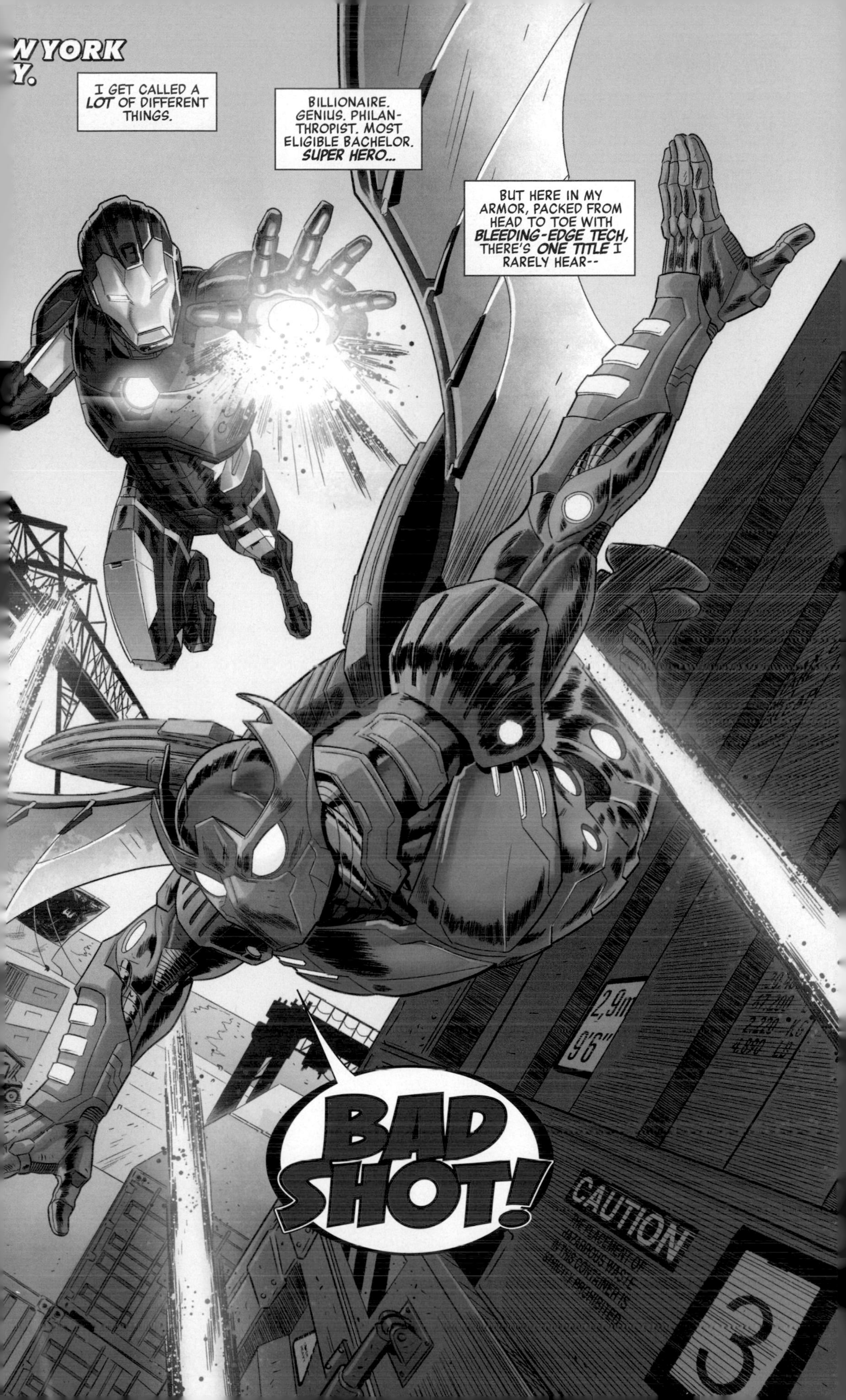
W YORK
Y.
I GET CALLED A LOT OF DIFFERENT THINGS.
BILLIONAIRE. GENIUS. PHILAN-THROPIST. MOST ELIGIBLE BACHELOR. SUPER HERO...
BUT HERE IN MY ARMOR, PACKED FROM HEAD TO TOE WITH BLEEDING-EDGE TECH, THERE'S ONE TITLE I RARELY HEAR--
BAD SHOT!
2,9m
9'6"
CAUTION
3

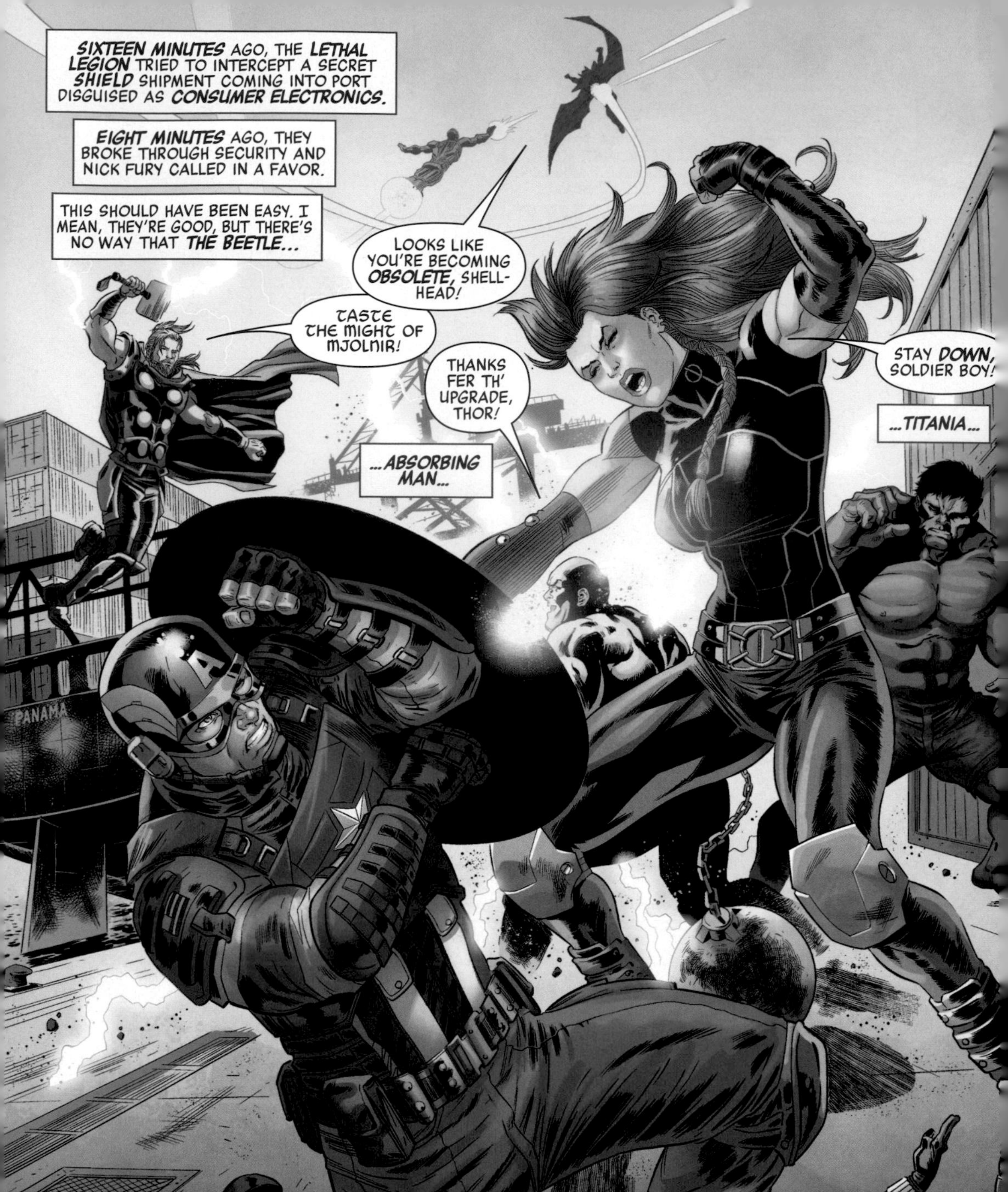
SIXTEEN MINUTES AGO, THE LETHAL LEGION TRIED TO INTERCEPT A SECRET SHIELD SHIPMENT COMING INTO PORT DISGUISED AS CONSUMER ELECTRONICS.
EIGHT MINUTES AGO, THEY BROKE THROUGH SECURITY AND NICK FURY CALLED IN A FAVOR.
THIS SHOULD HAVE BEEN EASY. I MEAN, THEY'RE GOOD, BUT THERE'S NO WAY THAT THE BEETLE...
LOOKS LIKE YOU'RE BECOMING OBSOLETE, SHELL-HEAD!
TASTE THE MIGHT OF MJOLNIR!
THANKS FER TH' UPGRADE, THOR!
...ABSORBING MAN...
STAY DOWN, SOLDIER BOY!
...TITANIA...
PANAMA

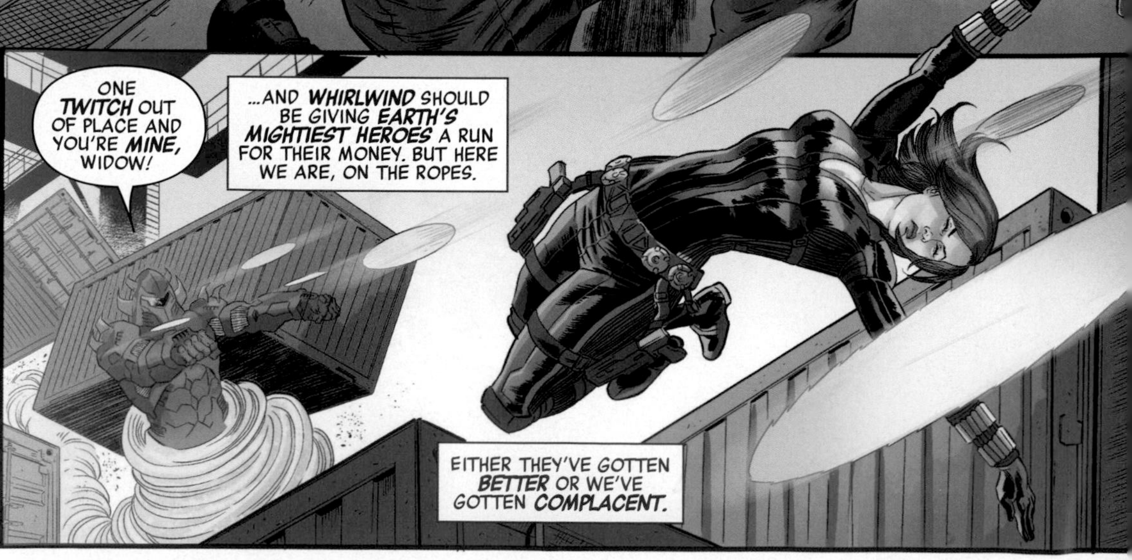
ONE TWITCH OUT OF PLACE AND YOU'RE MINE, WIDOW!
...AND WHIRLWIND SHOULD BE GIVING EARTH'S MIGHTIEST HEROES A RUN FOR THEIR MONEY. BUT HERE WE ARE, ON THE ROPES.
EITHER THEY'VE GOTTEN BETTER OR WE'VE GOTTEN COMPLACENT.

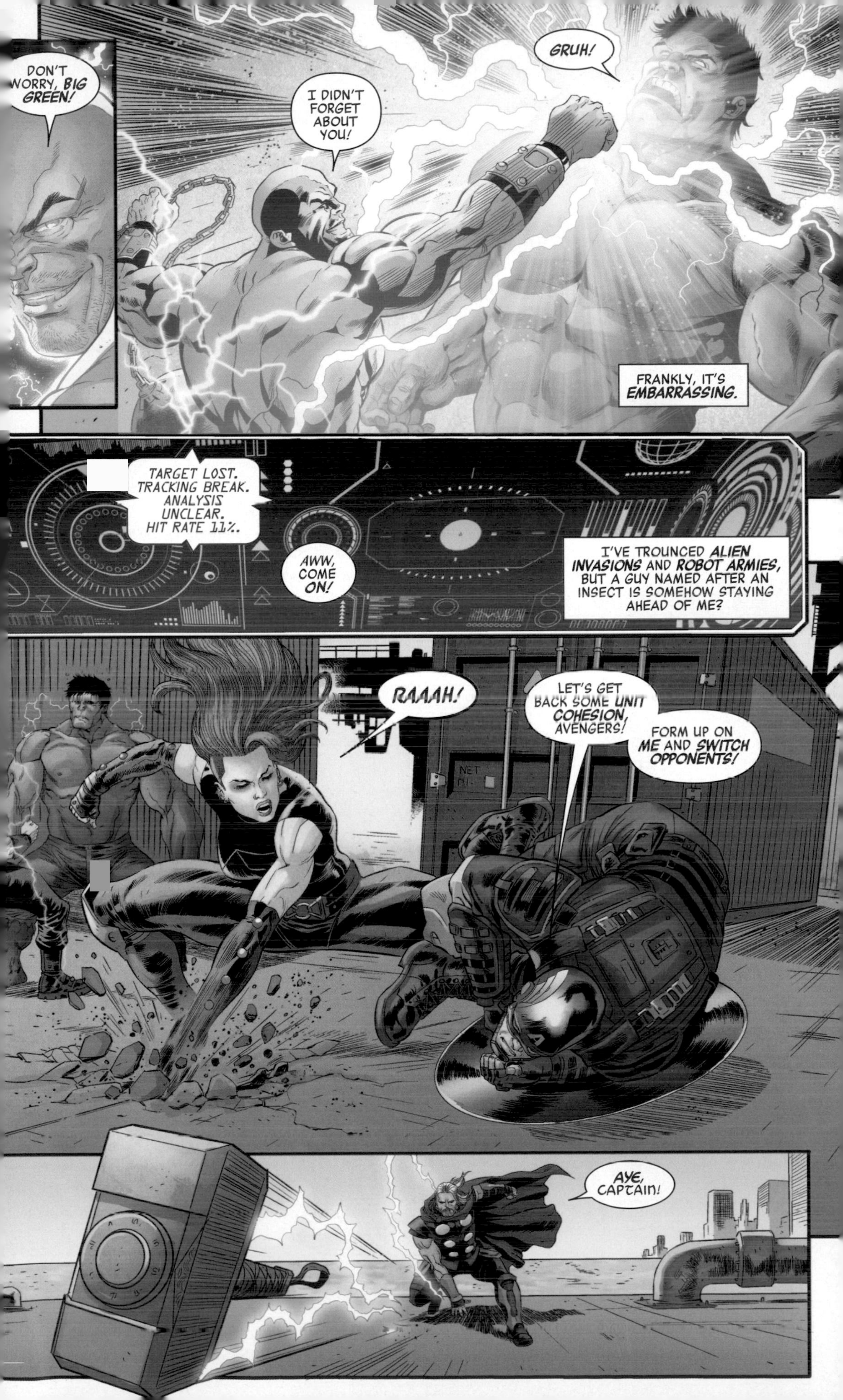
DON'T WORRY, BIG GREEN!
I DIDN'T FORGET ABOUT YOU!
GRUH!
FRANKLY, IT'S EMBARRASSING.
TARGET LOST. TRACKING BREAK. ANALYSIS UNCLEAR. HIT RATE 11%.
AWW, COME ON!
I'VE TROUNCED ALIEN INVASIONS AND ROBOT ARMIES, BUT A GUY NAMED AFTER AN INSECT IS SOMEHOW STAYING AHEAD OF ME?
RAAAH!
LET'S GET BACK SOME UNIT COHESION, AVENGERS!
FORM UP ON ME AND SWITCH OPPONENTS!
AYE, CAPTAIN!

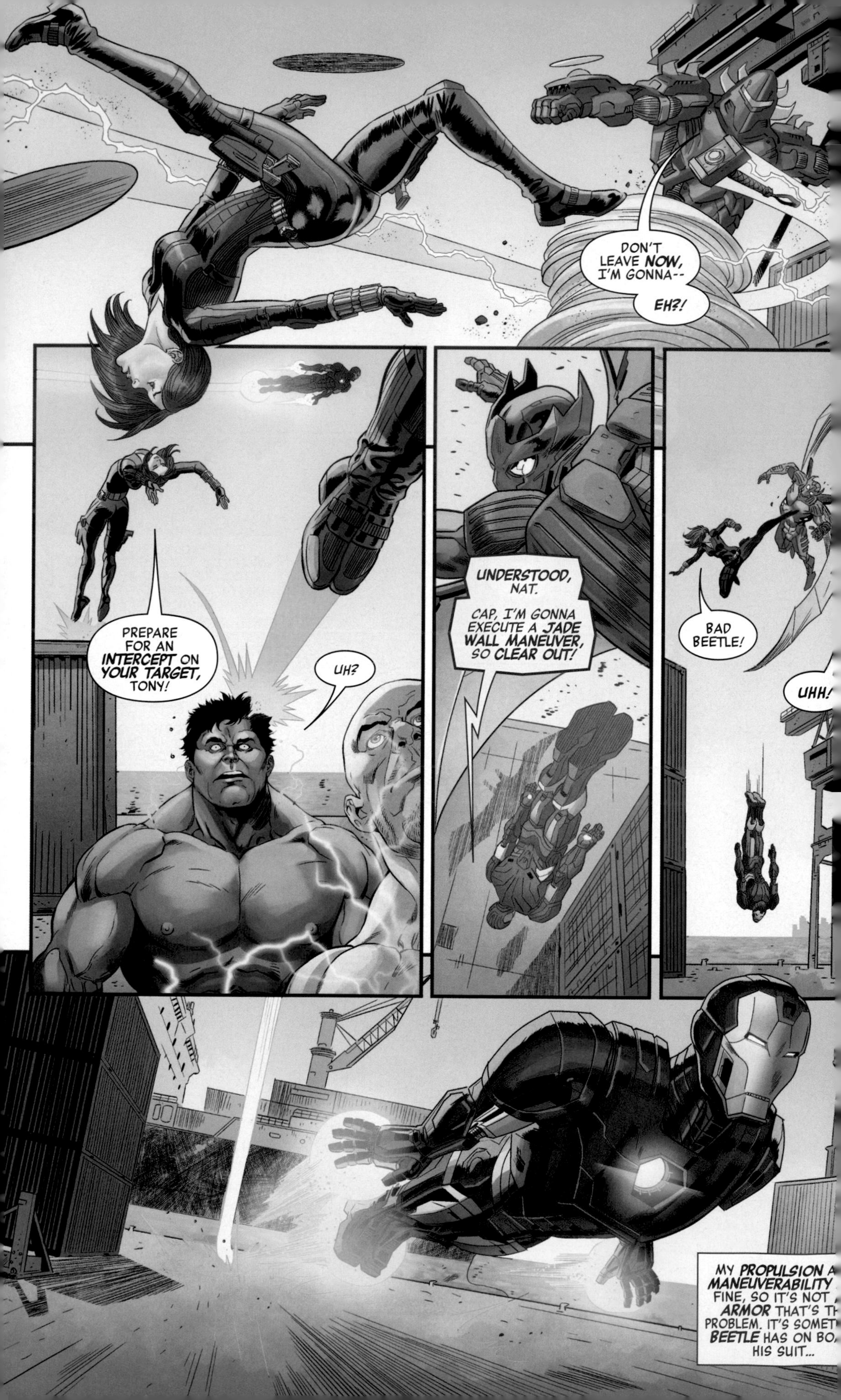

DON'T LEAVE NOW, I'M GONNA--
EH?!
PREPARE FOR AN INTERCEPT ON YOUR TARGET, TONY!
UH?
UNDERSTOOD, NAT.
CAP, I'M GONNA EXECUTE A JADE WALL MANEUVER, SO CLEAR OUT!
BAD BEETLE!
UHH!
MY PROPULSION A
MANEUVERABILITY
FINE, SO IT'S NOT
ARMOR THAT'S TH
PROBLEM. IT'S SOMET
BEETLE HAS ON BO
HIS SUIT...

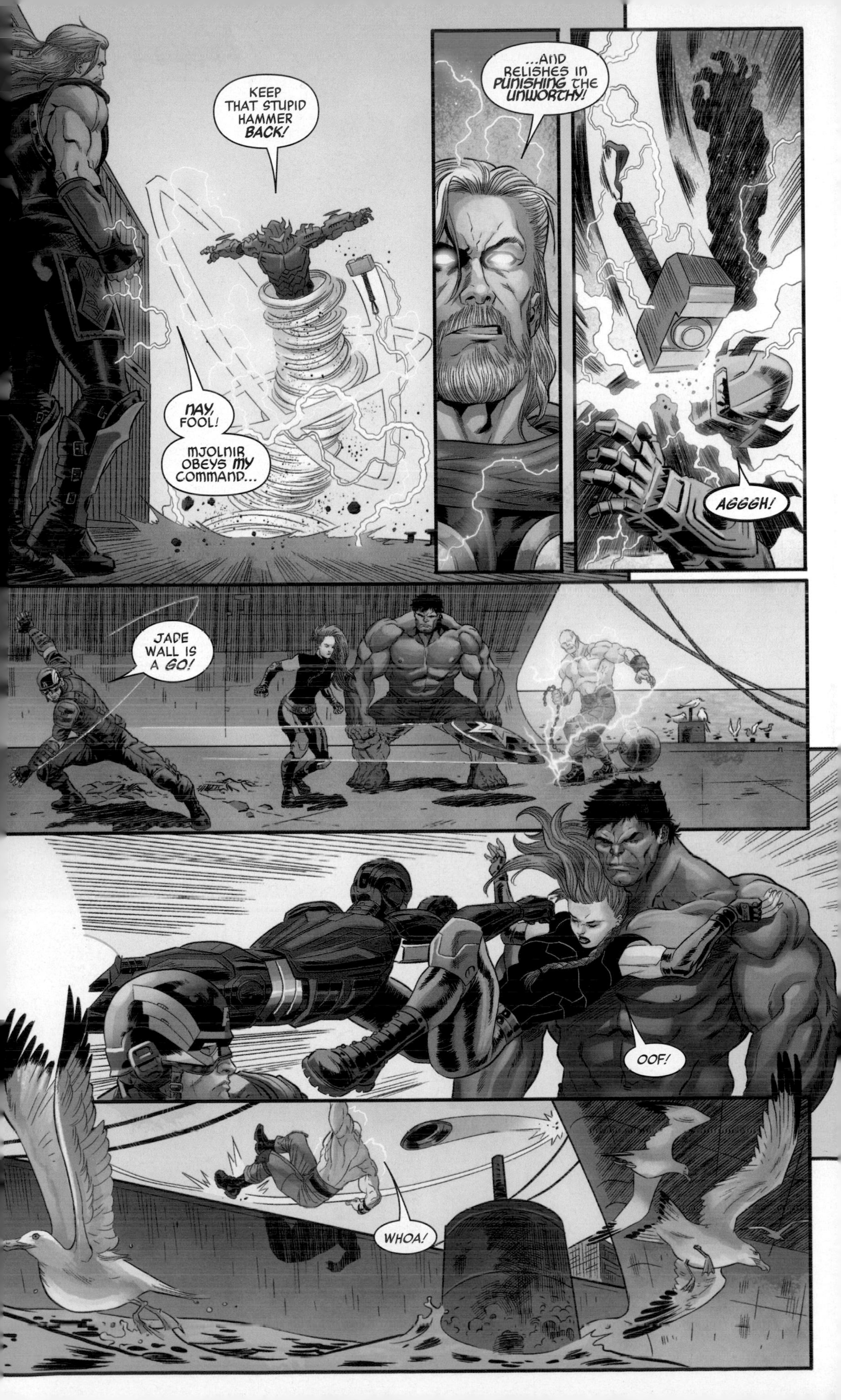

KEEP THAT STUPID HAMMER BACK!
NAY, FOOL!
MJOLNIR OBEYS MY COMMAND...
...AND RELISHES IN PUNISHING THE UNWORTHY!
AGGGH!
JADE WALL IS A GO!
OOF!
WHOA!

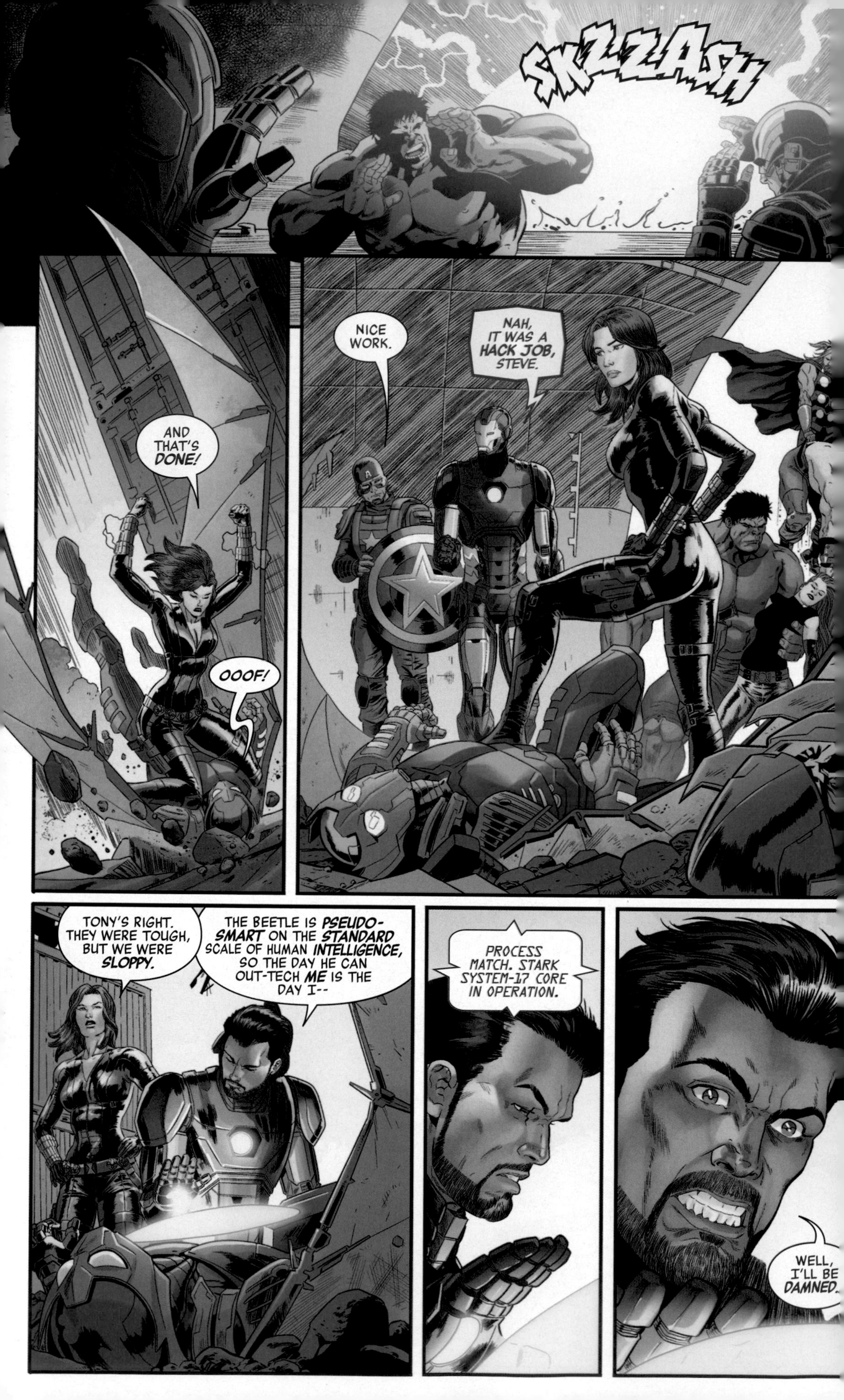
SKZZASH
AND THAT'S DONE!
OOOF!
NICE WORK.
NAH, IT WAS A HACK JOB, STEVE.
TONY'S RIGHT. THEY WERE TOUGH, BUT WE WERE SLOPPY.
THE BEETLE IS PSEUDO-SMART ON THE STANDARD SCALE OF HUMAN INTELLIGENCE, SO THE DAY HE CAN OUT-TECH ME IS THE DAY I--
PROCESS MATCH. STARK SYSTEM-17 CORE IN OPERATION.
WELL, I'LL BE DAMNED...

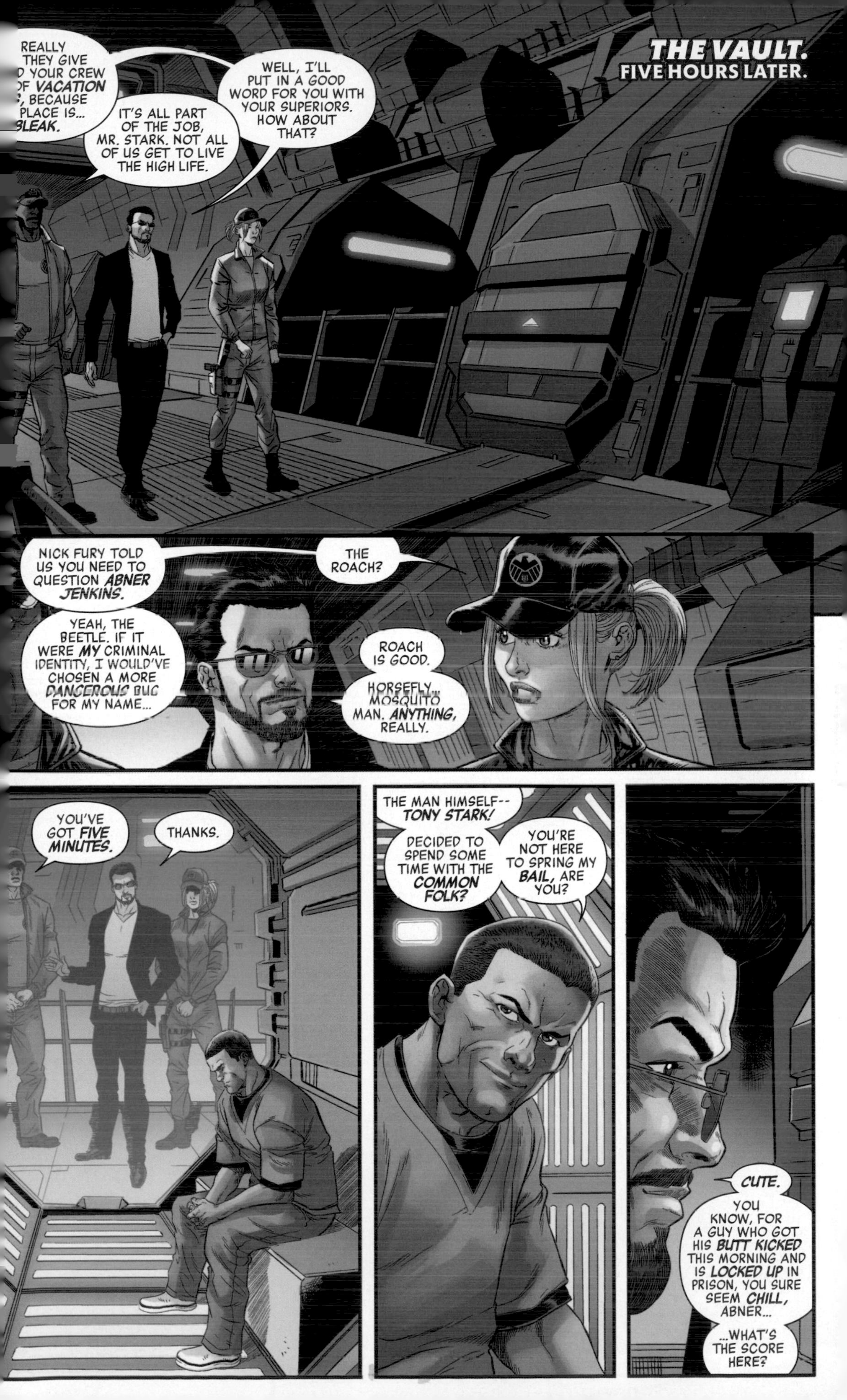
THE VAULT.
FIVE HOURS LATER.
REALLY THEY GIVE D YOUR CREW OF VACATION S, BECAUSE PLACE IS... BLEAK.
IT'S ALL PART OF THE JOB, MR. STARK. NOT ALL OF US GET TO LIVE THE HIGH LIFE.
WELL, I'LL PUT IN A GOOD WORD FOR YOU WITH YOUR SUPERIORS. HOW ABOUT THAT?
NICK FURY TOLD US YOU NEED TO QUESTION ABNER JENKINS.
THE ROACH?
YEAH, THE BEETLE. IF IT WERE MY CRIMINAL IDENTITY, I WOULD'VE CHOSEN A MORE DANGEROUS BUG FOR MY NAME...
ROACH IS GOOD.
HORSEFLY... MOSQUITO MAN. ANYTHING, REALLY.
YOU'VE GOT FIVE MINUTES.
THANKS.
THE MAN HIMSELF-- TONY STARK!
DECIDED TO SPEND SOME TIME WITH THE COMMON FOLK?
YOU'RE NOT HERE TO SPRING MY BAIL, ARE YOU?
CUTE.
YOU KNOW, FOR A GUY WHO GOT HIS BUTT KICKED THIS MORNING AND IS LOCKED UP IN PRISON, YOU SURE SEEM CHILL, ABNER...
...WHAT'S THE SCORE HERE?

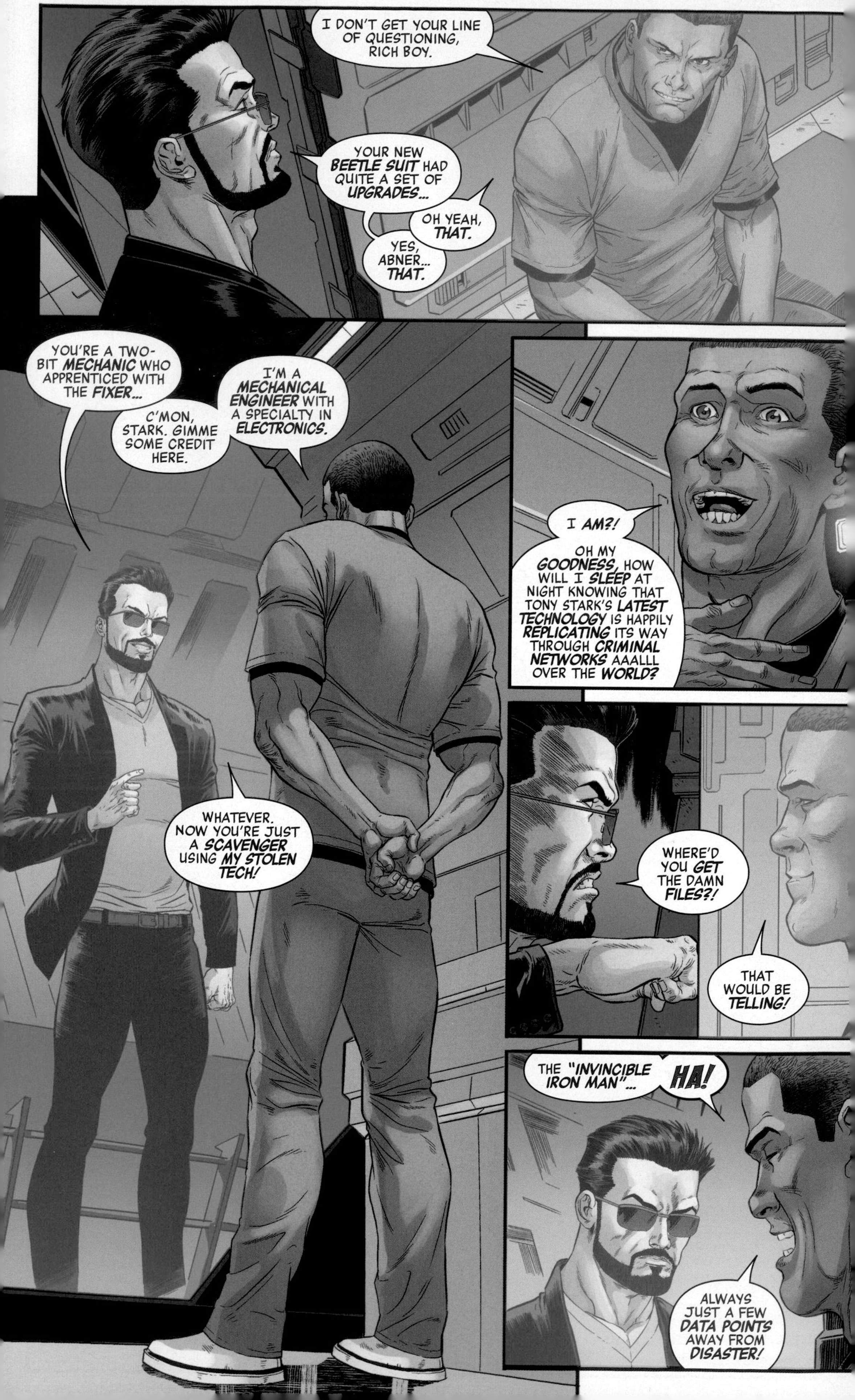
I DON'T GET YOUR LINE OF QUESTIONING, RICH BOY.
YOUR NEW BEETLE SUIT HAD QUITE A SET OF UPGRADES...
OH YEAH, THAT.
YES, ABNER... THAT.
YOU'RE A TWO-BIT MECHANIC WHO APPRENTICED WITH THE FIXER...
C'MON, STARK. GIMME SOME CREDIT HERE.
I'M A MECHANICAL ENGINEER WITH A SPECIALTY IN ELECTRONICS.
WHATEVER. NOW YOU'RE JUST A SCAVENGER USING MY STOLEN TECH!
I AM?!
OH MY GOODNESS, HOW WILL I SLEEP AT NIGHT KNOWING THAT TONY STARK'S LATEST TECHNOLOGY IS HAPPILY REPLICATING ITS WAY THROUGH CRIMINAL NETWORKS AAALLL OVER THE WORLD?
WHERE'D YOU GET THE DAMN FILES?!
THAT WOULD BE TELLING!
THE "INVINCIBLE IRON MAN"...
HA!
ALWAYS JUST A FEW DATA POINTS AWAY FROM DISASTER!

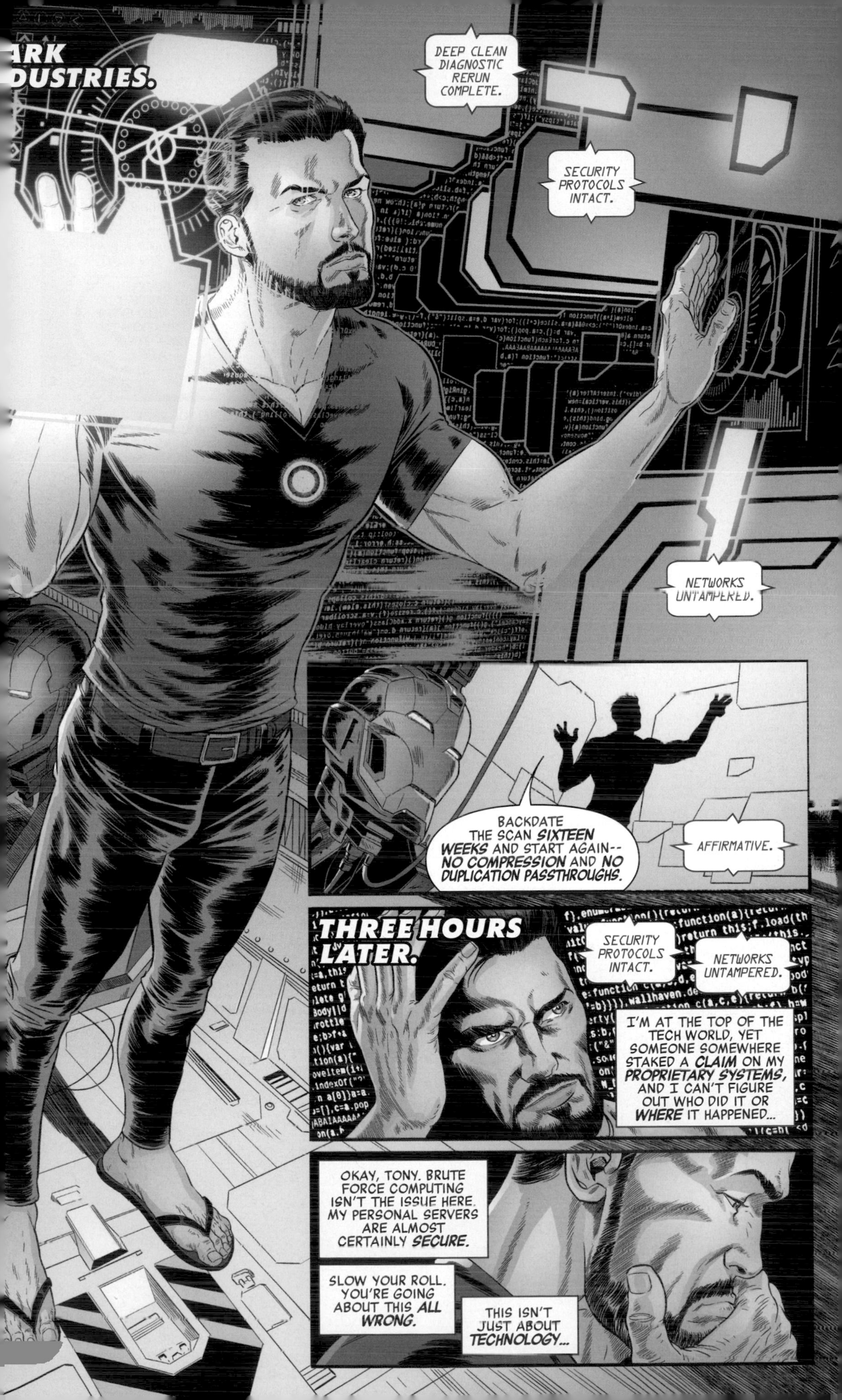
ARK
DUSTRIES.
DEEP CLEAN DIAGNOSTIC RERUN COMPLETE.
SECURITY PROTOCOLS INTACT.
NETWORKS UNTAMPERED.
BACKDATE THE SCAN SIXTEEN WEEKS AND START AGAIN-- NO COMPRESSION AND NO DUPLICATION PASSTHROUGHS.
AFFIRMATIVE.
THREE HOURS LATER.
SECURITY PROTOCOLS INTACT.
NETWORKS UNTAMPERED.
I'M AT THE TOP OF THE TECH WORLD, YET SOMEONE SOMEWHERE STAKED A CLAIM ON MY PROPRIETARY SYSTEMS, AND I CAN'T FIGURE OUT WHO DID IT OR WHERE IT HAPPENED...
OKAY, TONY. BRUTE FORCE COMPUTING ISN'T THE ISSUE HERE. MY PERSONAL SERVERS ARE ALMOST CERTAINLY SECURE.
SLOW YOUR ROLL. YOU'RE GOING ABOUT THIS ALL WRONG.
THIS ISN'T JUST ABOUT TECHNOLOGY...

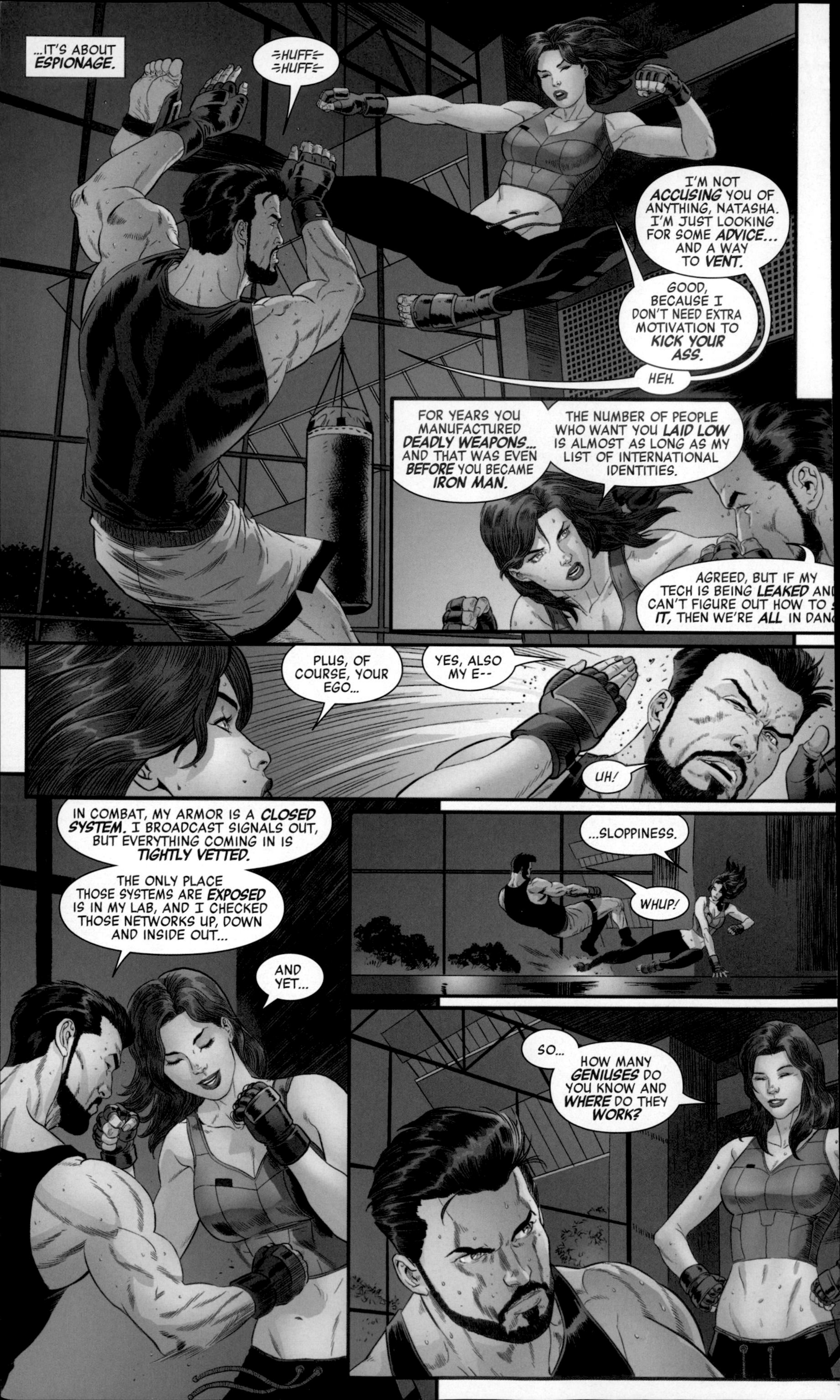

...IT'S ABOUT ESPIONAGE.
HUFF HUFF
I'M NOT ACCUSING YOU OF ANYTHING, NATASHA. I'M JUST LOOKING FOR SOME ADVICE... AND A WAY TO VENT.
GOOD, BECAUSE I DON'T NEED EXTRA MOTIVATION TO KICK YOUR ASS.
HEH.
FOR YEARS YOU MANUFACTURED DEADLY WEAPONS... AND THAT WAS EVEN BEFORE YOU BECAME IRON MAN.
THE NUMBER OF PEOPLE WHO WANT YOU LAID LOW IS ALMOST AS LONG AS MY LIST OF INTERNATIONAL IDENTITIES.
AGREED, BUT IF MY TECH IS BEING LEAKED AN
CAN'T FIGURE OUT HOW TO
IT, THEN WE'RE ALL IN DAN
PLUS, OF COURSE, YOUR EGO...
YES, ALSO MY E--
UH!
IN COMBAT, MY ARMOR IS A CLOSED SYSTEM. I BROADCAST SIGNALS OUT, BUT EVERYTHING COMING IN IS TIGHTLY VETTED.
THE ONLY PLACE THOSE SYSTEMS ARE EXPOSED IS IN MY LAB, AND I CHECKED THOSE NETWORKS UP, DOWN AND INSIDE OUT...
AND YET...
...SLOPPINESS.
WHUP!
SO...
HOW MANY GENIUSES DO YOU KNOW AND WHERE DO THEY WORK?

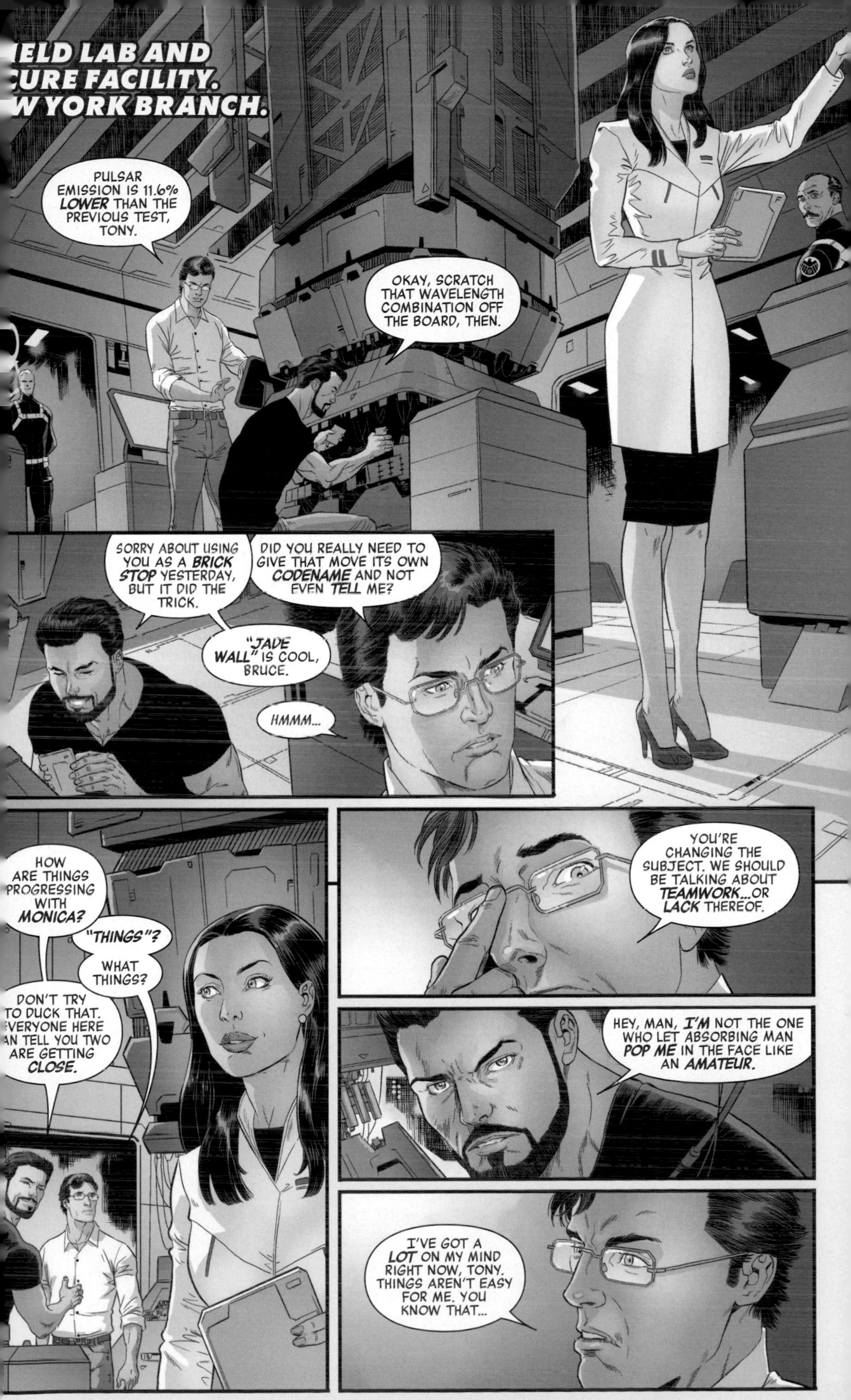

IELD LAB AND CURE FACILITY. W YORK BRANCH.
PULSAR EMISSION IS 11.6% LOWER THAN THE PREVIOUS TEST, TONY.
OKAY, SCRATCH THAT WAVELENGTH COMBINATION OFF THE BOARD, THEN.
SORRY ABOUT USING YOU AS A BRICK STOP YESTERDAY, BUT IT DID THE TRICK.
"JADE WALL" IS COOL, BRUCE.
DID YOU REALLY NEED TO GIVE THAT MOVE ITS OWN CODENAME AND NOT EVEN TELL ME?
HMMM...
HOW ARE THINGS PROGRESSING WITH MONICA?
"THINGS"?
WHAT THINGS?
DON'T TRY TO DUCK THAT. EVERYONE HERE AN TELL YOU TWO ARE GETTING CLOSE.
YOU'RE CHANGING THE SUBJECT. WE SHOULD BE TALKING ABOUT TEAMWORK...OR LACK THEREOF.
HEY, MAN, I'M NOT THE ONE WHO LET ABSORBING MAN POP ME IN THE FACE LIKE AN AMATEUR.
I'VE GOT A LOT ON MY MIND RIGHT NOW, TONY. THINGS AREN'T EASY FOR ME. YOU KNOW THAT...

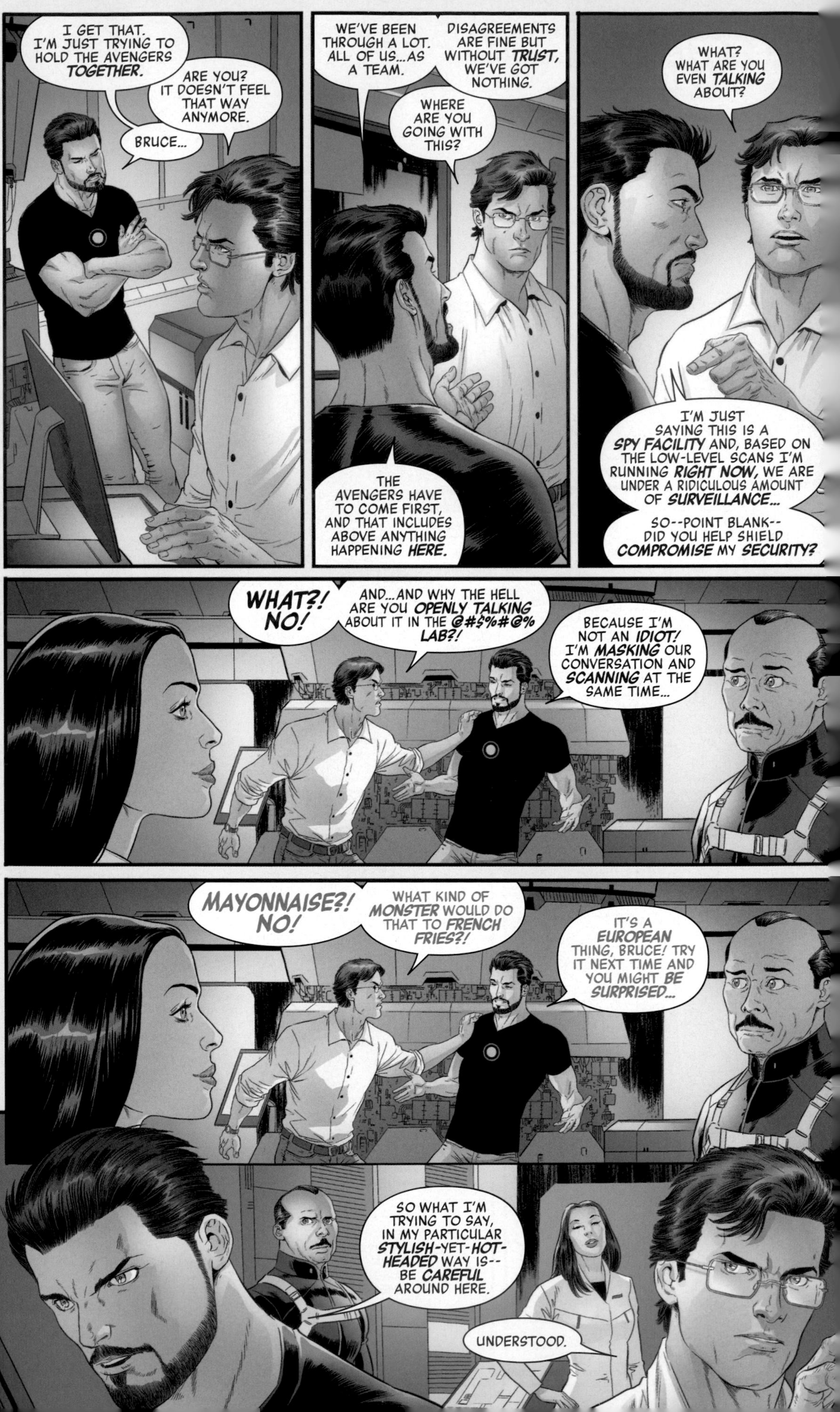

I GET THAT. I'M JUST TRYING TO HOLD THE AVENGERS TOGETHER.
ARE YOU? IT DOESN'T FEEL THAT WAY ANYMORE.
BRUCE...
WE'VE BEEN THROUGH A LOT. ALL OF US...AS A TEAM.
DISAGREEMENTS ARE FINE BUT WITHOUT TRUST, WE'VE GOT NOTHING.
WHERE ARE YOU GOING WITH THIS?
THE AVENGERS HAVE TO COME FIRST, AND THAT INCLUDES ABOVE ANYTHING HAPPENING HERE.
WHAT? WHAT ARE YOU EVEN TALKING ABOUT?
I'M JUST SAYING THIS IS A SPY FACILITY AND, BASED ON THE LOW-LEVEL SCANS I'M RUNNING RIGHT NOW, WE ARE UNDER A RIDICULOUS AMOUNT OF SURVEILLANCE...
SO--POINT BLANK--DID YOU HELP SHIELD COMPROMISE MY SECURITY?
WHAT?! NO!
AND...AND WHY THE HELL ARE YOU OPENLY TALKING ABOUT IT IN THE @#$%#@% LAB?!
BECAUSE I'M NOT AN IDIOT! I'M MASKING OUR CONVERSATION AND SCANNING AT THE SAME TIME...
MAYONNAISE?! NO!
WHAT KIND OF MONSTER WOULD DO THAT TO FRENCH FRIES?!
IT'S A EUROPEAN THING, BRUCE! TRY IT NEXT TIME AND YOU MIGHT BE SURPRISED...
SO WHAT I'M TRYING TO SAY, IN MY PARTICULAR STYLISH-YET-HOT-HEADED WAY IS--BE CAREFUL AROUND HERE.
UNDERSTOOD.

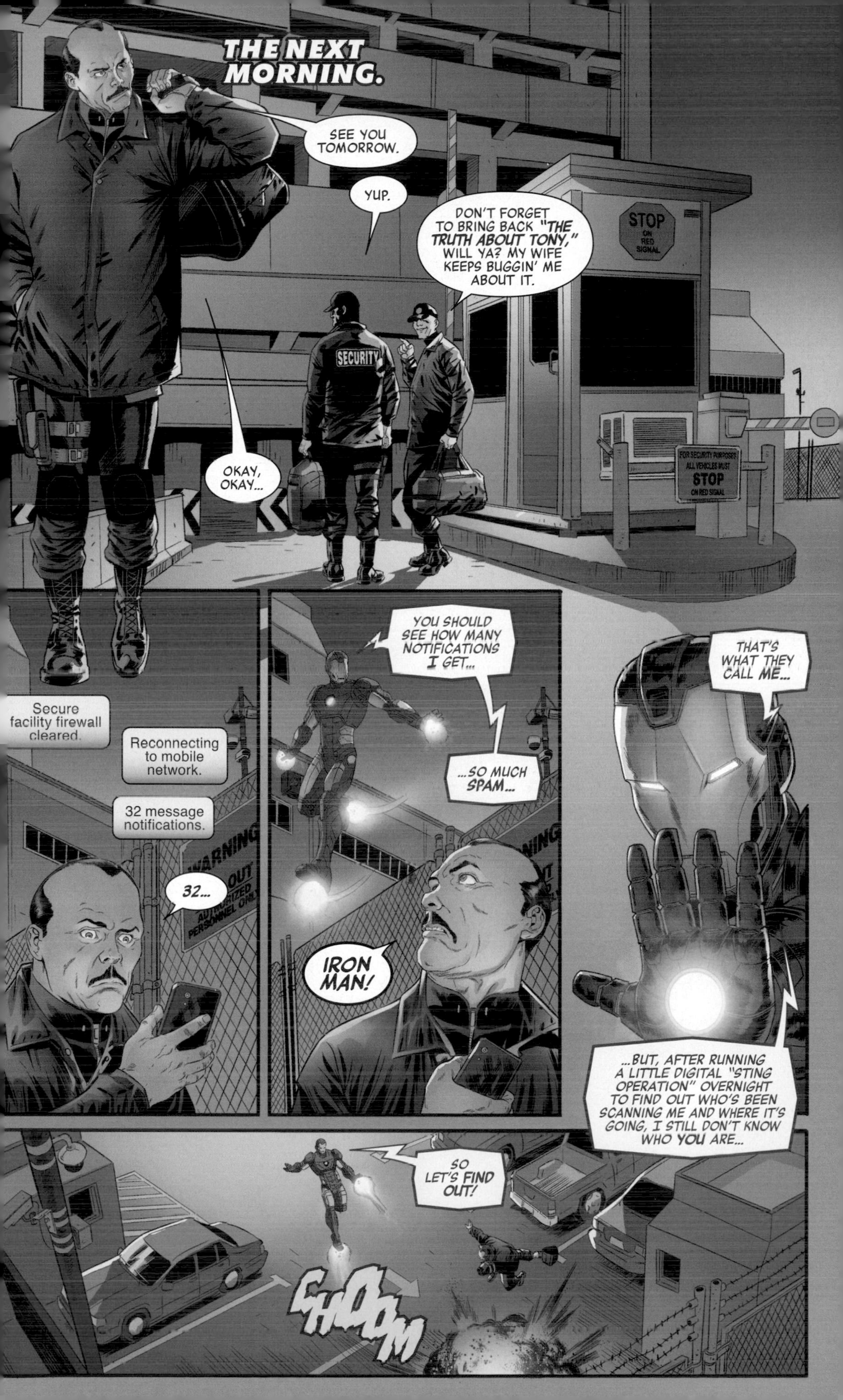
THE NEXT MORNING.
SEE YOU TOMORROW.
YUP.
DON'T FORGET TO BRING BACK "THE TRUTH ABOUT TONY," WILL YA? MY WIFE KEEPS BUGGIN' ME ABOUT IT.
STOP ON RED SIGNAL
SECURITY
OKAY, OKAY...
FOR SECURITY PURPOSES ALL VEHICLES MUST STOP ON RED SIGNAL
Secure facility firewall cleared.
Reconnecting to mobile network.
32 message notifications.
32...
YOU SHOULD SEE HOW MANY NOTIFICATIONS I GET...
...SO MUCH SPAM...
IRON MAN!
THAT'S WHAT THEY CALL ME...
...BUT, AFTER RUNNING A LITTLE DIGITAL "STING OPERATION" OVERNIGHT TO FIND OUT WHO'S BEEN SCANNING ME AND WHERE IT'S GOING, I STILL DON'T KNOW WHO YOU ARE...
SO LET'S FIND OUT!
CHOOOM

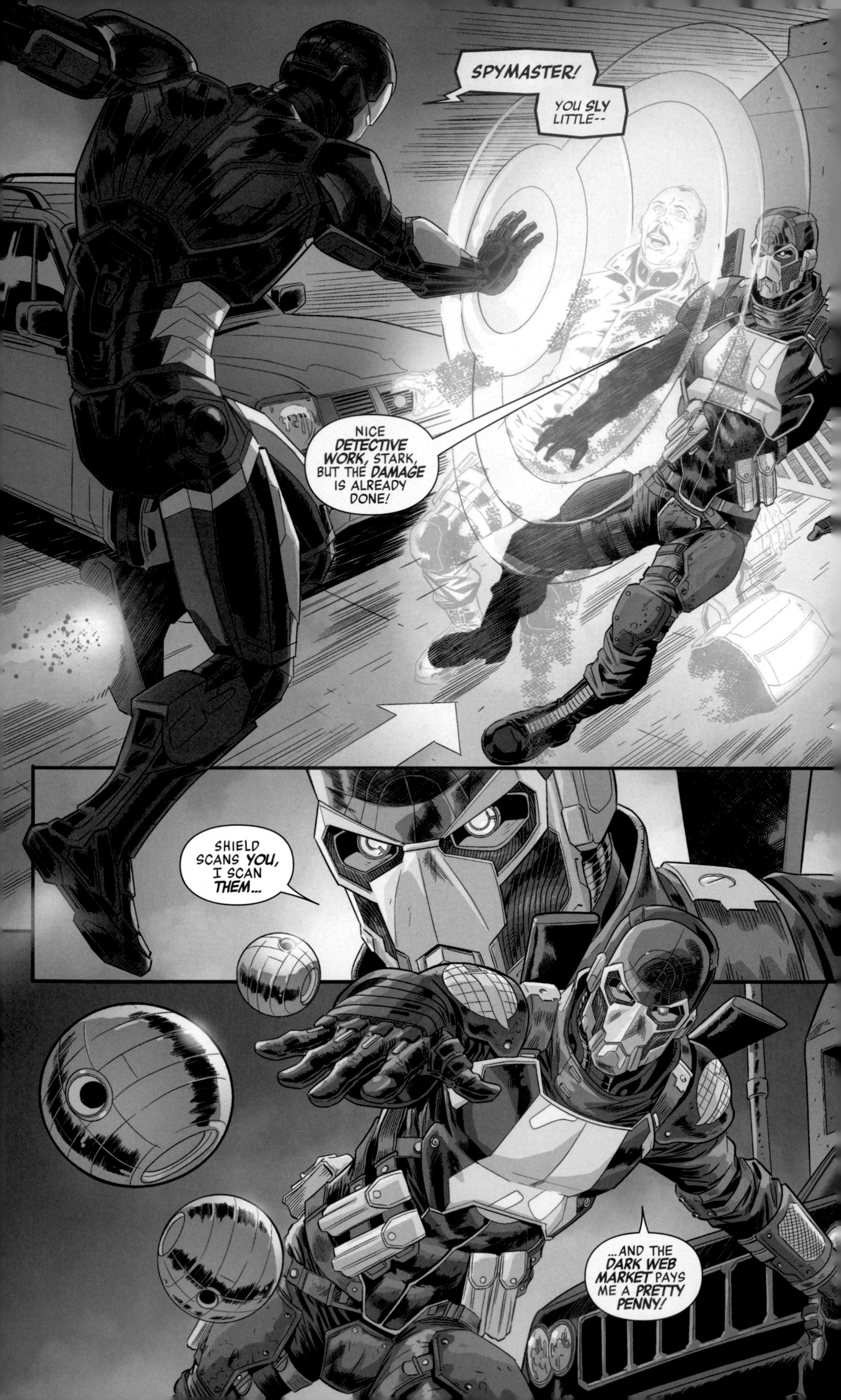
SPYMASTER!
YOU SLY LITTLE--
NICE DETECTIVE WORK, STARK, BUT THE DAMAGE IS ALREADY DONE!
SHIELD SCANS YOU, I SCAN THEM...
...AND THE DARK WEB MARKET PAYS ME A PRETTY PENNY!

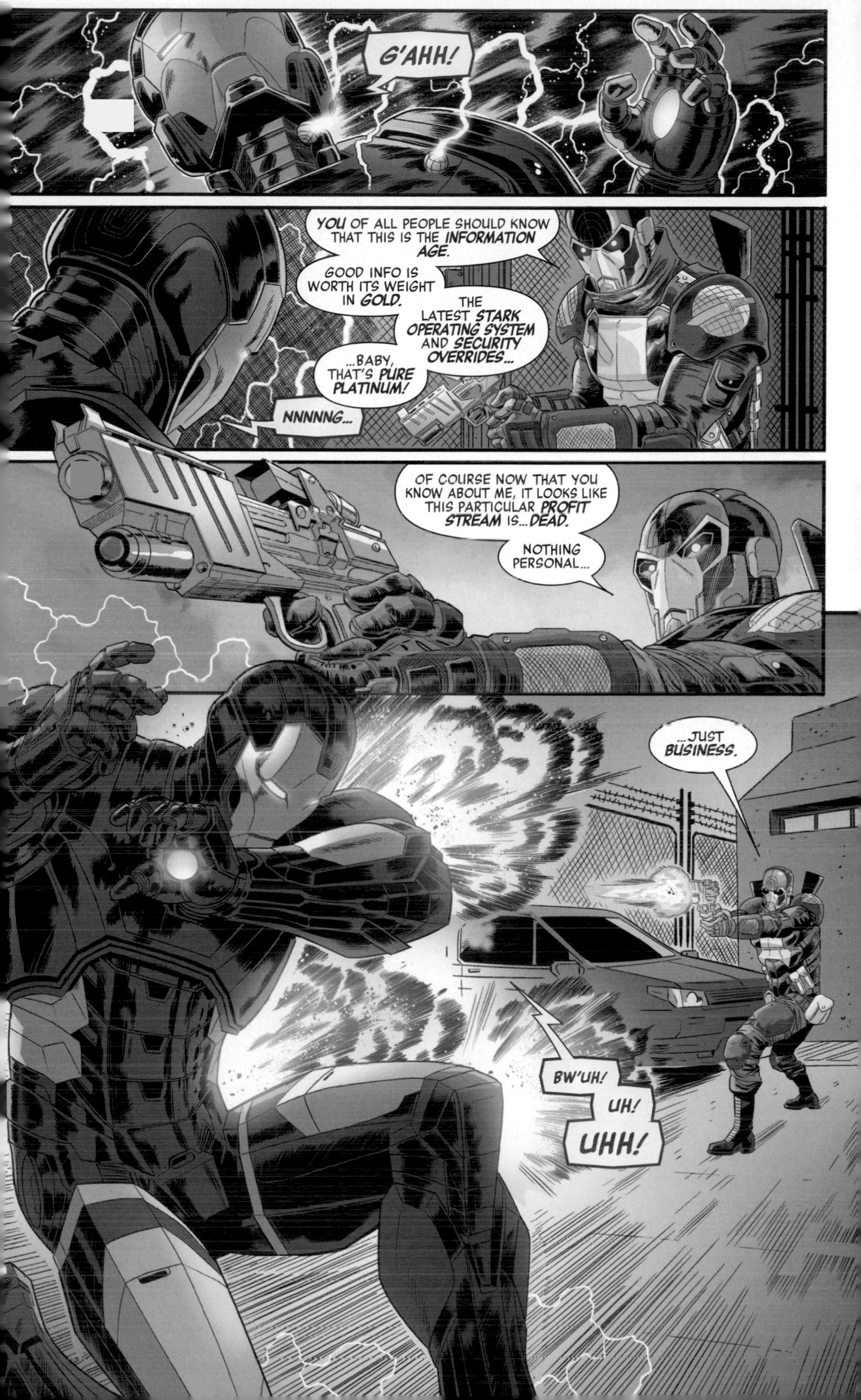
G'AHH!
YOU OF ALL PEOPLE SHOULD KNOW THAT THIS IS THE INFORMATION AGE.
GOOD INFO IS WORTH ITS WEIGHT IN GOLD.
THE LATEST STARK OPERATING SYSTEM AND SECURITY OVERRIDES...
...BABY, THAT'S PURE PLATINUM!
NNNNNG...
OF COURSE NOW THAT YOU KNOW ABOUT ME, IT LOOKS LIKE THIS PARTICULAR PROFIT STREAM IS...DEAD.
NOTHING PERSONAL...
...JUST BUSINESS.
BW'UH!
UH!
UHH!

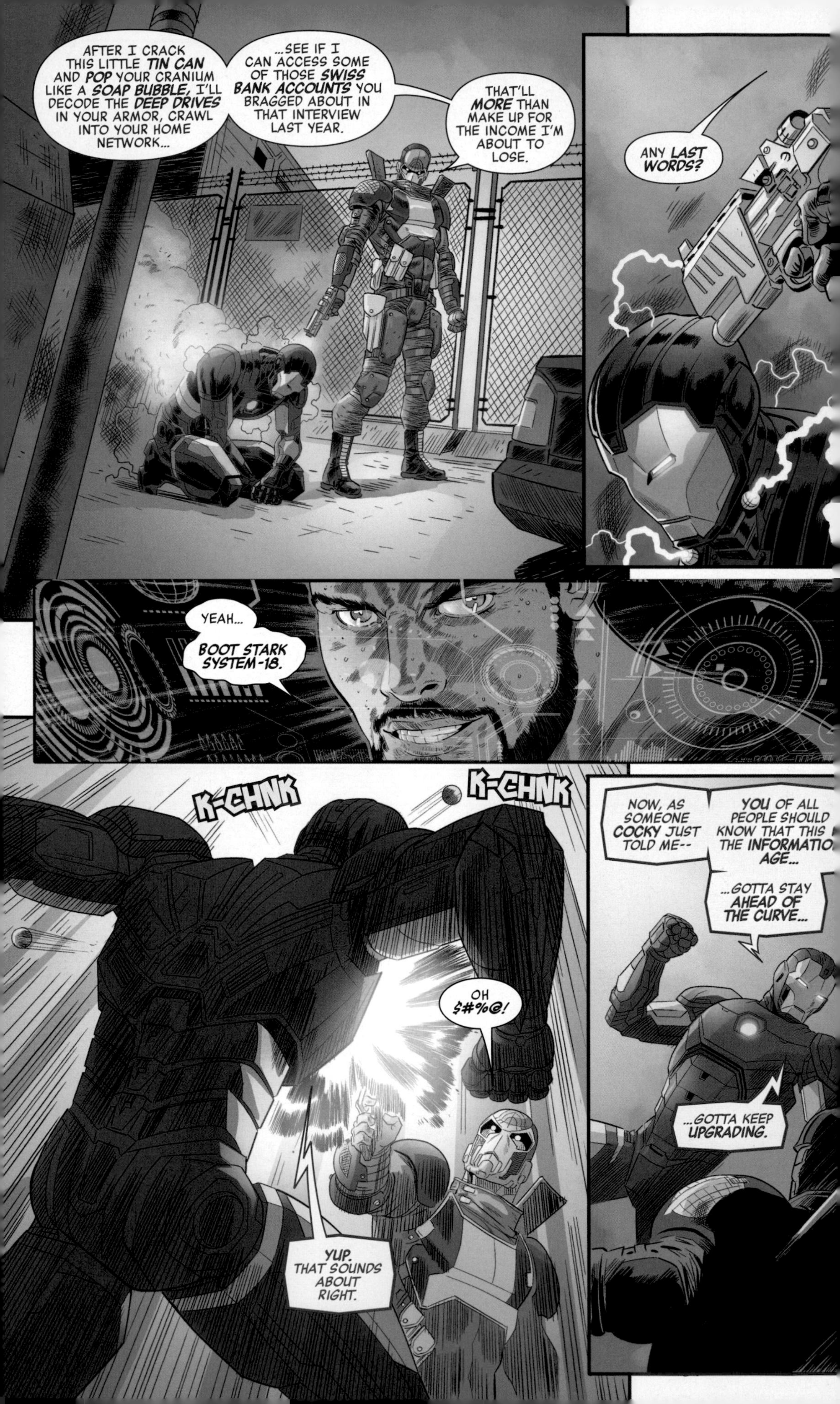
AFTER I CRACK THIS LITTLE TIN CAN AND POP YOUR CRANIUM LIKE A SOAP BUBBLE, I'LL DECODE THE DEEP DRIVES IN YOUR ARMOR, CRAWL INTO YOUR HOME NETWORK...
...SEE IF I CAN ACCESS SOME OF THOSE SWISS BANK ACCOUNTS YOU BRAGGED ABOUT IN THAT INTERVIEW LAST YEAR.
THAT'LL MORE THAN MAKE UP FOR THE INCOME I'M ABOUT TO LOSE.
ANY LAST WORDS?
YEAH...
BOOT STARK SYSTEM-18.
K-CHNK
K-CHNK
OH $#%@!
YUP. THAT SOUNDS ABOUT RIGHT.
NOW, AS SOMEONE COCKY JUST TOLD ME--
YOU OF ALL PEOPLE SHOULD KNOW THAT THIS THE INFORMATIO AGE...
...GOTTA STAY AHEAD OF THE CURVE...
...GOTTA KEEP UPGRADING.

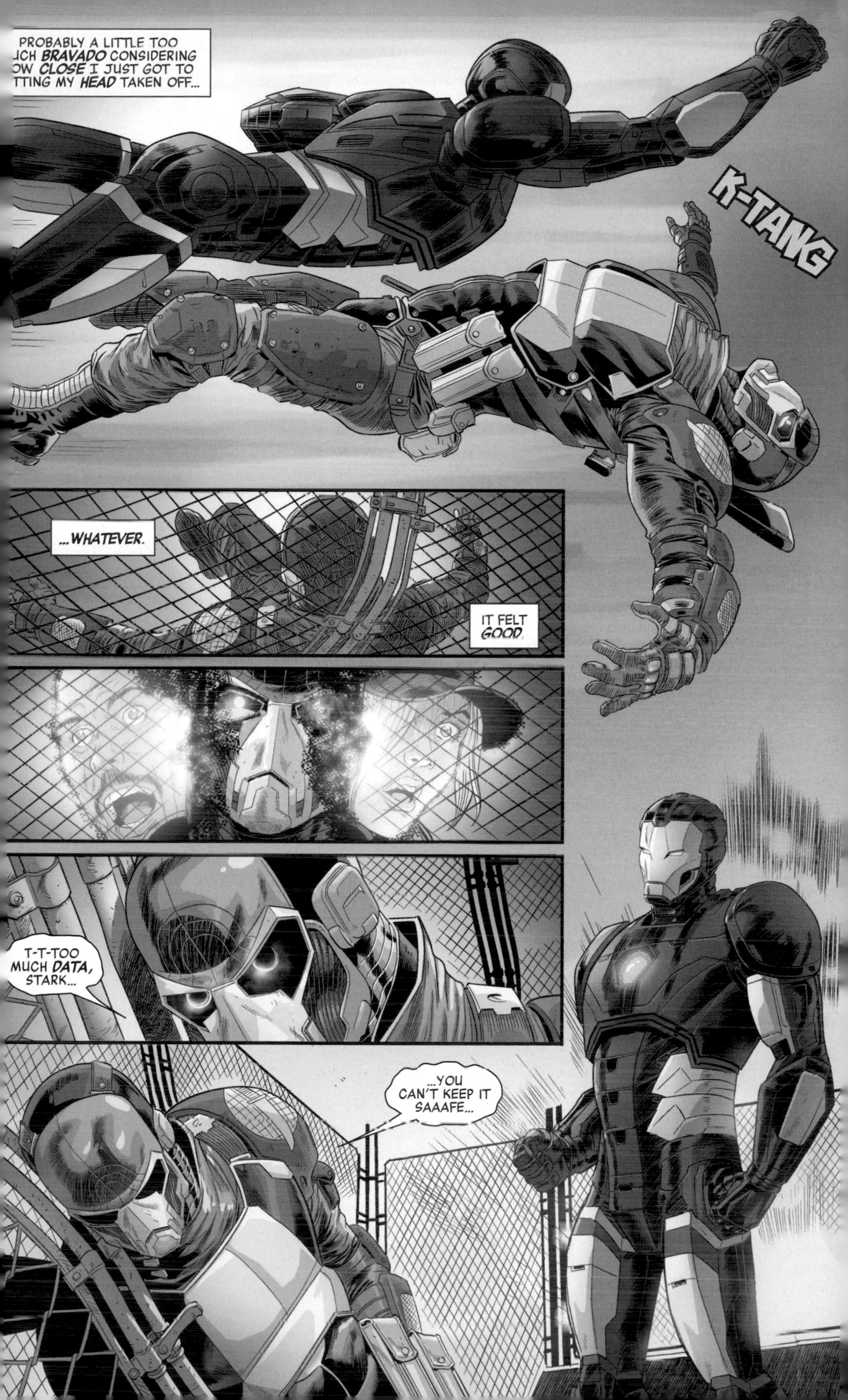
PROBABLY A LITTLE TOO
...UCH BRAVADO CONSIDERING
...OW CLOSE I JUST GOT TO
...TTING MY HEAD TAKEN OFF...
K-TANG
...WHATEVER.
IT FELT GOOD.
T-T-TOO MUCH DATA, STARK...
...YOU CAN'T KEEP IT SAAAFE...

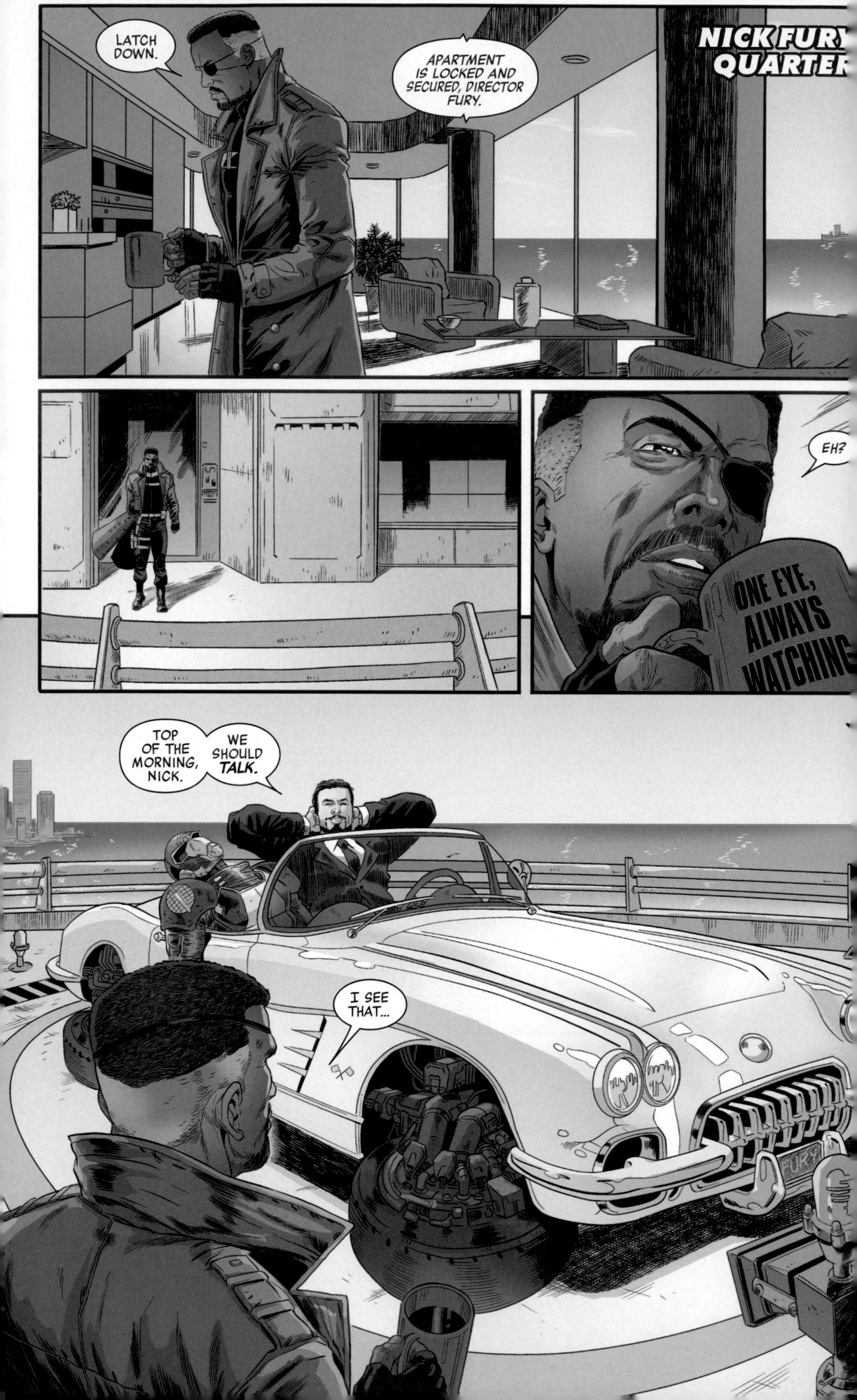
NICK FURY'S QUARTERS
LATCH DOWN.
APARTMENT IS LOCKED AND SECURED, DIRECTOR FURY.
EH?
ONE EYE, ALWAYS WATCHING
TOP OF THE MORNING, NICK.
WE SHOULD TALK.
I SEE THAT...
FURY

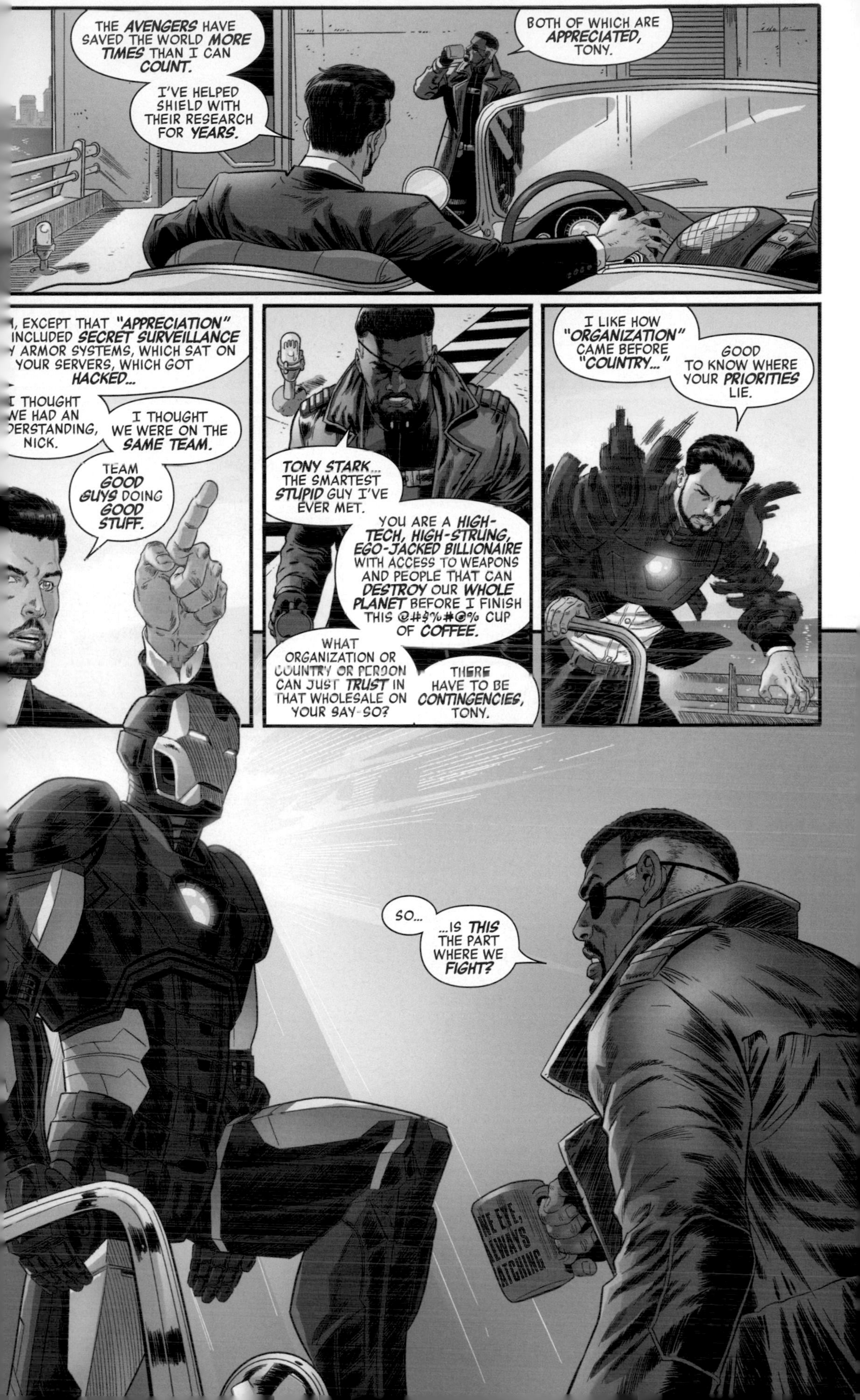
THE AVENGERS HAVE SAVED THE WORLD MORE TIMES THAN I CAN COUNT.
I'VE HELPED SHIELD WITH THEIR RESEARCH FOR YEARS.
BOTH OF WHICH ARE APPRECIATED, TONY.
, EXCEPT THAT "APPRECIATION" INCLUDED SECRET SURVEILLANCE ARMOR SYSTEMS, WHICH SAT ON YOUR SERVERS, WHICH GOT HACKED...
THOUGHT WE HAD AN ERSTANDING, NICK.
I THOUGHT WE WERE ON THE SAME TEAM.
TEAM GOOD GUYS DOING GOOD STUFF.
TONY STARK... THE SMARTEST STUPID GUY I'VE EVER MET.
YOU ARE A HIGH-TECH, HIGH-STRUNG, EGO-JACKED BILLIONAIRE WITH ACCESS TO WEAPONS AND PEOPLE THAT CAN DESTROY OUR WHOLE PLANET BEFORE I FINISH THIS @#$%#@% CUP OF COFFEE.
WHAT ORGANIZATION OR COUNTRY OR PERSON CAN JUST TRUST IN THAT WHOLESALE ON YOUR SAY-SO?
THERE HAVE TO BE CONTINGENCIES, TONY.
I LIKE HOW "ORGANIZATION" CAME BEFORE "COUNTRY..."
GOOD TO KNOW WHERE YOUR PRIORITIES LIE.
SO...
...IS THIS THE PART WHERE WE FIGHT?
NE EYE, ALWAYS ATCHING

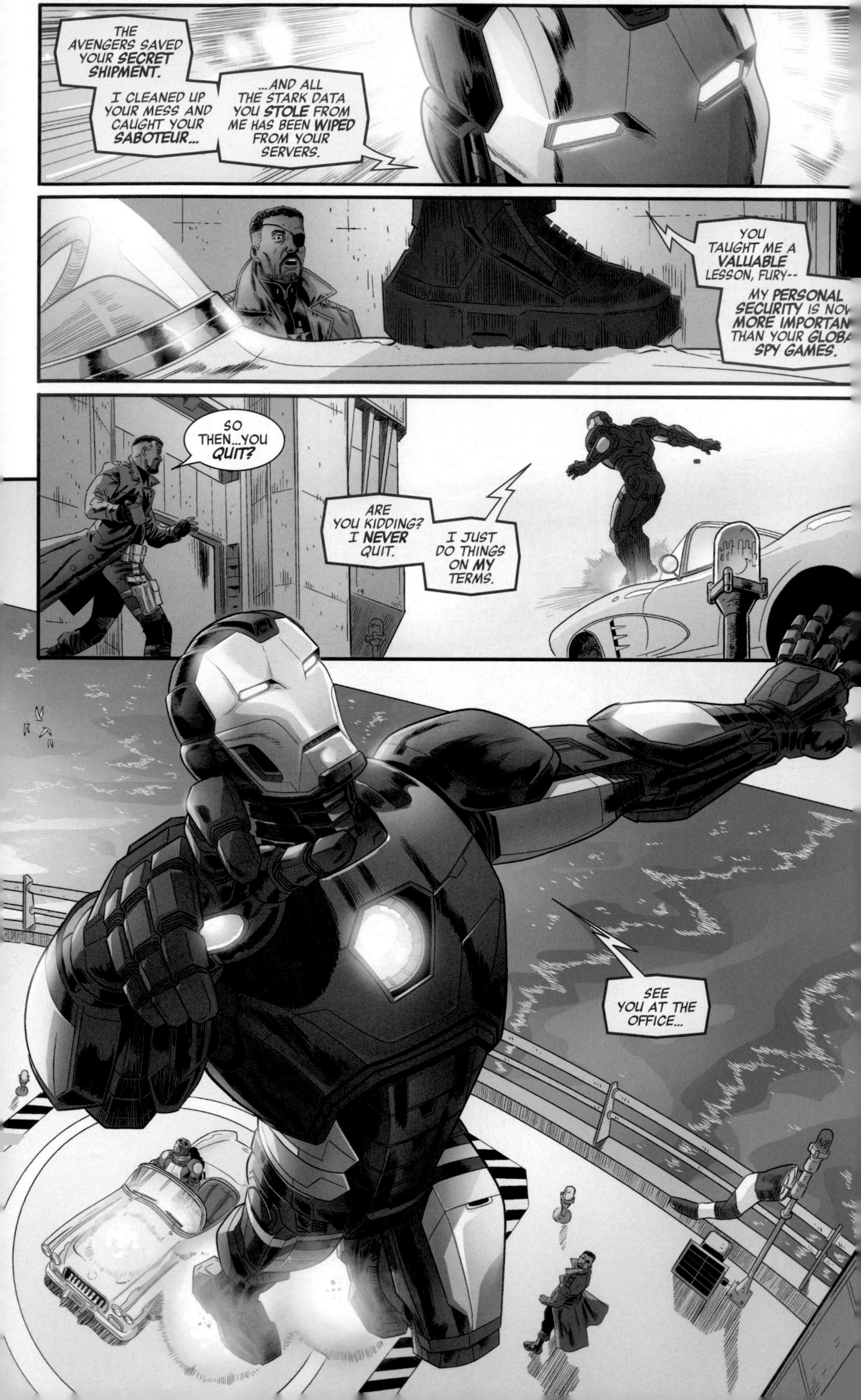

THE AVENGERS SAVED YOUR SECRET SHIPMENT.
I CLEANED UP YOUR MESS AND CAUGHT YOUR SABOTEUR...
...AND ALL THE STARK DATA YOU STOLE FROM ME HAS BEEN WIPED FROM YOUR SERVERS.
YOU TAUGHT ME A VALUABLE LESSON, FURY--
MY PERSONAL SECURITY IS NOW MORE IMPORTANT THAN YOUR GLOBAL SPY GAMES.
SO THEN...YOU QUIT?
ARE YOU KIDDING? I NEVER QUIT.
I JUST DO THINGS ON MY TERMS.
SEE YOU AT THE OFFICE...

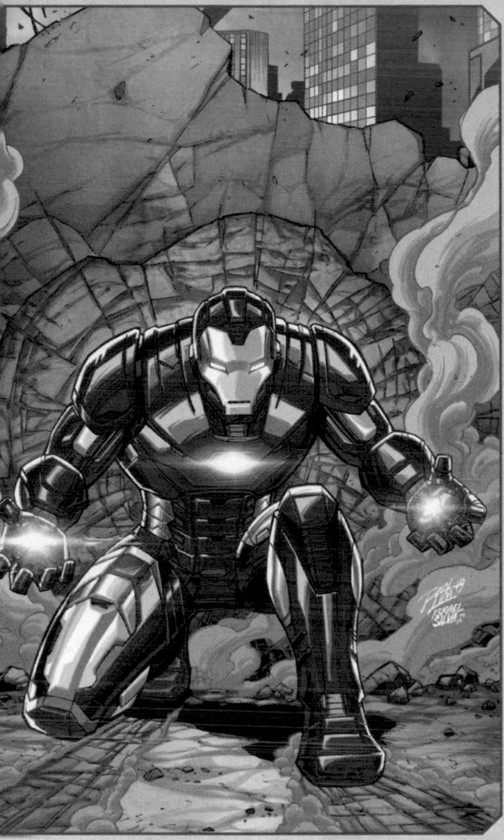

IRON MAN VARIANT BY **RON LIM** & **ISRAEL SILVA**

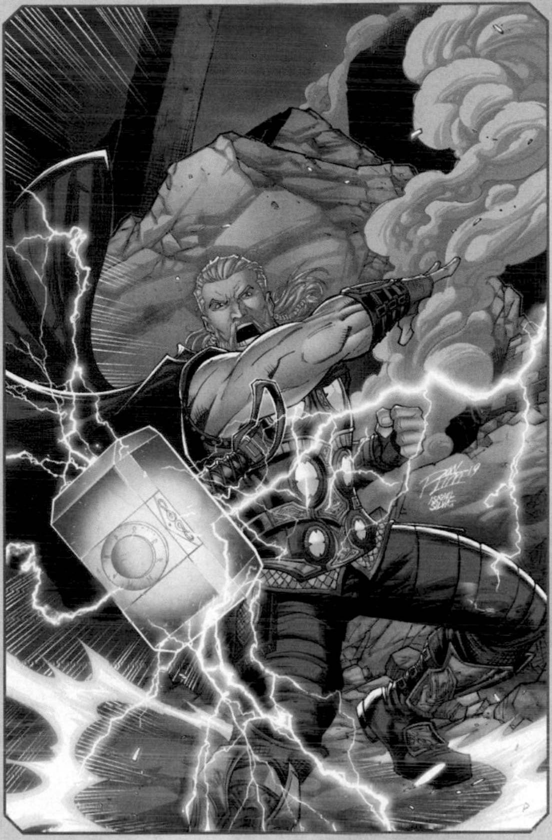

THOR VARIANT BY **RON LIM** & **ISRAEL SILVA**

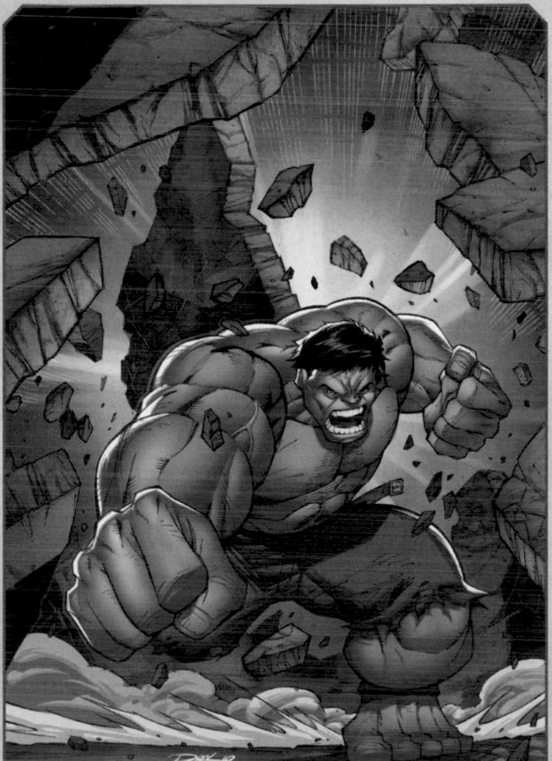

HULK VARIANT BY **RON LIM** & **ISRAEL SILVA**

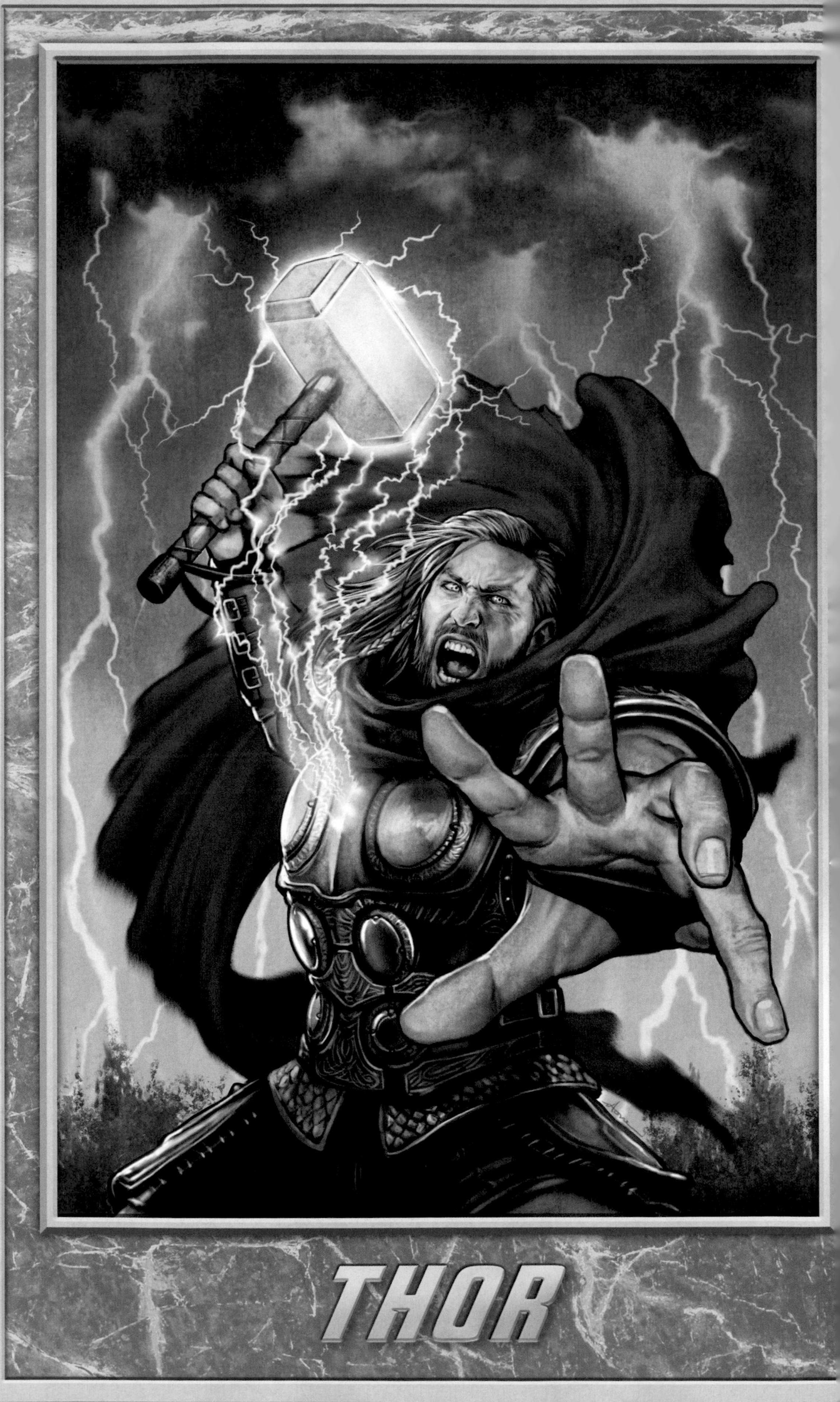
THOR

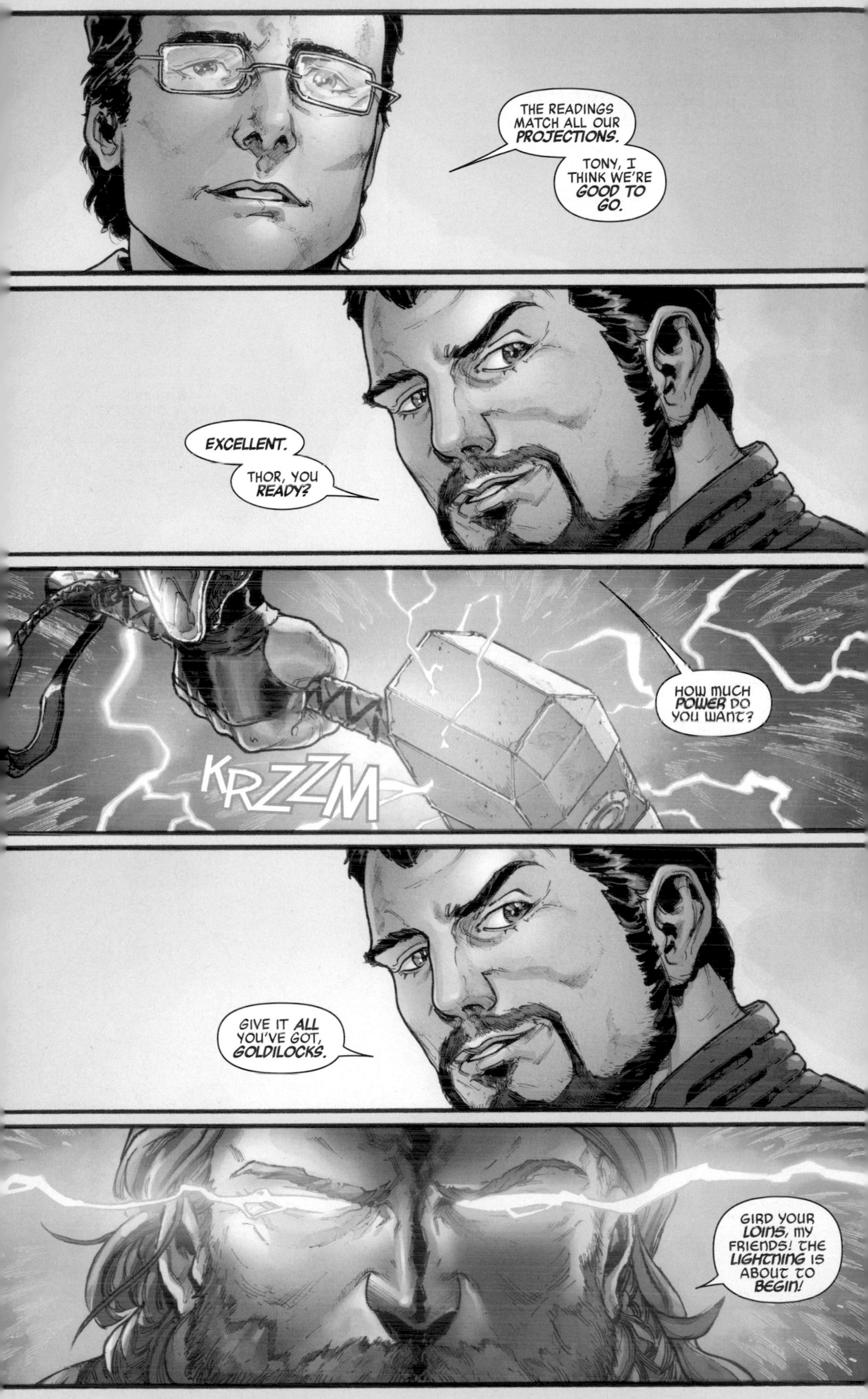
THE READINGS MATCH ALL OUR PROJECTIONS.
TONY, I THINK WE'RE GOOD TO GO.
EXCELLENT.
THOR, YOU READY?
HOW MUCH POWER DO YOU WANT?
KRZZM
GIVE IT ALL YOU'VE GOT, GOLDILOCKS.
GIRD YOUR LOINS, MY FRIENDS! THE LIGHTNING IS ABOUT TO BEGIN!

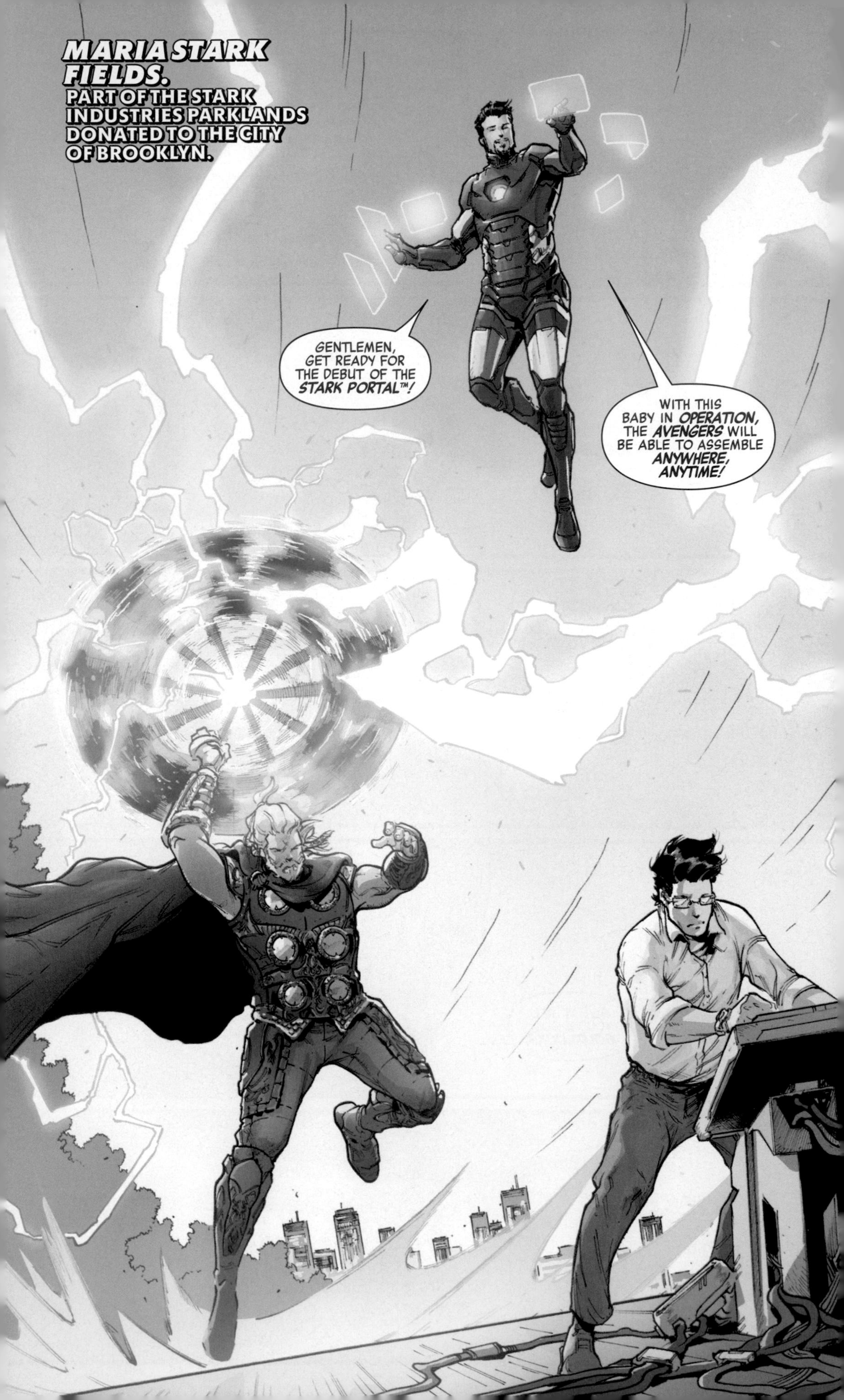
MARIA STARK FIELDS.
PART OF THE STARK INDUSTRIES PARKLANDS DONATED TO THE CITY OF BROOKLYN.
GENTLEMEN, GET READY FOR THE DEBUT OF THE STARK PORTAL™!
WITH THIS BABY IN OPERATION, THE AVENGERS WILL BE ABLE TO ASSEMBLE ANYWHERE, ANYTIME!

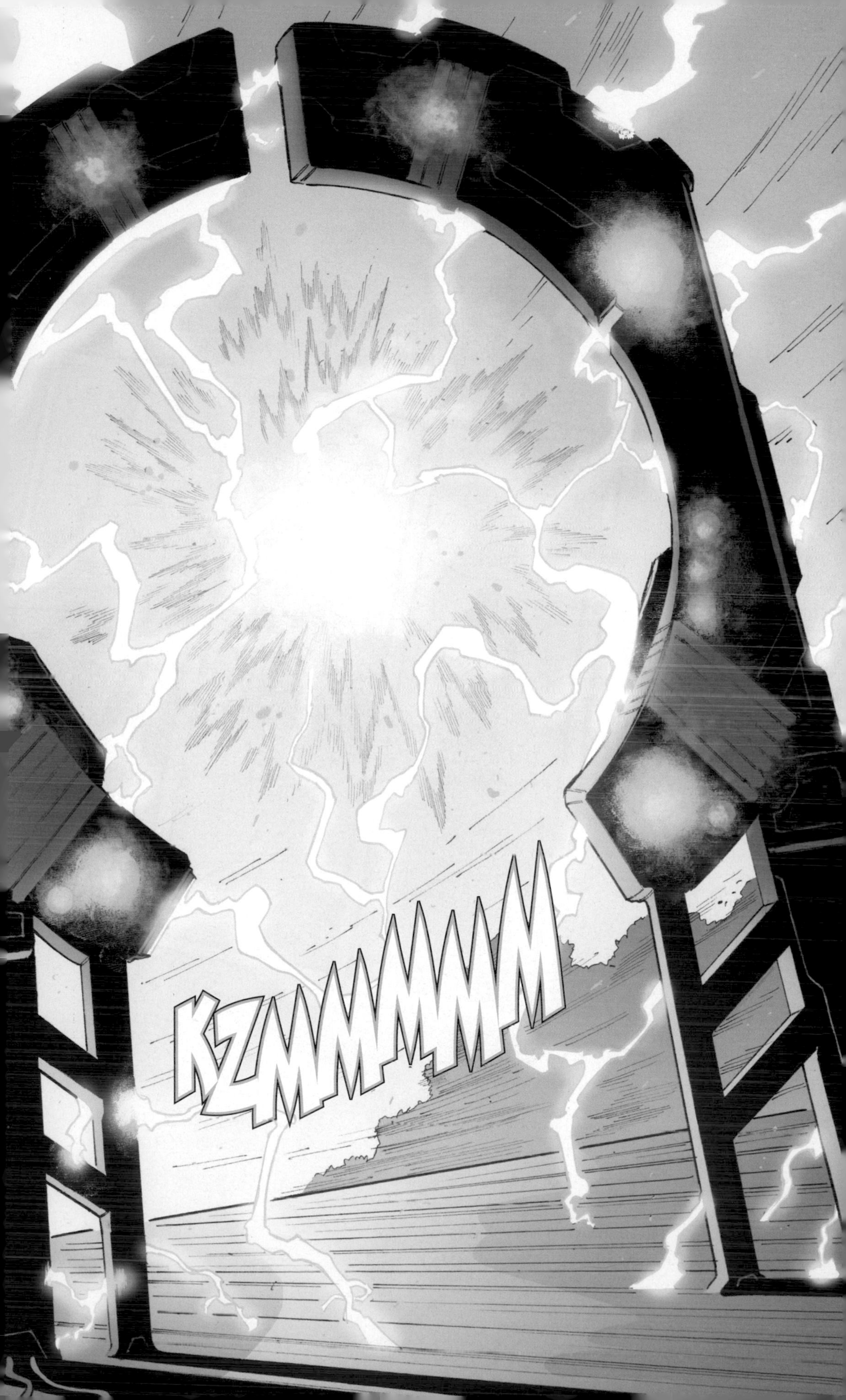
KZMMMMMMM

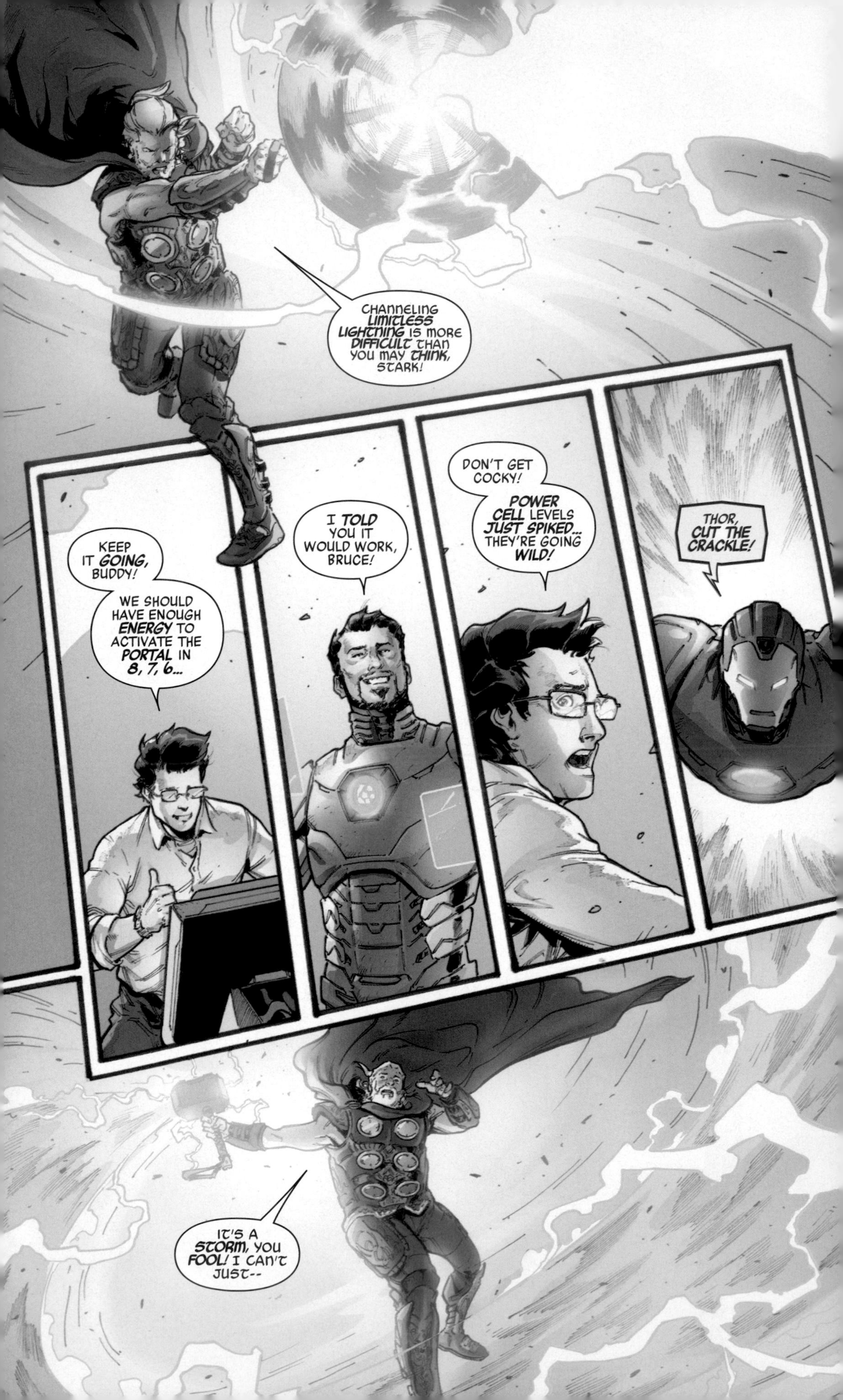

CHANNELING LIMITLESS LIGHTNING IS MORE DIFFICULT THAN YOU MAY THINK, STARK!
KEEP IT GOING, BUDDY!
WE SHOULD HAVE ENOUGH ENERGY TO ACTIVATE THE PORTAL IN 8, 7, 6...
I TOLD YOU IT WOULD WORK, BRUCE!
DON'T GET COCKY!
POWER CELL LEVELS JUST SPIKED... THEY'RE GOING WILD!
THOR, CUT THE CRACKLE!
IT'S A STORM, YOU FOOL! I CAN'T JUST--

BOOM
BANNER?
STARK?
WHAT THE HELL WAS THAT?!
I BELIEVE THAT'S WHAT WE GENIUSES CALL A "MISCALCULATION."
WERE YOU TOO BUSY PARTYING WITH SUPERMODELS AND TECH BROS TO CHECK YOUR NUMBERS?
SLOW YOUR ROLL, BRUCE. YOU SAW THE SAME SIMULATIONS I DID.
BESIDES, THAT'S NOT IMPORTANT. ARE YOU OKAY? THAT BLAST WAS PRETTY CLO--
I'M FINE, TONY.

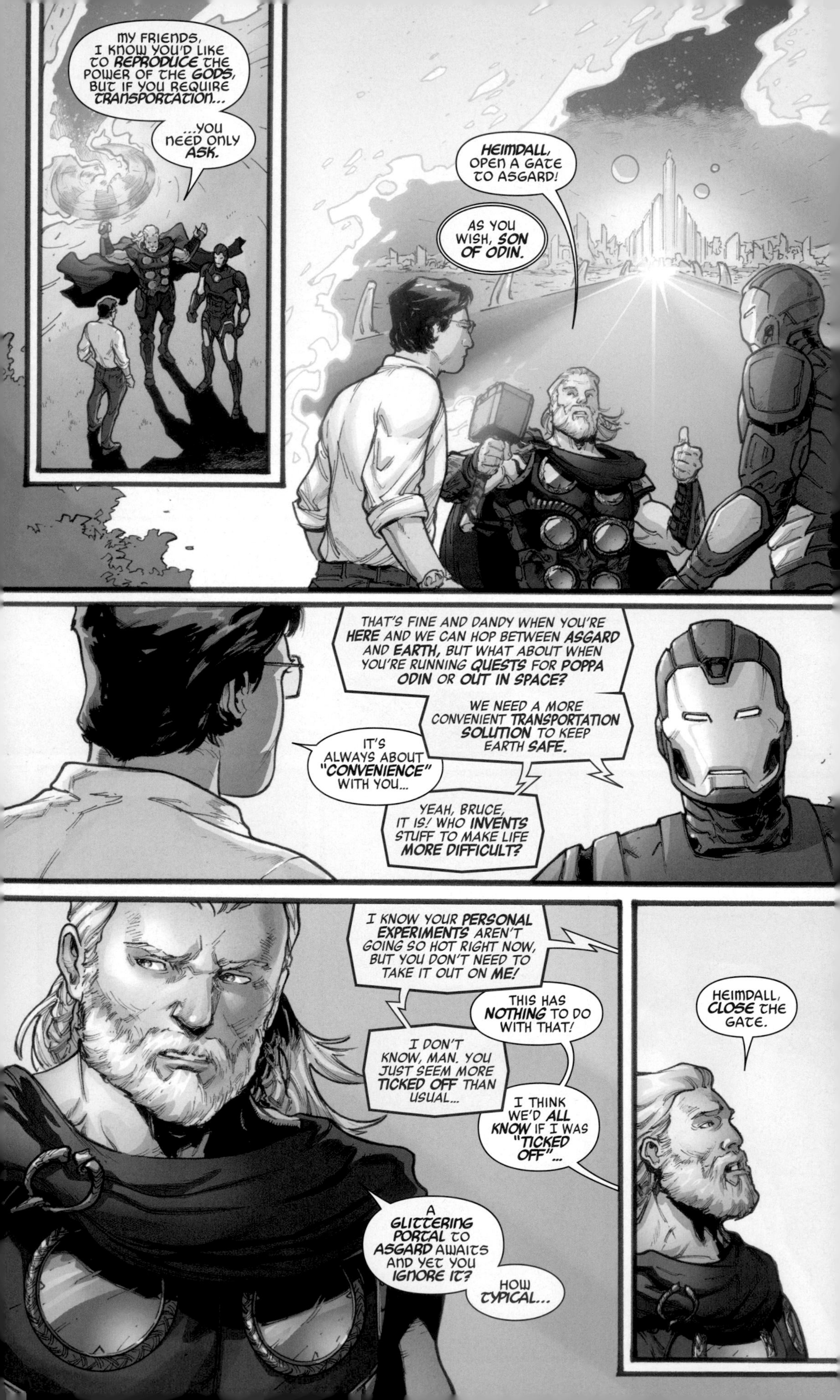

MY FRIENDS, I KNOW YOU'D LIKE TO REPRODUCE THE POWER OF THE GODS, BUT IF YOU REQUIRE TRANSPORTATION...
...YOU NEED ONLY ASK.
HEIMDALL, OPEN A GATE TO ASGARD!
AS YOU WISH, SON OF ODIN.
THAT'S FINE AND DANDY WHEN YOU'RE HERE AND WE CAN HOP BETWEEN ASGARD AND EARTH, BUT WHAT ABOUT WHEN YOU'RE RUNNING QUESTS FOR POPPA ODIN OR OUT IN SPACE?
WE NEED A MORE CONVENIENT TRANSPORTATION SOLUTION TO KEEP EARTH SAFE.
IT'S ALWAYS ABOUT "CONVENIENCE" WITH YOU...
YEAH, BRUCE, IT IS! WHO INVENTS STUFF TO MAKE LIFE MORE DIFFICULT?
I KNOW YOUR PERSONAL EXPERIMENTS AREN'T GOING SO HOT RIGHT NOW, BUT YOU DON'T NEED TO TAKE IT OUT ON ME!
THIS HAS NOTHING TO DO WITH THAT!
I DON'T KNOW, MAN. YOU JUST SEEM MORE TICKED OFF THAN USUAL...
I THINK WE'D ALL KNOW IF I WAS "TICKED OFF"...
A GLITTERING PORTAL TO ASGARD AWAITS AND YET YOU IGNORE IT?
HOW TYPICAL...
HEIMDALL, CLOSE THE GATE.

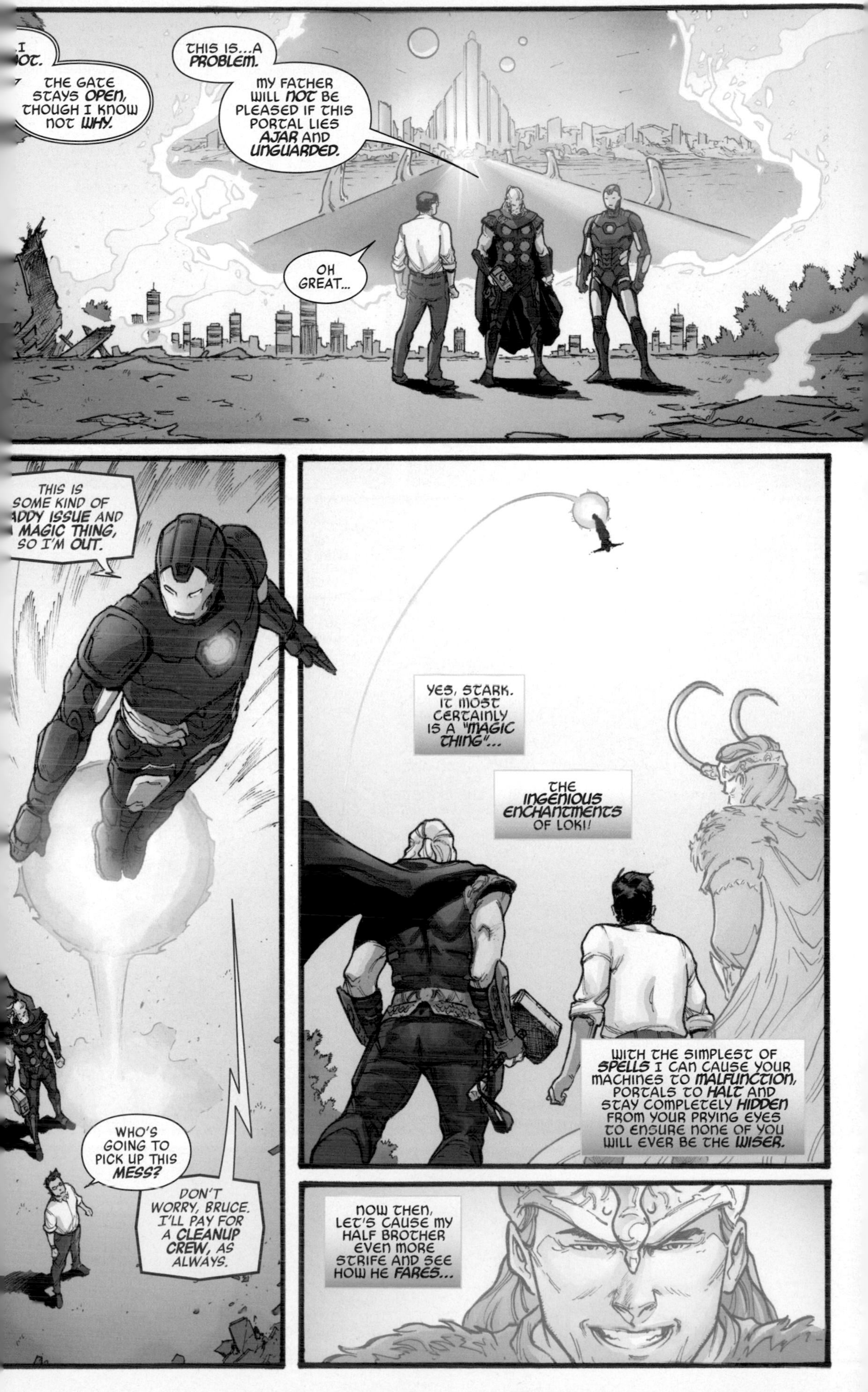
THE GATE STAYS OPEN, THOUGH I KNOW NOT WHY.
THIS IS...A PROBLEM.
MY FATHER WILL NOT BE PLEASED IF THIS PORTAL LIES AJAR AND UNGUARDED.
OH GREAT...
THIS IS SOME KIND OF ADDY ISSUE AND MAGIC THING, SO I'M OUT.
WHO'S GOING TO PICK UP THIS MESS?
DON'T WORRY, BRUCE. I'LL PAY FOR A CLEANUP CREW, AS ALWAYS.
YES, STARK. IT MOST CERTAINLY IS A "MAGIC THING"...
THE INGENIOUS ENCHANTMENTS OF LOKI!
WITH THE SIMPLEST OF SPELLS I CAN CAUSE YOUR MACHINES TO MALFUNCTION, PORTALS TO HALT AND STAY COMPLETELY HIDDEN FROM YOUR PRYING EYES TO ENSURE NONE OF YOU WILL EVER BE THE WISER.
NOW THEN, LET'S CAUSE MY HALF BROTHER EVEN MORE STRIFE AND SEE HOW HE FARES...

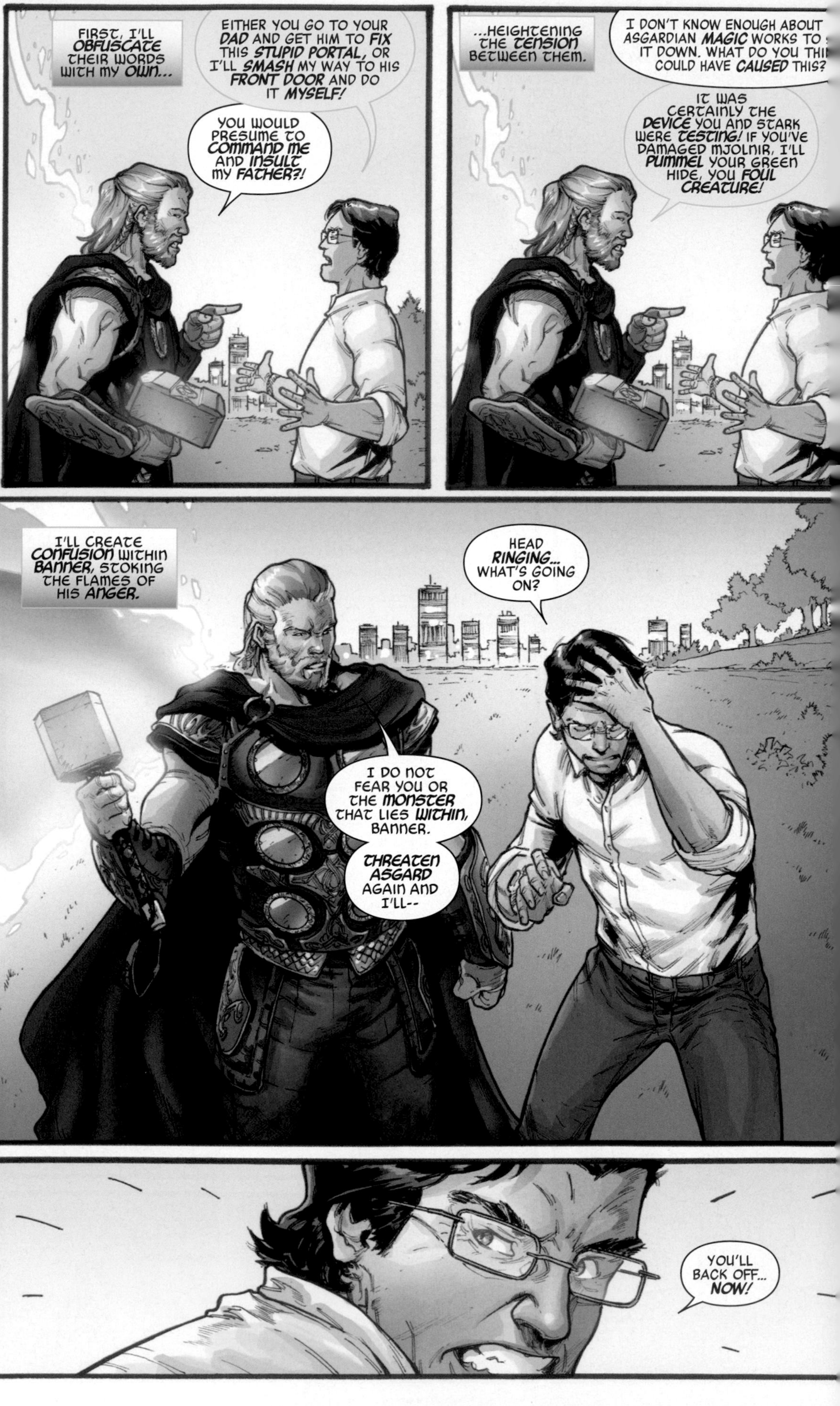
FIRST, I'LL OBFUSCATE THEIR WORDS WITH MY OWN...
EITHER YOU GO TO YOUR DAD AND GET HIM TO FIX THIS STUPID PORTAL, OR I'LL SMASH MY WAY TO HIS FRONT DOOR AND DO IT MYSELF!
YOU WOULD PRESUME TO COMMAND ME AND INSULT MY FATHER?!
...HEIGHTENING THE TENSION BETWEEN THEM.
I DON'T KNOW ENOUGH ABOUT ASGARDIAN MAGIC WORKS TO
IT DOWN. WHAT DO YOU THI
COULD HAVE CAUSED THIS?
IT WAS CERTAINLY THE DEVICE YOU AND STARK WERE TESTING! IF YOU'VE DAMAGED MJOLNIR, I'LL PUMMEL YOUR GREEN HIDE, YOU FOUL CREATURE!
I'LL CREATE CONFUSION WITHIN BANNER, STOKING THE FLAMES OF HIS ANGER.
HEAD RINGING... WHAT'S GOING ON?
I DO NOT FEAR YOU OR THE MONSTER THAT LIES WITHIN, BANNER.
THREATEN ASGARD AGAIN AND I'LL--
YOU'LL BACK OFF... NOW!

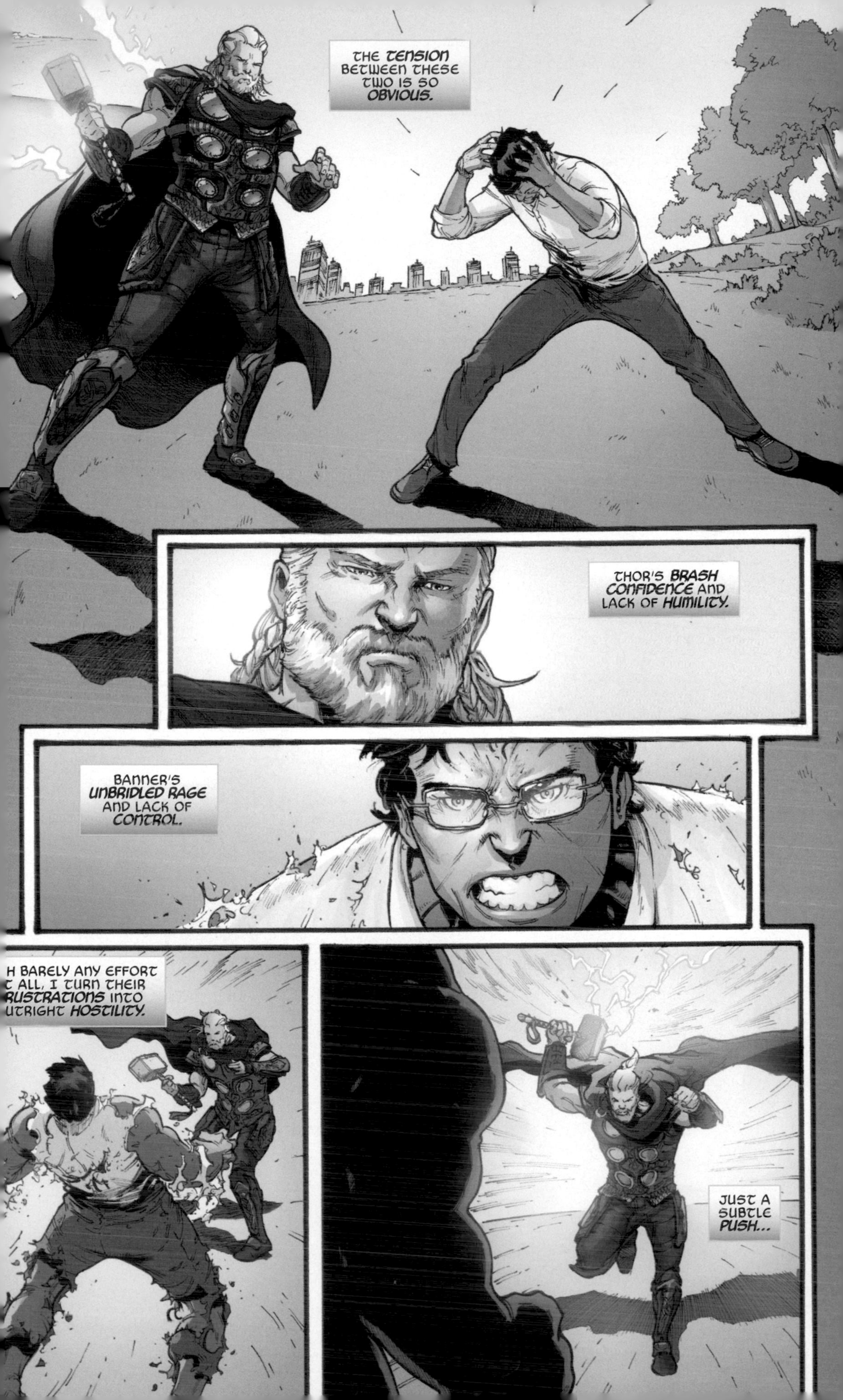
THE TENSION BETWEEN THESE TWO IS SO OBVIOUS.
THOR'S BRASH CONFIDENCE AND LACK OF HUMILITY.
BANNER'S UNBRIDLED RAGE AND LACK OF CONTROL.
H BARELY ANY EFFORT
T ALL, I TURN THEIR
RUSTRATIONS INTO
UTRIGHT HOSTILITY.
JUST A SUBTLE PUSH...

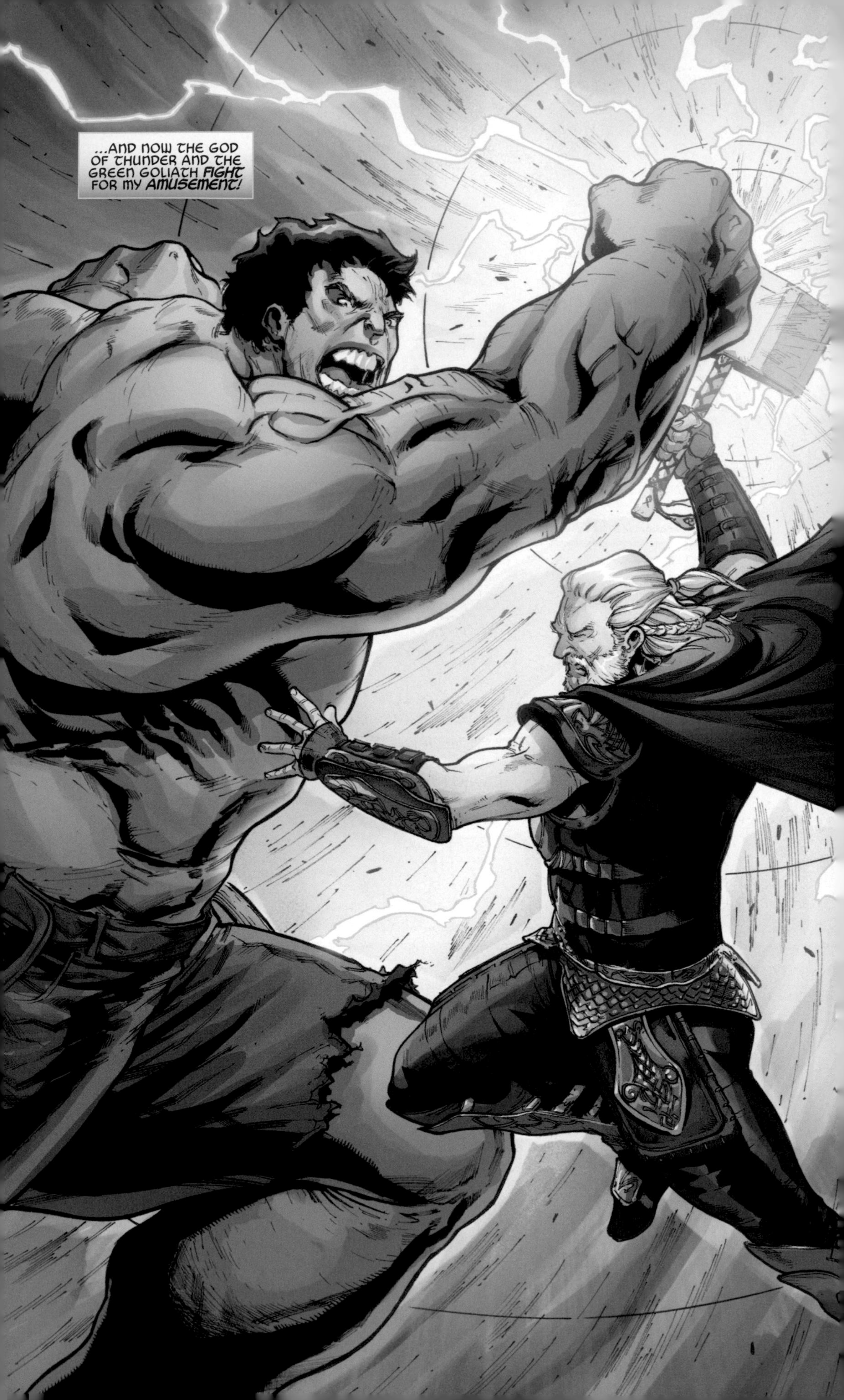
...AND NOW THE GOD OF THUNDER AND THE GREEN GOLIATH FIGHT FOR MY AMUSEMENT!

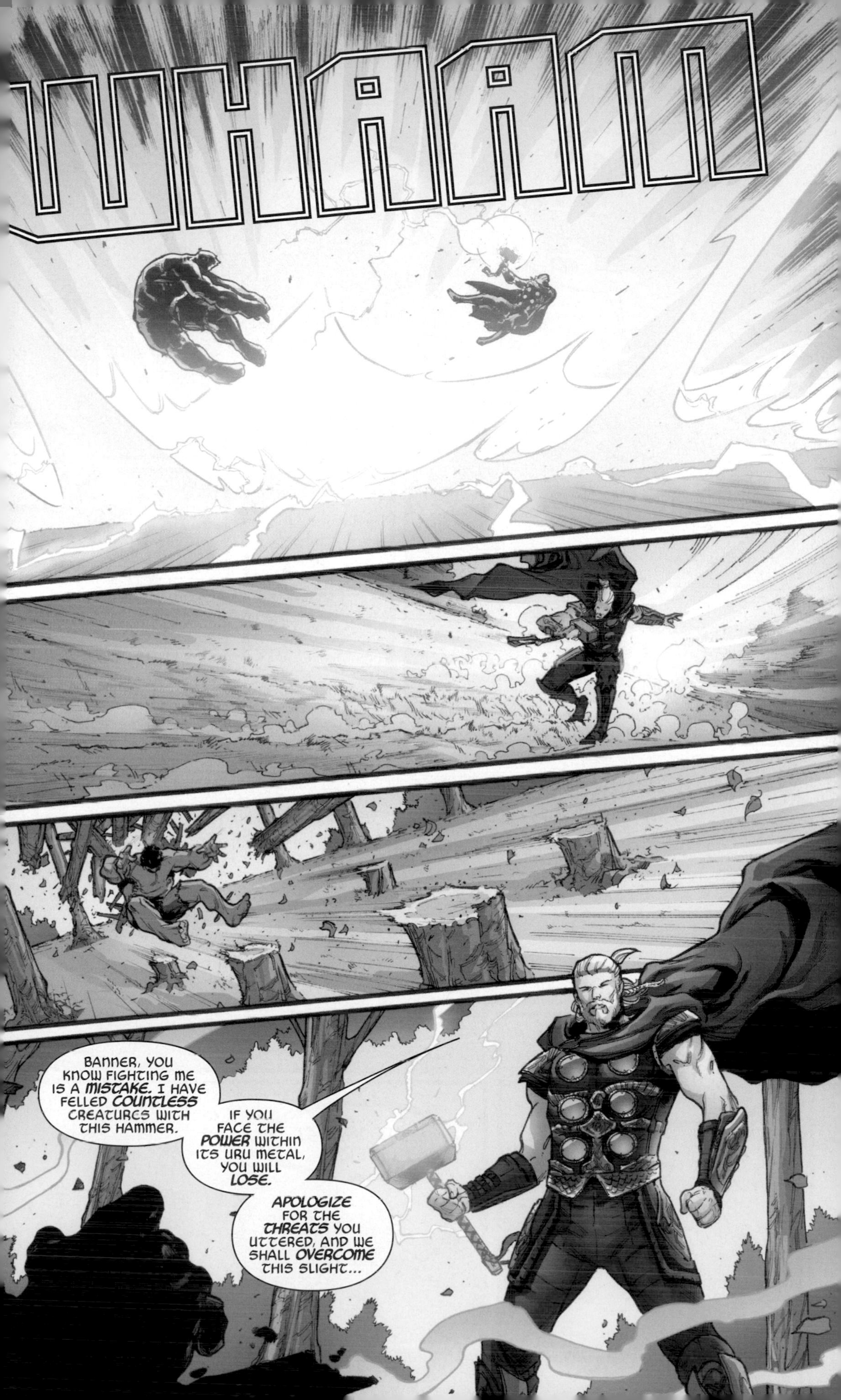

WHAAM
BANNER, YOU KNOW FIGHTING ME IS A MISTAKE. I HAVE FELLED COUNTLESS CREATURES WITH THIS HAMMER.
IF YOU FACE THE POWER WITHIN ITS URU METAL, YOU WILL LOSE.
APOLOGIZE FOR THE THREATS YOU UTTERED, AND WE SHALL OVERCOME THIS SLIGHT...

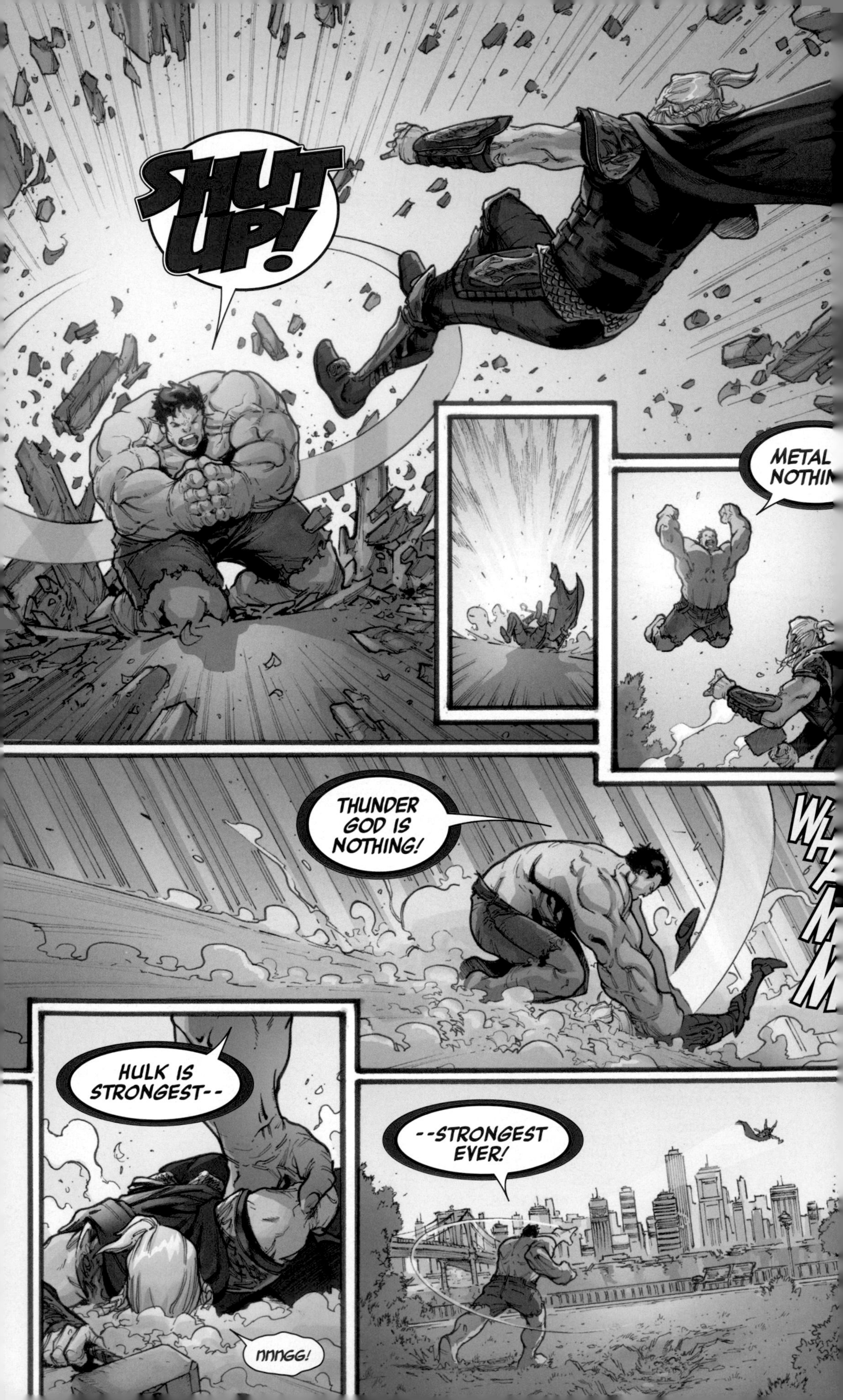
SHUT UP!
METAL NOTHIN
THUNDER GOD IS NOTHING!
HULK IS STRONGEST--
nnngg!
--STRONGEST EVER!

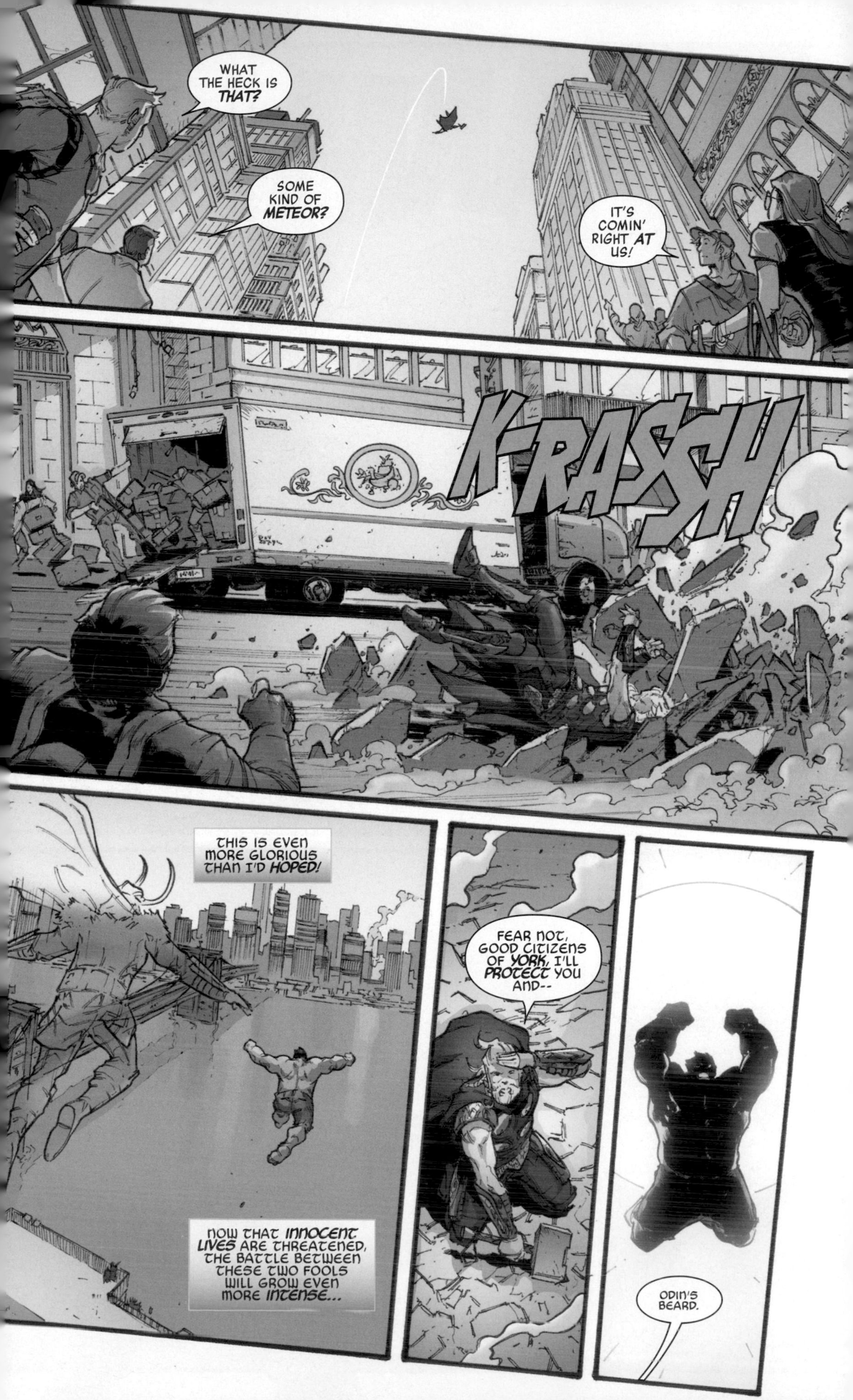
WHAT THE HECK IS THAT?
SOME KIND OF METEOR?
IT'S COMIN' RIGHT AT US!
K-RASSH
THIS IS EVEN MORE GLORIOUS THAN I'D HOPED!
NOW THAT INNOCENT LIVES ARE THREATENED, THE BATTLE BETWEEN THESE TWO FOOLS WILL GROW EVEN MORE INTENSE...
FEAR NOT, GOOD CITIZENS OF YORK, I'LL PROTECT YOU AND--
ODIN'S BEARD.

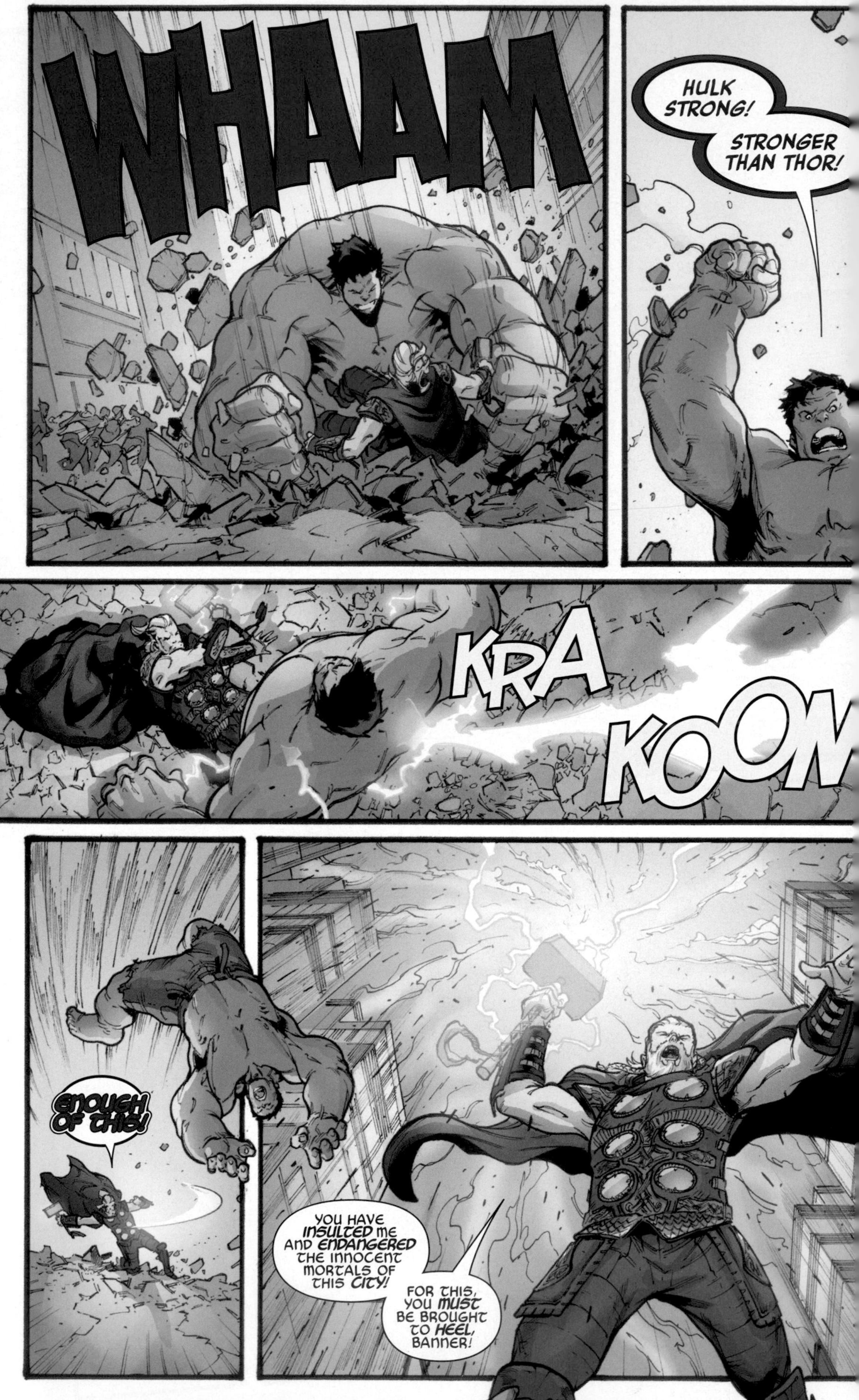
WHAAM
HULK STRONG!
STRONGER THAN THOR!
KRA
KOOM
ENOUGH OF THIS!
YOU HAVE INSULTED ME AND ENDANGERED THE INNOCENT MORTALS OF THIS CITY!
FOR THIS, YOU MUST BE BROUGHT TO HEEL, BANNER!

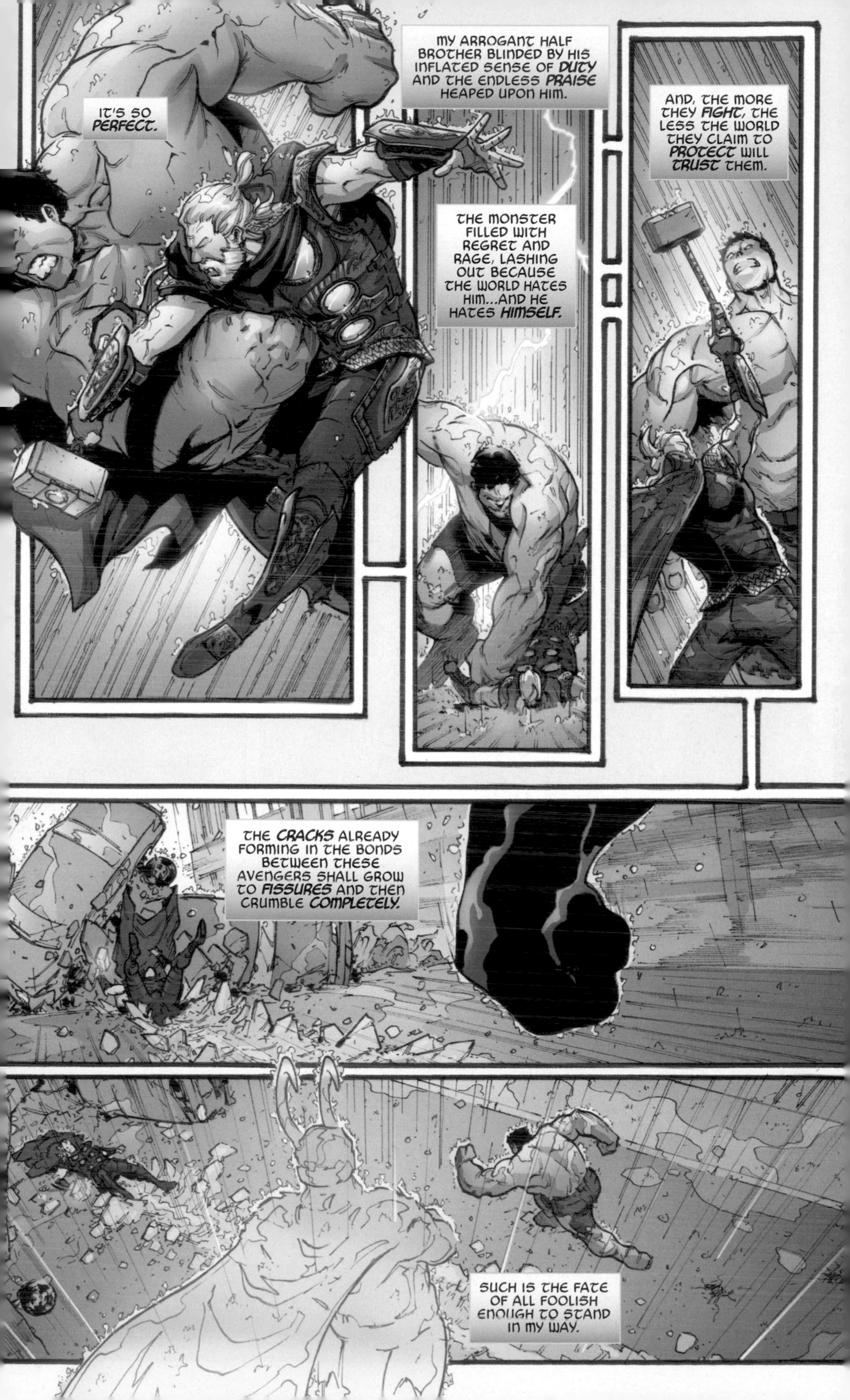
IT'S SO PERFECT.
MY ARROGANT HALF BROTHER BLINDED BY HIS INFLATED SENSE OF DUTY AND THE ENDLESS PRAISE HEAPED UPON HIM.
THE MONSTER FILLED WITH REGRET AND RAGE, LASHING OUT BECAUSE THE WORLD HATES HIM...AND HE HATES HIMSELF.
AND, THE MORE THEY FIGHT, THE LESS THE WORLD THEY CLAIM TO PROTECT WILL TRUST THEM.
THE CRACKS ALREADY FORMING IN THE BONDS BETWEEN THESE AVENGERS SHALL GROW TO FISSURES AND THEN CRUMBLE COMPLETELY.
SUCH IS THE FATE OF ALL FOOLISH ENOUGH TO STAND IN MY WAY.

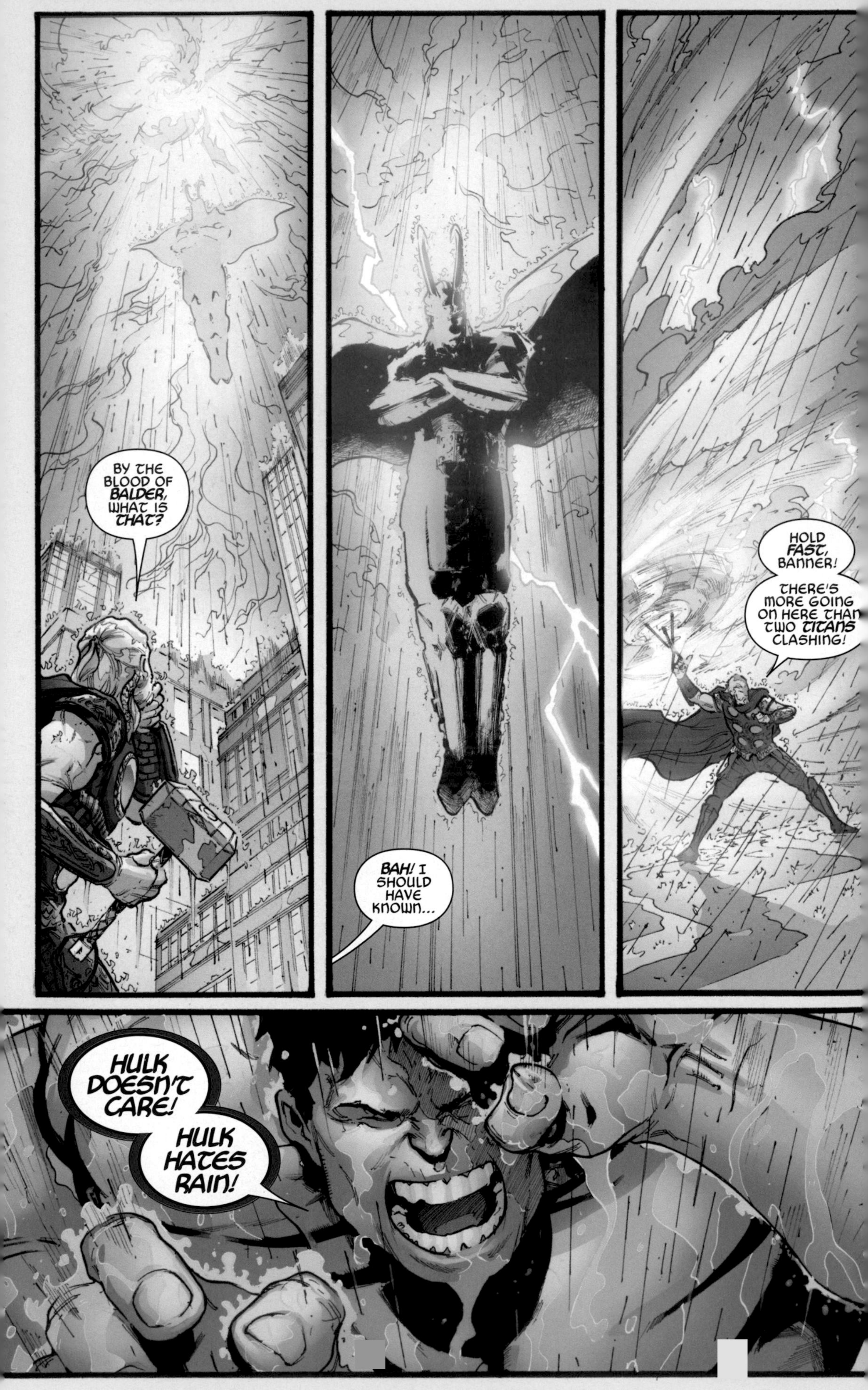

BY THE BLOOD OF BALDER, WHAT IS THAT?
BAH! I SHOULD HAVE KNOWN...
HOLD FAST, BANNER!
THERE'S MORE GOING ON HERE THAN TWO TITANS CLASHING!
HULK DOESN'T CARE!
HULK HATES RAIN!

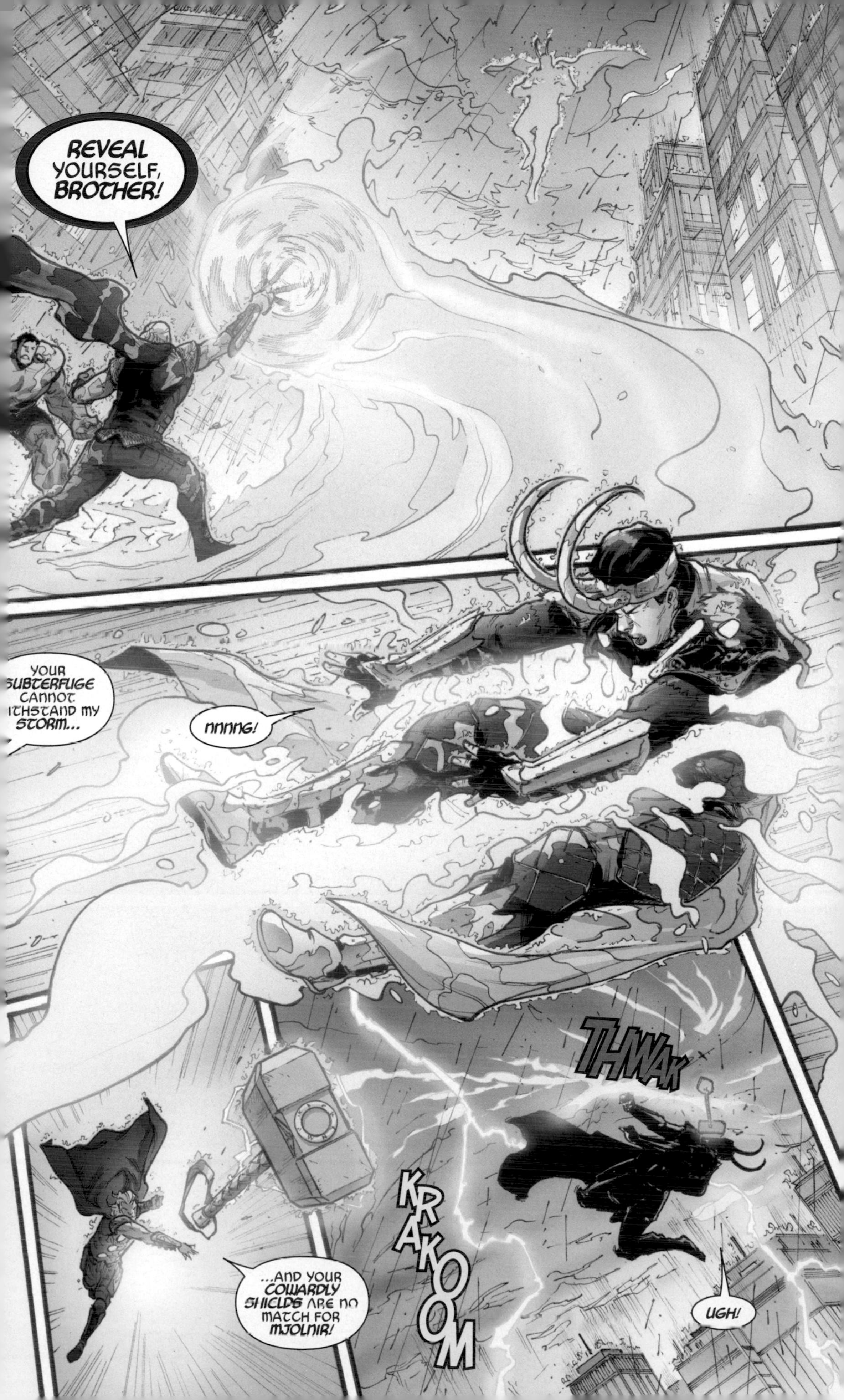
REVEAL YOURSELF, BROTHER!
YOUR SUBTERFUGE CANNOT WITHSTAND MY STORM...
NNNNG!
THWAK
KRAKOOM
...AND YOUR COWARDLY SHIELDS ARE NO MATCH FOR MJOLNIR!
UGH!

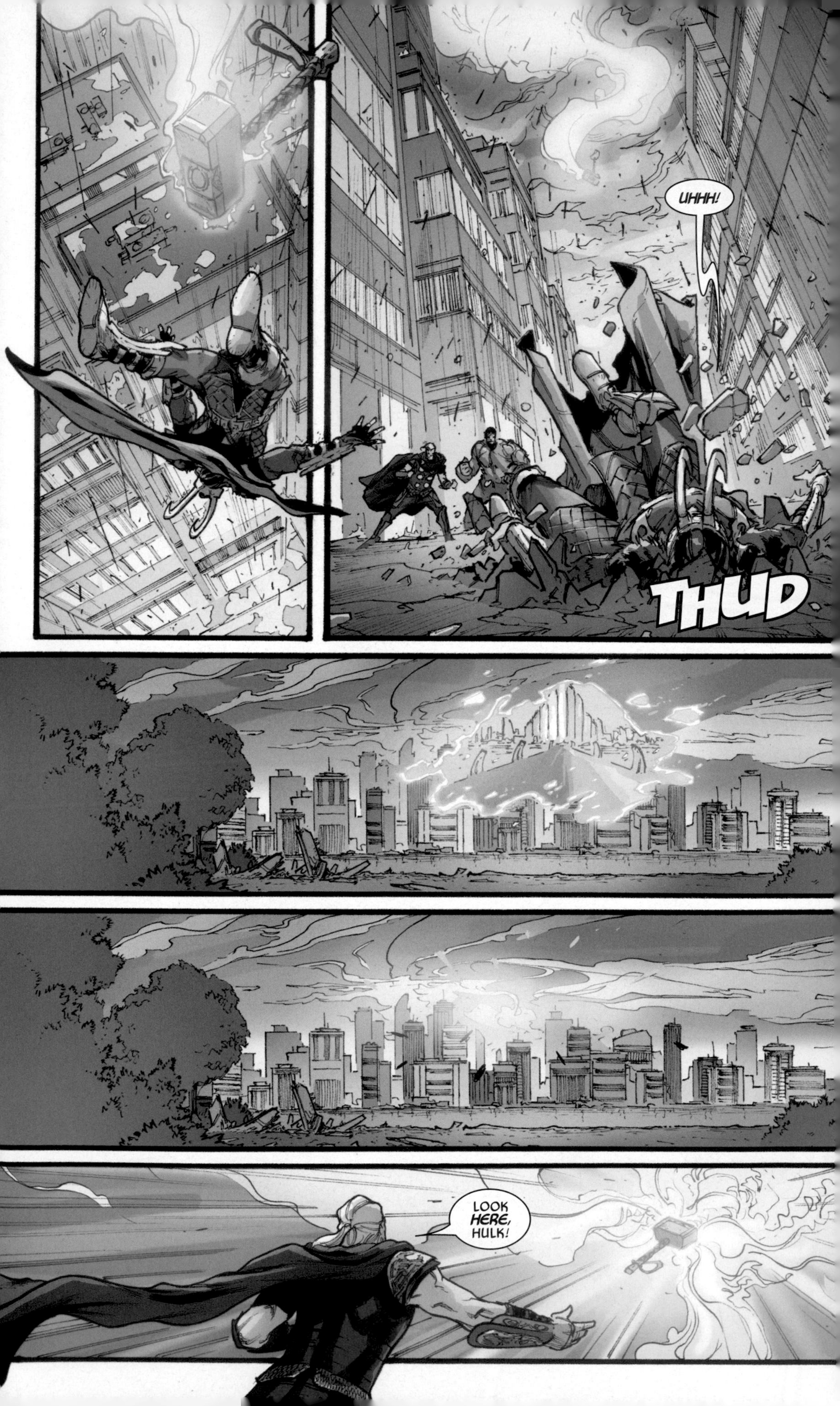
UHHH!
THUD
LOOK HERE, HULK!

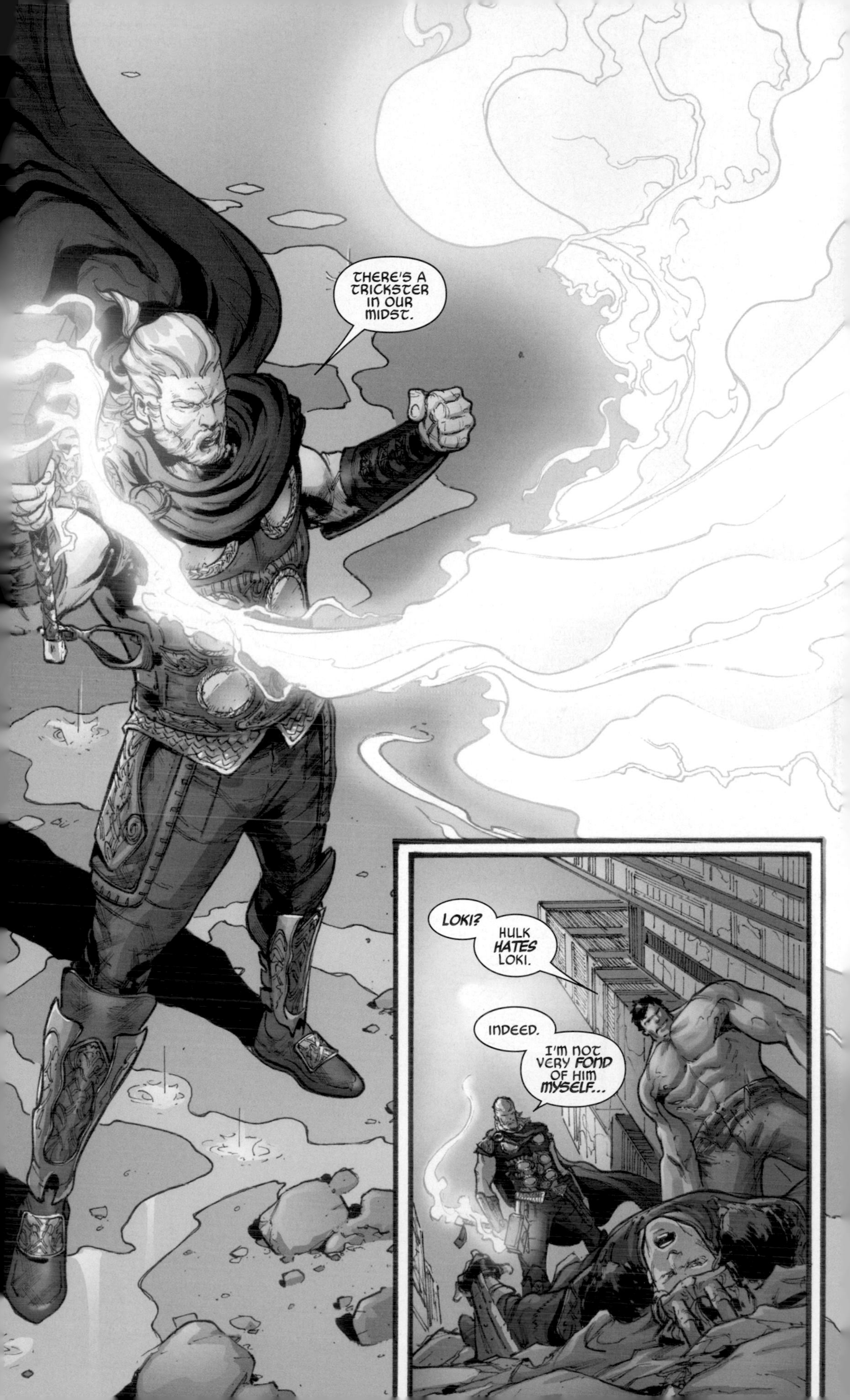
THERE'S A TRICKSTER IN OUR MIDST.
LOKI?
HULK HATES LOKI.
INDEED.
I'M NOT VERY FOND OF HIM MYSELF...

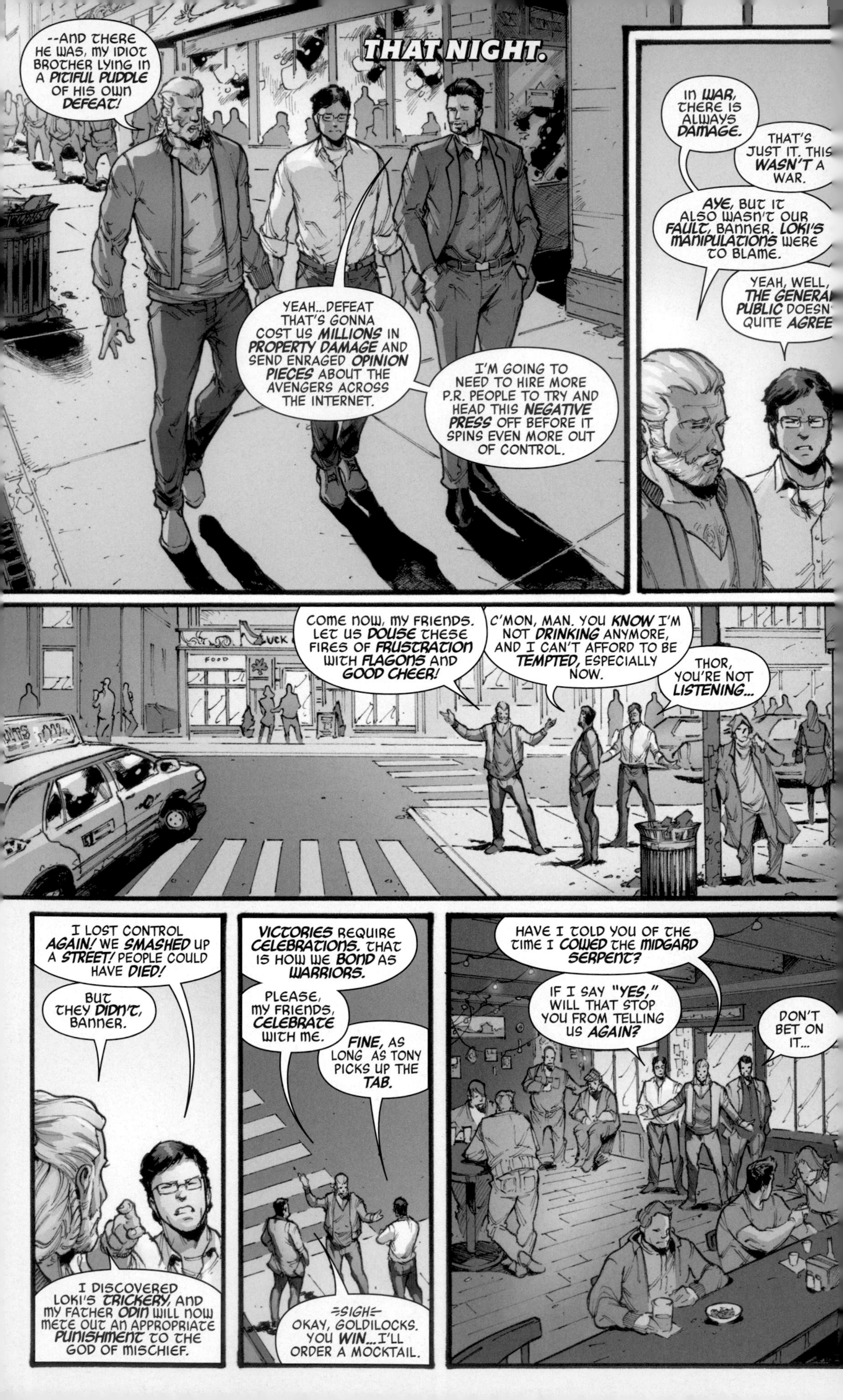
THAT NIGHT.
--AND THERE HE WAS, MY IDIOT BROTHER LYING IN A PITIFUL PUDDLE OF HIS OWN DEFEAT!
YEAH...DEFEAT THAT'S GONNA COST US MILLIONS IN PROPERTY DAMAGE AND SEND ENRAGED OPINION PIECES ABOUT THE AVENGERS ACROSS THE INTERNET.
I'M GOING TO NEED TO HIRE MORE P.R. PEOPLE TO TRY AND HEAD THIS NEGATIVE PRESS OFF BEFORE IT SPINS EVEN MORE OUT OF CONTROL.
IN WAR, THERE IS ALWAYS DAMAGE.
THAT'S JUST IT. THIS WASN'T A WAR.
AYE, BUT IT ALSO WASN'T OUR FAULT, BANNER. LOKI'S MANIPULATIONS WERE TO BLAME.
YEAH, WELL, THE GENERAL PUBLIC DOESN'T QUITE AGREE
COME NOW, MY FRIENDS. LET US DOUSE THESE FIRES OF FRUSTRATION WITH FLAGONS AND GOOD CHEER!
C'MON, MAN. YOU KNOW I'M NOT DRINKING ANYMORE, AND I CAN'T AFFORD TO BE TEMPTED, ESPECIALLY NOW.
THOR, YOU'RE NOT LISTENING...
I LOST CONTROL AGAIN! WE SMASHED UP A STREET! PEOPLE COULD HAVE DIED!
BUT THEY DIDN'T, BANNER.
I DISCOVERED LOKI'S TRICKERY, AND MY FATHER ODIN WILL NOW METE OUT AN APPROPRIATE PUNISHMENT TO THE GOD OF MISCHIEF.
VICTORIES REQUIRE CELEBRATIONS. THAT IS HOW WE BOND AS WARRIORS.
PLEASE, MY FRIENDS, CELEBRATE WITH ME.
FINE, AS LONG AS TONY PICKS UP THE TAB.
=SIGH= OKAY, GOLDILOCKS. YOU WIN...I'LL ORDER A MOCKTAIL.
HAVE I TOLD YOU OF THE TIME I COWED THE MIDGARD SERPENT?
IF I SAY "YES," WILL THAT STOP YOU FROM TELLING US AGAIN?
DON'T BET ON IT...

HULK

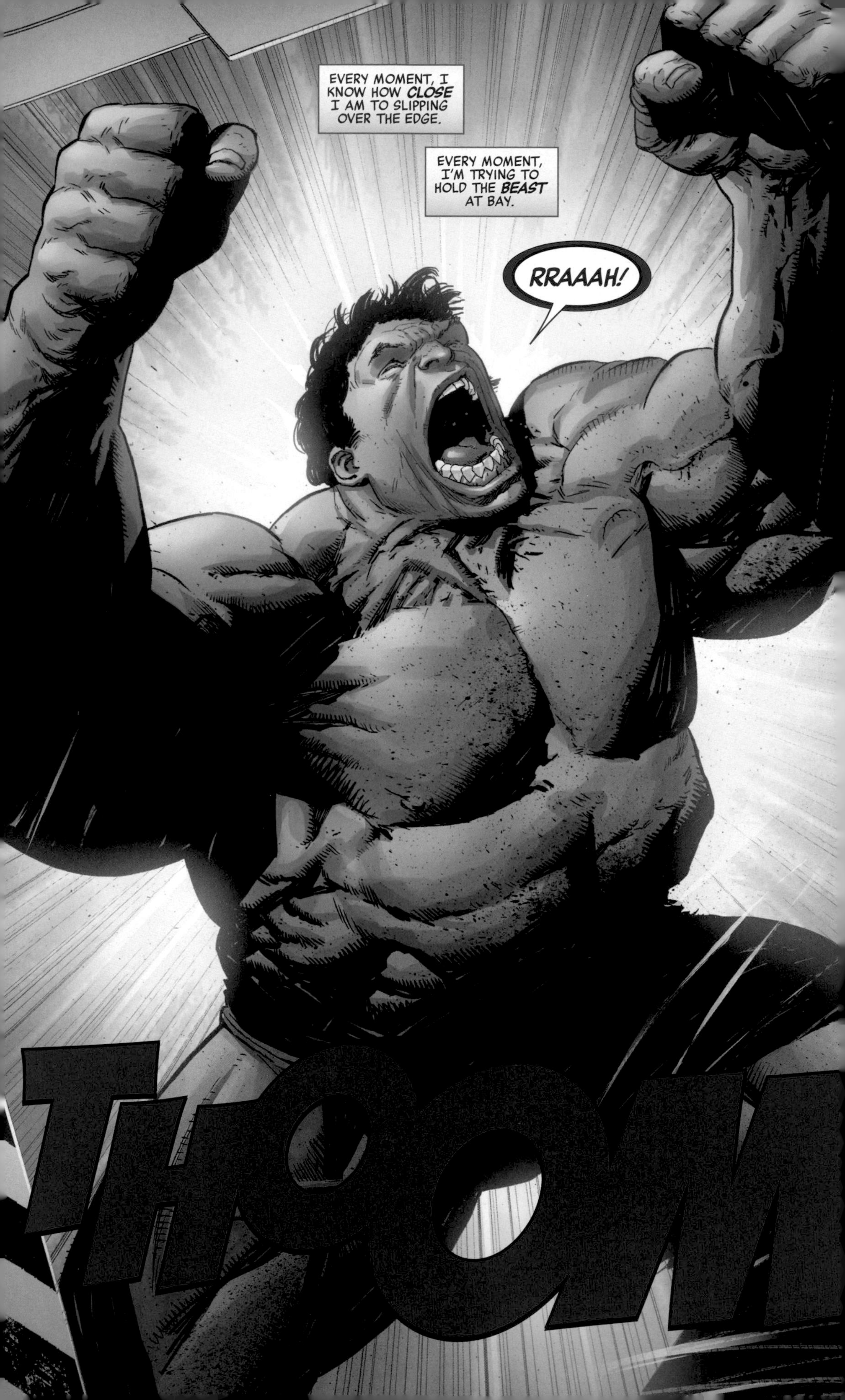
EVERY MOMENT, I KNOW HOW CLOSE I AM TO SLIPPING OVER THE EDGE.
EVERY MOMENT, I'M TRYING TO HOLD THE BEAST AT BAY.
RRAAAH!
THOOM

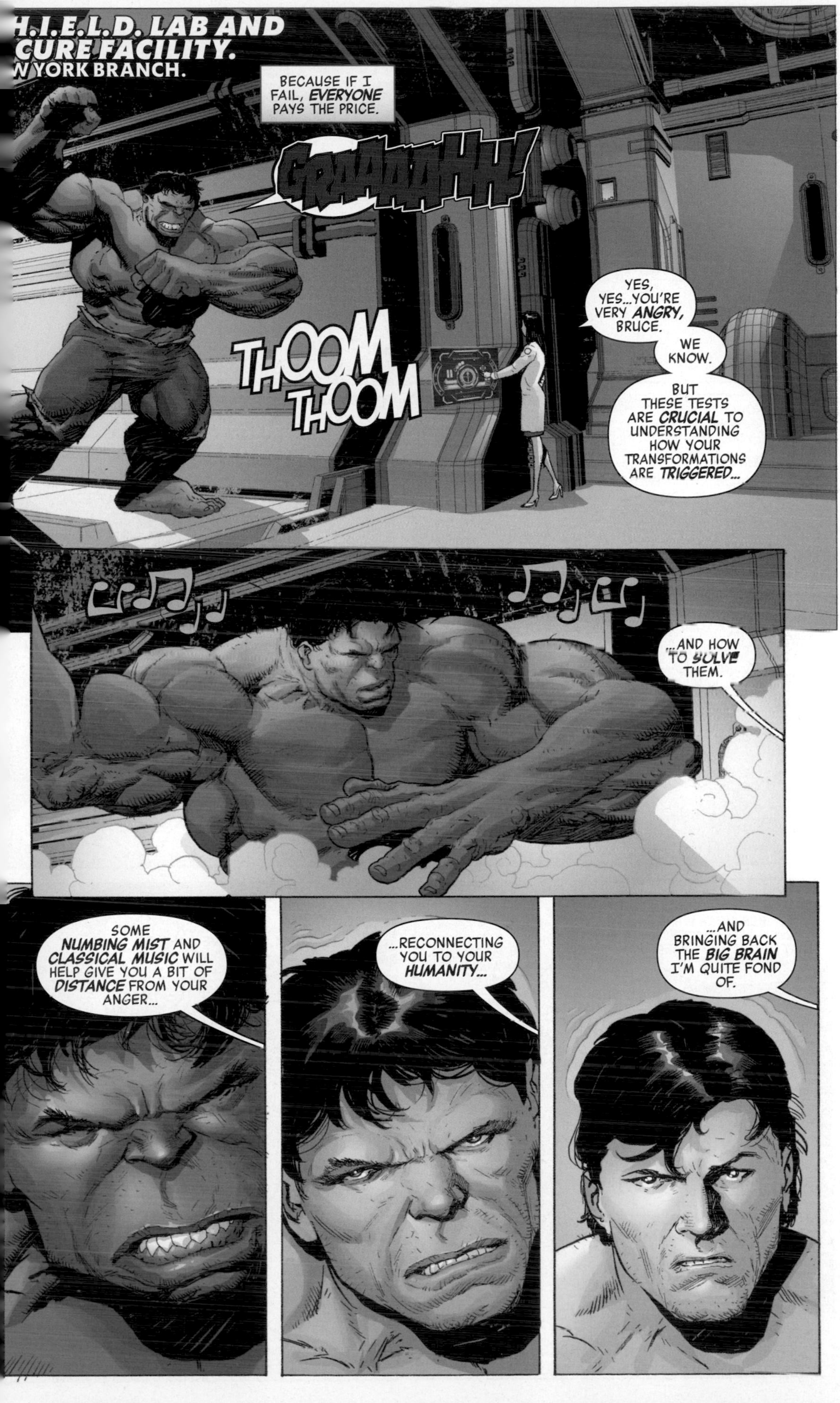
H.I.E.L.D. LAB AND
CURE FACILITY.
W YORK BRANCH.
BECAUSE IF I FAIL, EVERYONE PAYS THE PRICE.
GRAAAAHHH!
THOOM THOOM
YES, YES...YOU'RE VERY ANGRY, BRUCE.
WE KNOW.
BUT THESE TESTS ARE CRUCIAL TO UNDERSTANDING HOW YOUR TRANSFORMATIONS ARE TRIGGERED...
...AND HOW TO SOLVE THEM.
SOME NUMBING MIST AND CLASSICAL MUSIC WILL HELP GIVE YOU A BIT OF DISTANCE FROM YOUR ANGER...
...RECONNECTING YOU TO YOUR HUMANITY...
...AND BRINGING BACK THE BIG BRAIN I'M QUITE FOND OF.

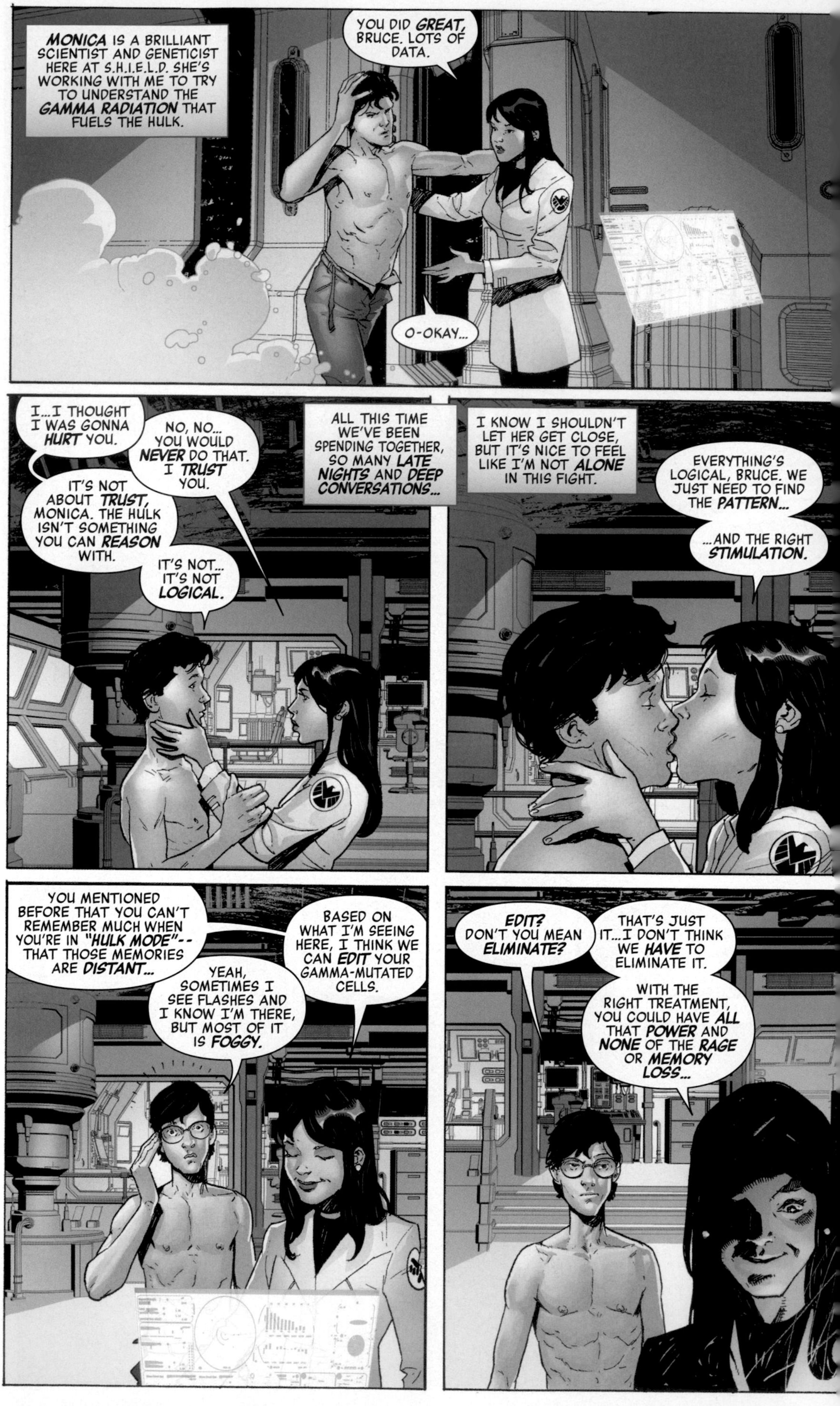
MONICA IS A BRILLIANT SCIENTIST AND GENETICIST HERE AT S.H.I.E.L.D. SHE'S WORKING WITH ME TO TRY TO UNDERSTAND THE GAMMA RADIATION THAT FUELS THE HULK.
YOU DID GREAT, BRUCE. LOTS OF DATA.
O-OKAY...
I...I THOUGHT I WAS GONNA HURT YOU.
NO, NO... YOU WOULD NEVER DO THAT. I TRUST YOU.
IT'S NOT ABOUT TRUST, MONICA. THE HULK ISN'T SOMETHING YOU CAN REASON WITH.
IT'S NOT... IT'S NOT LOGICAL.
ALL THIS TIME WE'VE BEEN SPENDING TOGETHER, SO MANY LATE NIGHTS AND DEEP CONVERSATIONS...
I KNOW I SHOULDN'T LET HER GET CLOSE, BUT IT'S NICE TO FEEL LIKE I'M NOT ALONE IN THIS FIGHT.
EVERYTHING'S LOGICAL, BRUCE. WE JUST NEED TO FIND THE PATTERN...
...AND THE RIGHT STIMULATION.
YOU MENTIONED BEFORE THAT YOU CAN'T REMEMBER MUCH WHEN YOU'RE IN "HULK MODE"-- THAT THOSE MEMORIES ARE DISTANT...
YEAH, SOMETIMES I SEE FLASHES AND I KNOW I'M THERE, BUT MOST OF IT IS FOGGY.
BASED ON WHAT I'M SEEING HERE, I THINK WE CAN EDIT YOUR GAMMA-MUTATED CELLS.
EDIT? DON'T YOU MEAN ELIMINATE?
THAT'S JUST IT...I DON'T THINK WE HAVE TO ELIMINATE IT.
WITH THE RIGHT TREATMENT, YOU COULD HAVE ALL THAT POWER AND NONE OF THE RAGE OR MEMORY LOSS...

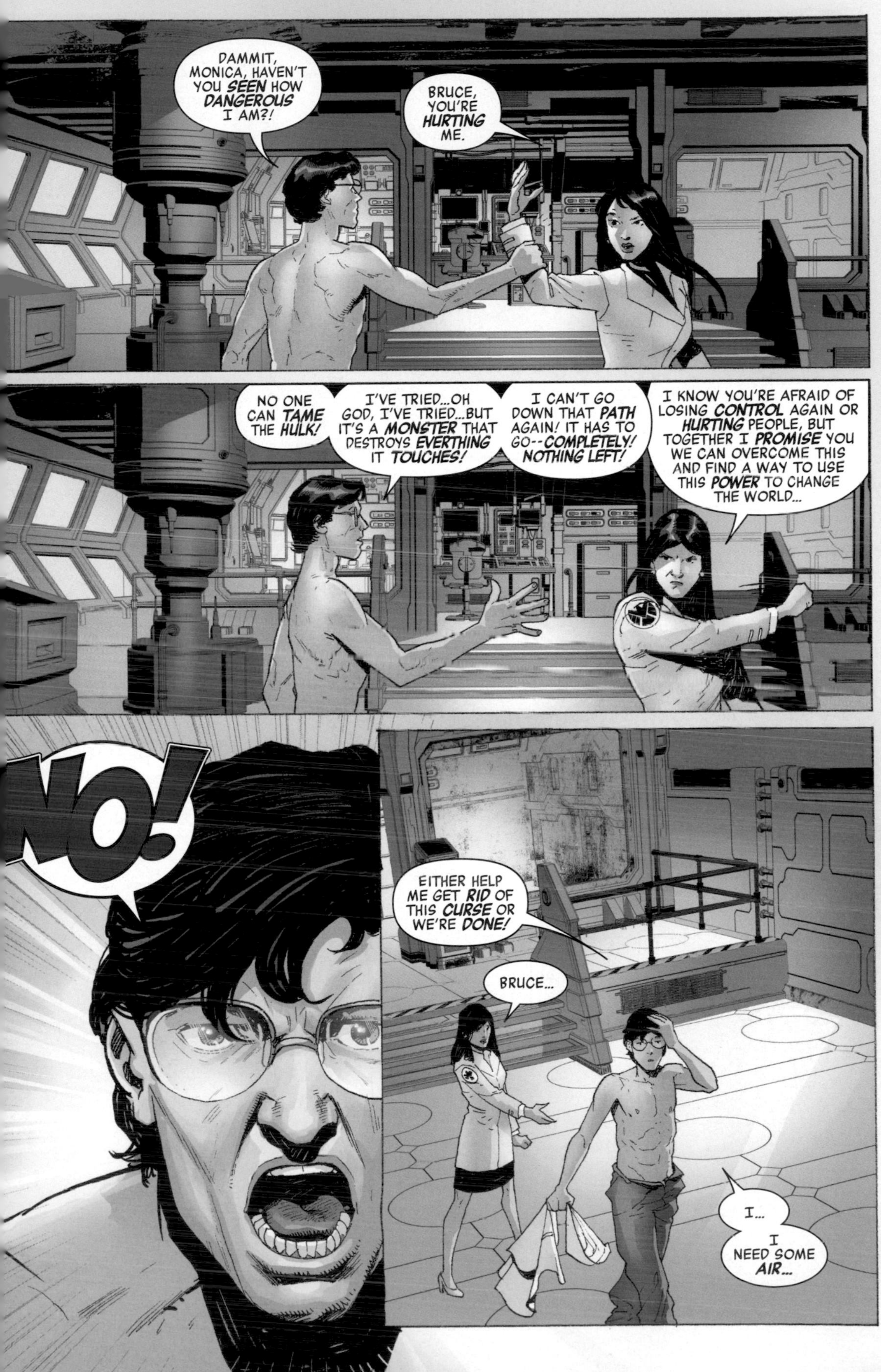
DAMMIT, MONICA, HAVEN'T YOU SEEN HOW DANGEROUS I AM?!
BRUCE, YOU'RE HURTING ME.
NO ONE CAN TAME THE HULK!
I'VE TRIED...OH GOD, I'VE TRIED...BUT IT'S A MONSTER THAT DESTROYS EVERTHING IT TOUCHES!
I CAN'T GO DOWN THAT PATH AGAIN! IT HAS TO GO--COMPLETELY! NOTHING LEFT!
I KNOW YOU'RE AFRAID OF LOSING CONTROL AGAIN OR HURTING PEOPLE, BUT TOGETHER I PROMISE YOU WE CAN OVERCOME THIS AND FIND A WAY TO USE THIS POWER TO CHANGE THE WORLD...
NO!
EITHER HELP ME GET RID OF THIS CURSE OR WE'RE DONE!
BRUCE...
I... I NEED SOME AIR...

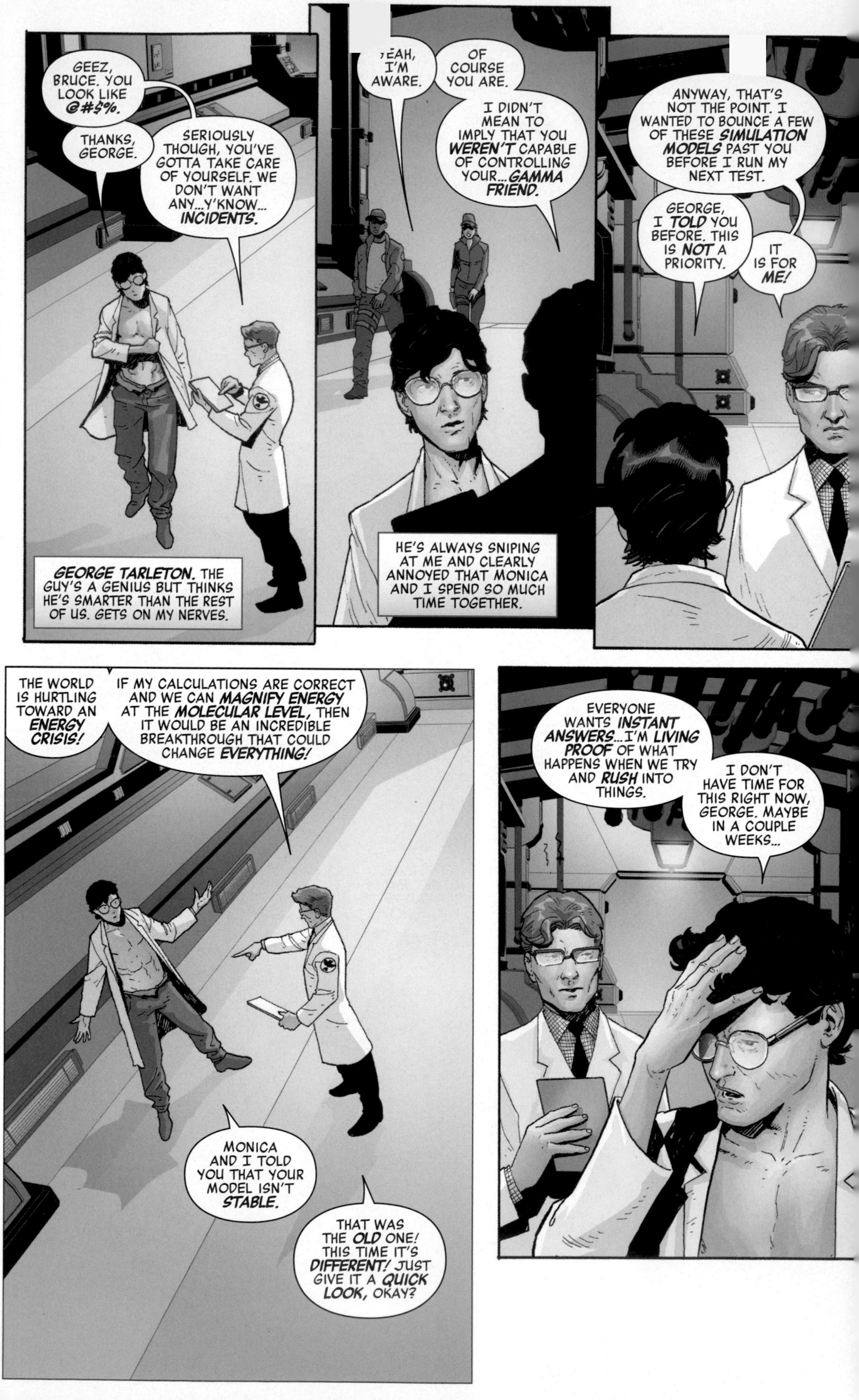
GEEZ, BRUCE. YOU LOOK LIKE @#$%.
THANKS, GEORGE.
SERIOUSLY THOUGH, YOU'VE GOTTA TAKE CARE OF YOURSELF. WE DON'T WANT ANY...Y'KNOW... INCIDENTS.
GEORGE TARLETON. THE GUY'S A GENIUS BUT THINKS HE'S SMARTER THAN THE REST OF US. GETS ON MY NERVES.
EAH, I'M AWARE.
OF COURSE YOU ARE.
I DIDN'T MEAN TO IMPLY THAT YOU WEREN'T CAPABLE OF CONTROLLING YOUR...GAMMA FRIEND.
HE'S ALWAYS SNIPING AT ME AND CLEARLY ANNOYED THAT MONICA AND I SPEND SO MUCH TIME TOGETHER.
ANYWAY, THAT'S NOT THE POINT. I WANTED TO BOUNCE A FEW OF THESE SIMULATION MODELS PAST YOU BEFORE I RUN MY NEXT TEST.
GEORGE, I TOLD YOU BEFORE. THIS IS NOT A PRIORITY.
IT IS FOR ME!
THE WORLD IS HURTLING TOWARD AN ENERGY CRISIS!
IF MY CALCULATIONS ARE CORRECT AND WE CAN MAGNIFY ENERGY AT THE MOLECULAR LEVEL, THEN IT WOULD BE AN INCREDIBLE BREAKTHROUGH THAT COULD CHANGE EVERYTHING!
MONICA AND I TOLD YOU THAT YOUR MODEL ISN'T STABLE.
THAT WAS THE OLD ONE! THIS TIME IT'S DIFFERENT! JUST GIVE IT A QUICK LOOK, OKAY?
EVERYONE WANTS INSTANT ANSWERS...I'M LIVING PROOF OF WHAT HAPPENS WHEN WE TRY AND RUSH INTO THINGS.
I DON'T HAVE TIME FOR THIS RIGHT NOW, GEORGE. MAYBE IN A COUPLE WEEKS...

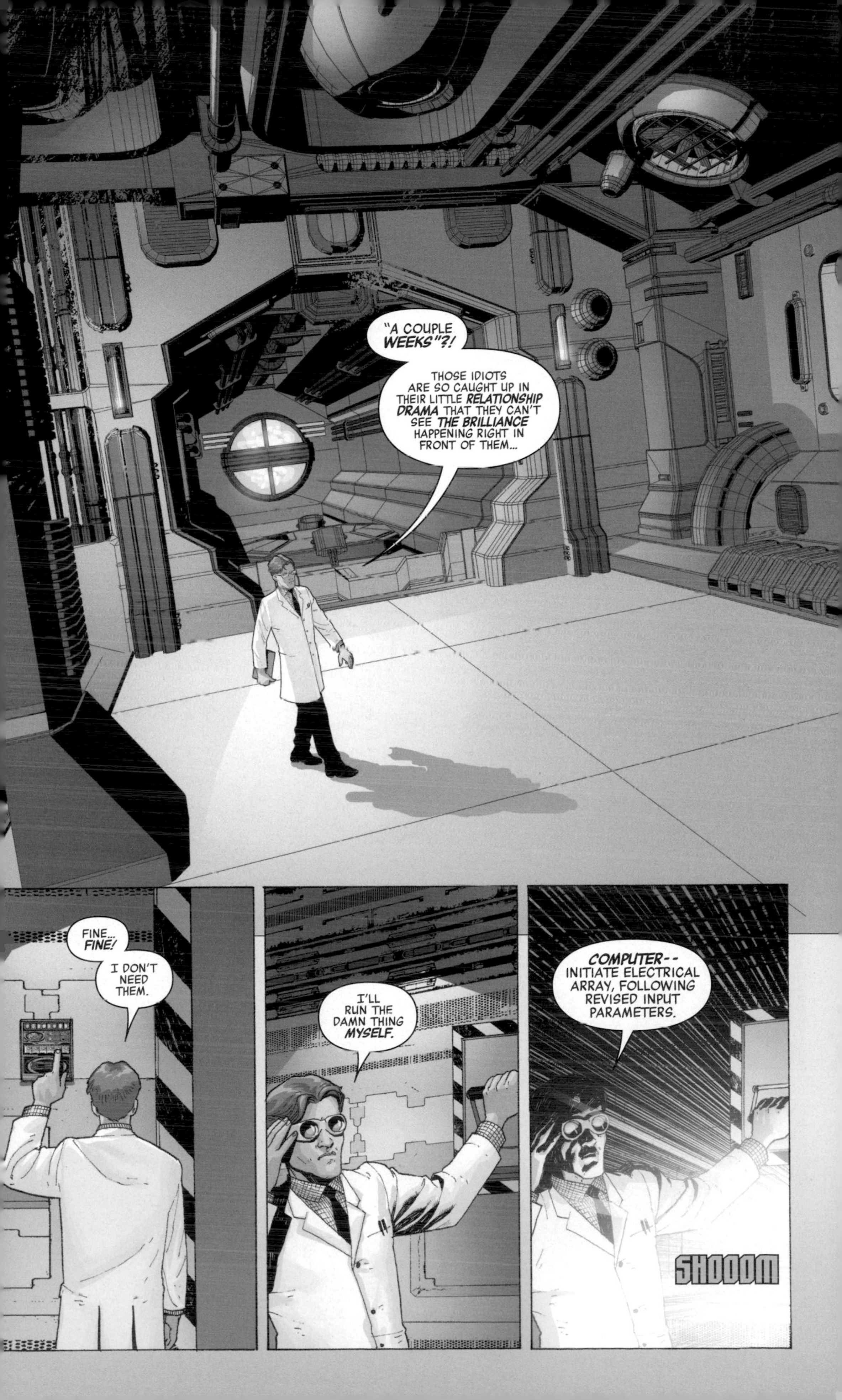
"A COUPLE WEEKS"?!
THOSE IDIOTS ARE SO CAUGHT UP IN THEIR LITTLE RELATIONSHIP DRAMA THAT THEY CAN'T SEE THE BRILLIANCE HAPPENING RIGHT IN FRONT OF THEM...
FINE... FINE!
I DON'T NEED THEM.
I'LL RUN THE DAMN THING MYSELF.
COMPUTER-- INITIATE ELECTRICAL ARRAY, FOLLOWING REVISED INPUT PARAMETERS.
SHOOOM

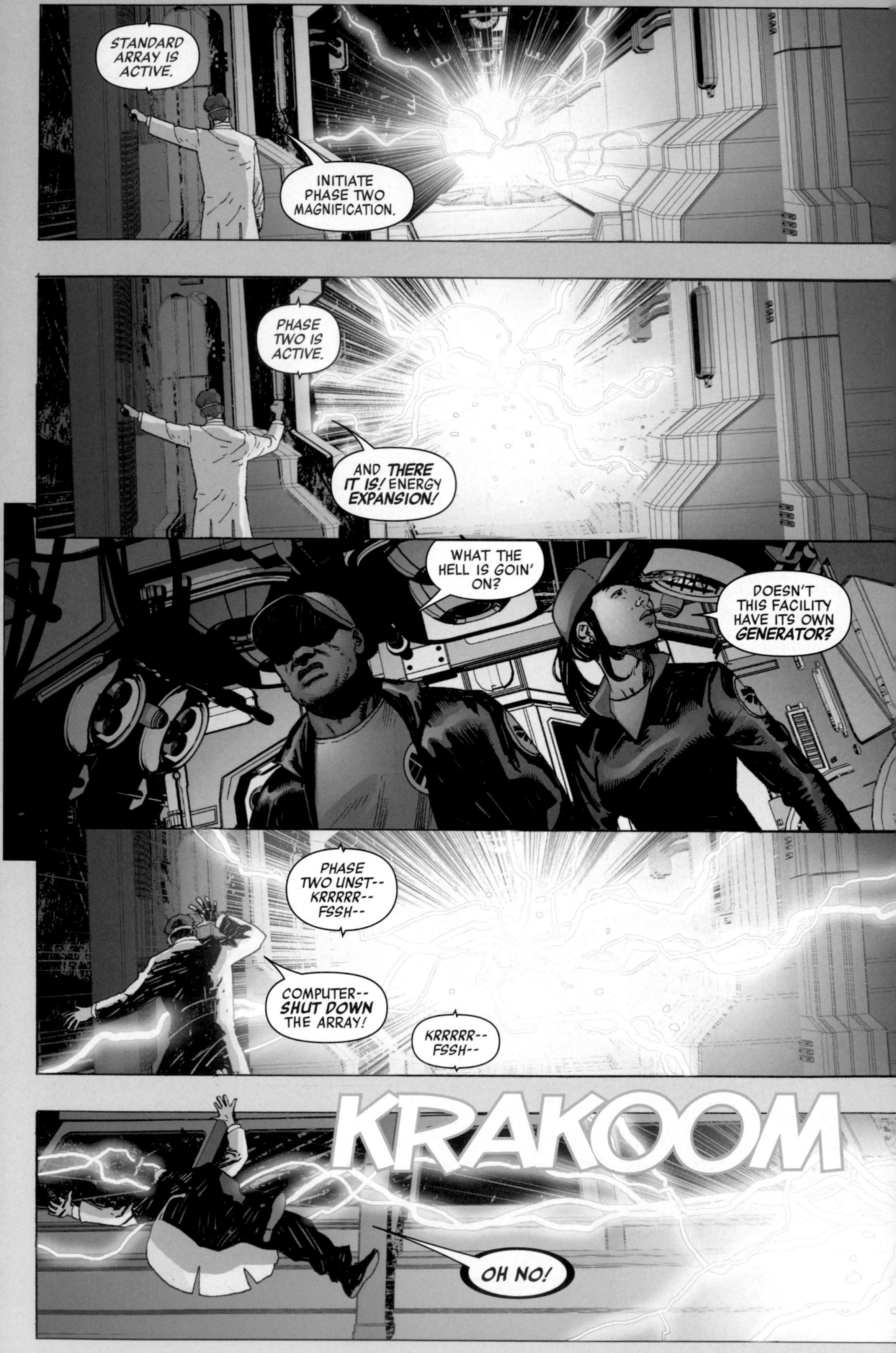
STANDARD ARRAY IS ACTIVE.
INITIATE PHASE TWO MAGNIFICATION.
PHASE TWO IS ACTIVE.
AND THERE IT IS! ENERGY EXPANSION!
WHAT THE HELL IS GOIN' ON?
DOESN'T THIS FACILITY HAVE ITS OWN GENERATOR?
PHASE TWO UNST-- KRRRRR-- FSSH--
COMPUTER-- SHUT DOWN THE ARRAY!
KRRRRR-- FSSH--
KRAKOOM
OH NO!

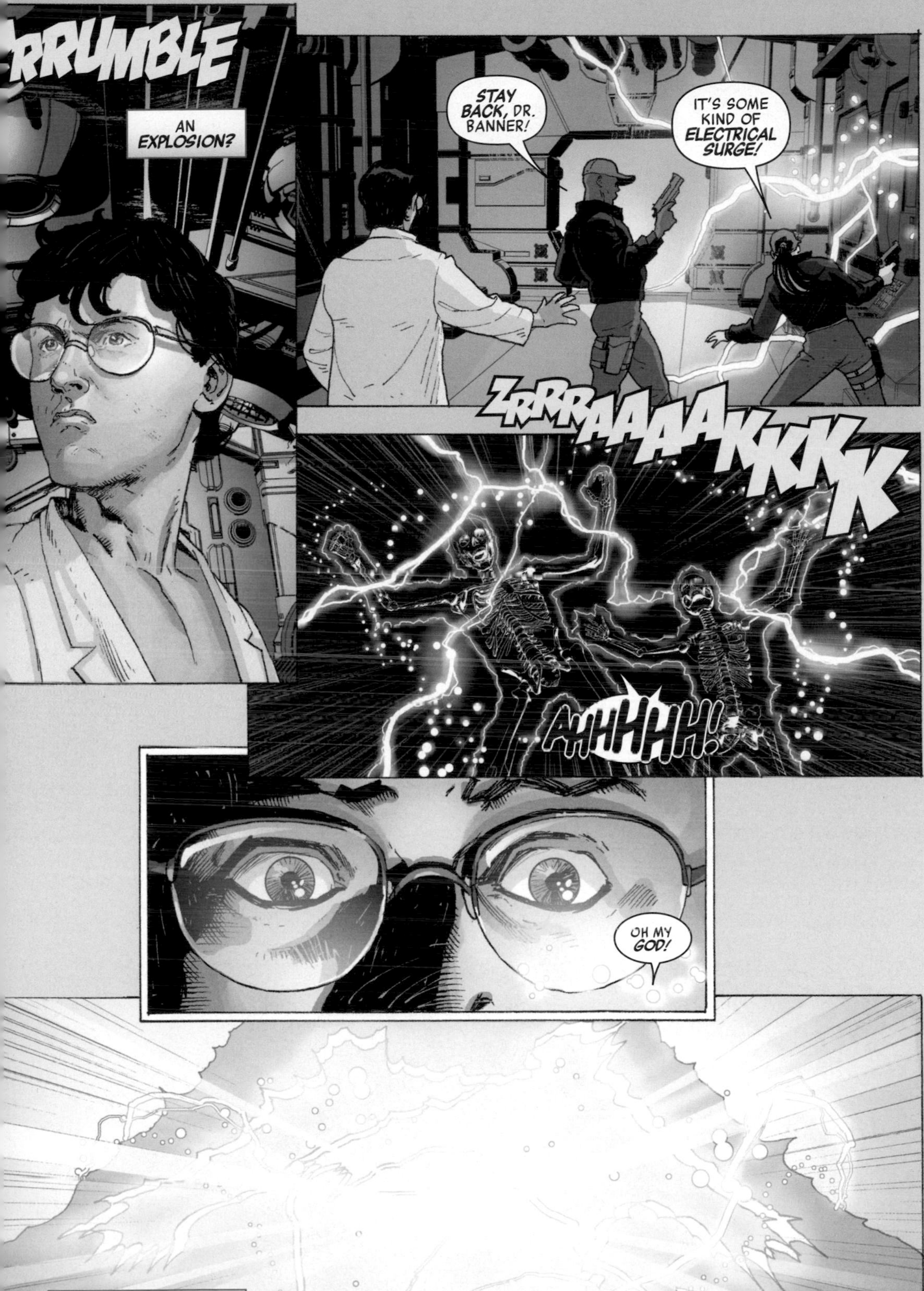
RRUMBLE
AN EXPLOSION?
STAY BACK, DR. BANNER!
IT'S SOME KIND OF ELECTRICAL SURGE!
ZRRRAAAAKKKK
AHHHH!
OH MY GOD!
THE GUARDS... THEIR BODIES MERGE WITH THE ELECTRICITY AND THEIR SCREAMS BECOME PULSES OF STATIC.

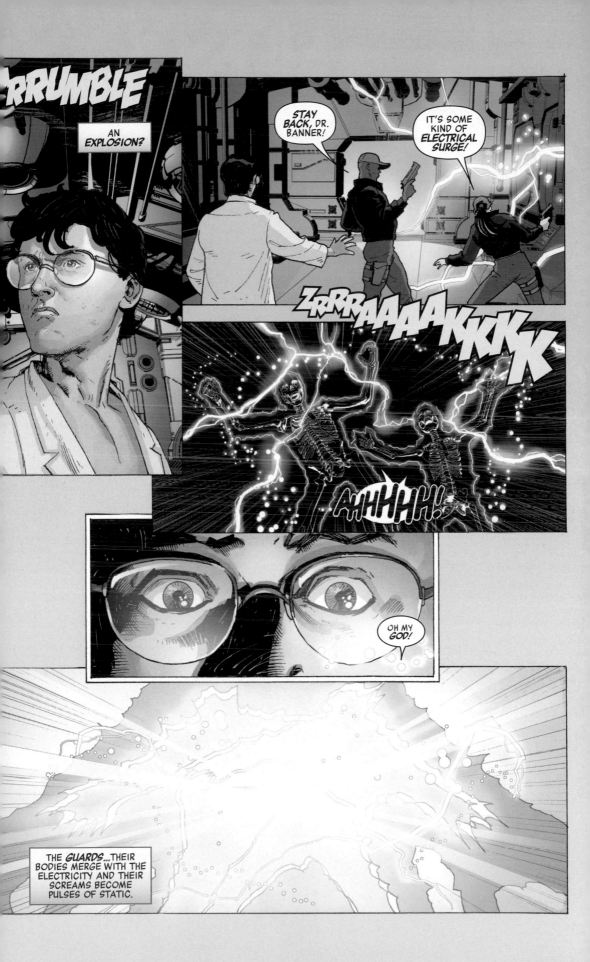

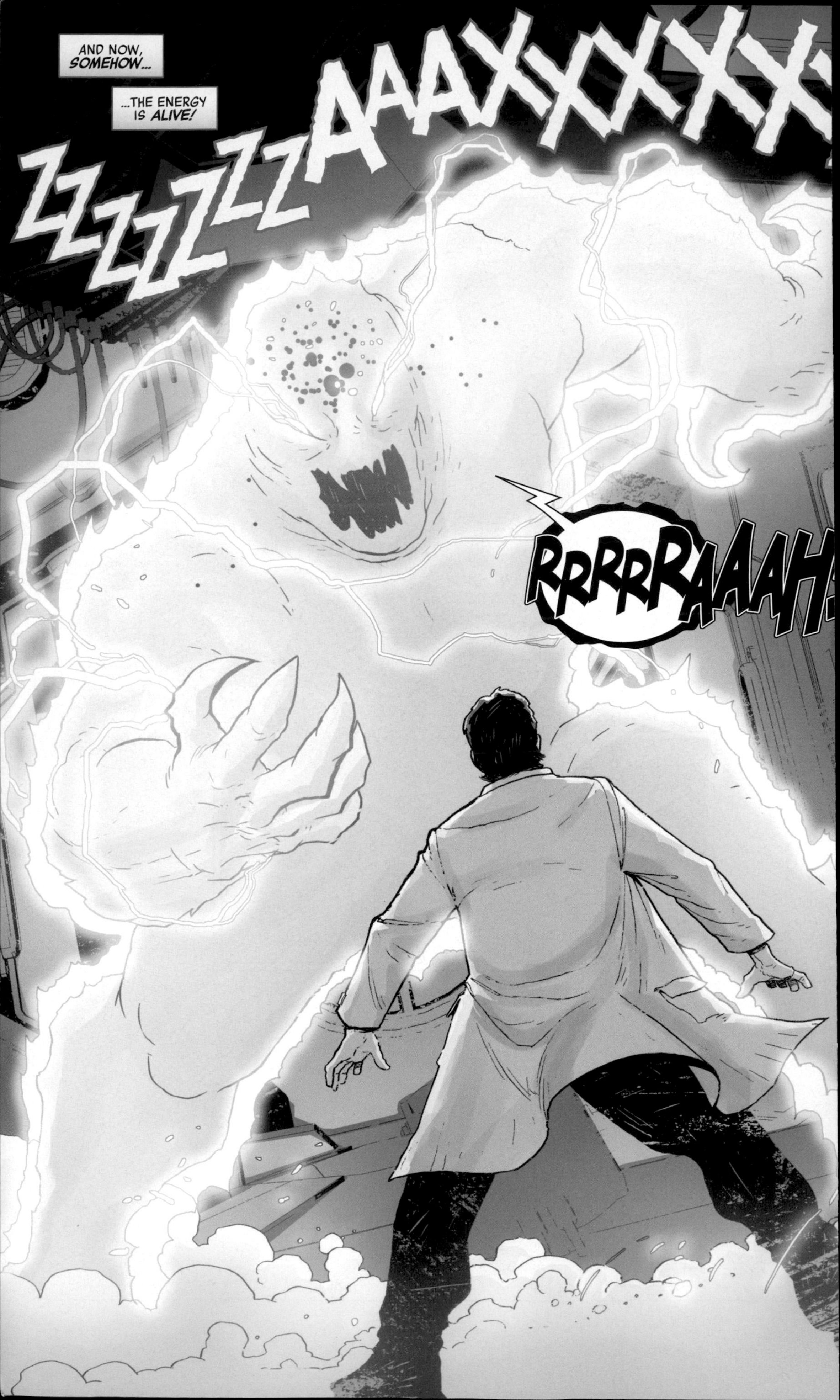
AND NOW, SOMEHOW...
...THE ENERGY IS ALIVE!
ZZZZZZZZAAAXXXX
RRRRRAAAH!

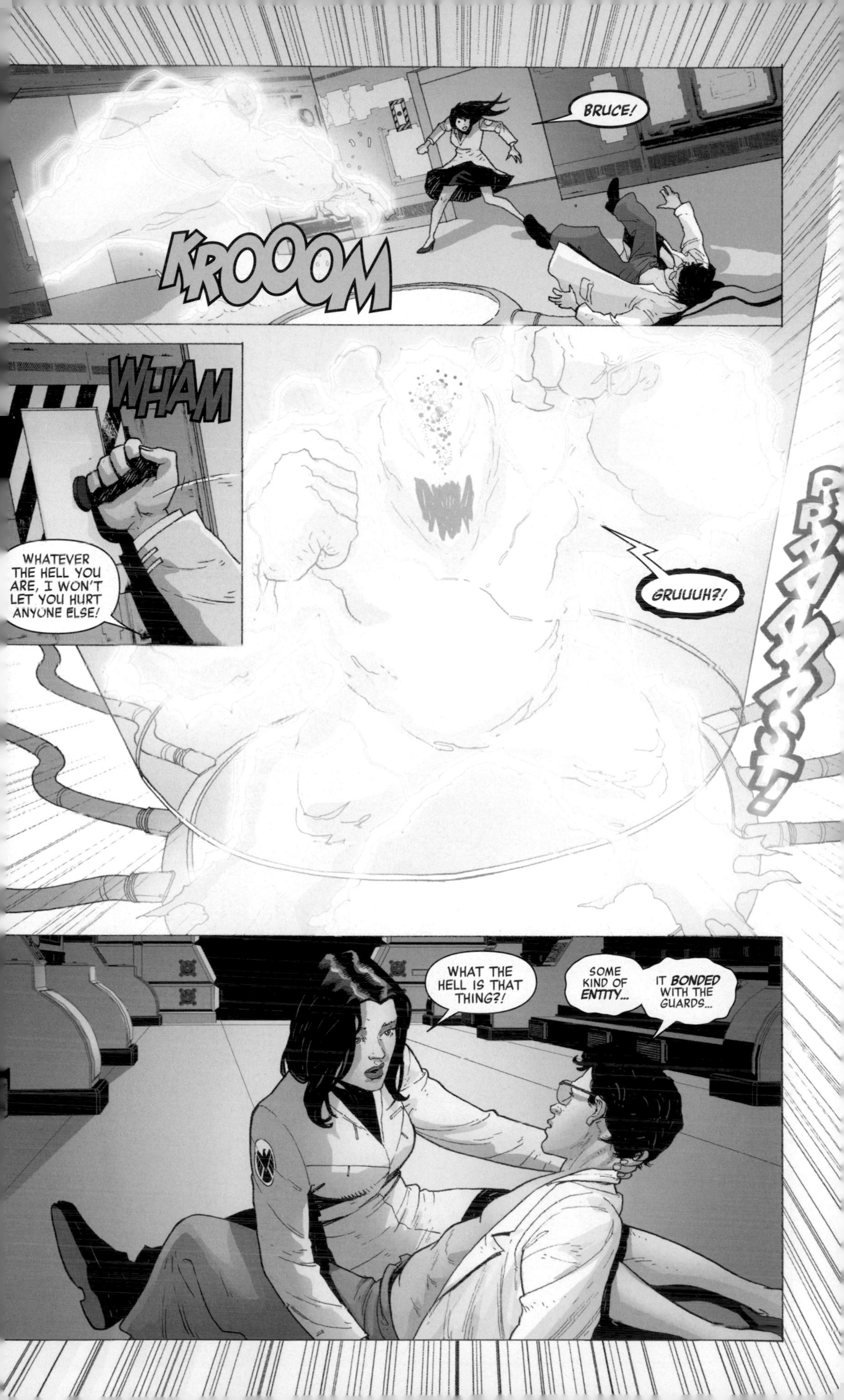
BRUCE!
KROOOOM
WHAM
WHATEVER THE HELL YOU ARE, I WON'T LET YOU HURT ANYONE ELSE!
GRUUUH?!
RRAAAASH!
WHAT THE HELL IS THAT THING?!
SOME KIND OF ENTITY...
IT BONDED WITH THE GUARDS...

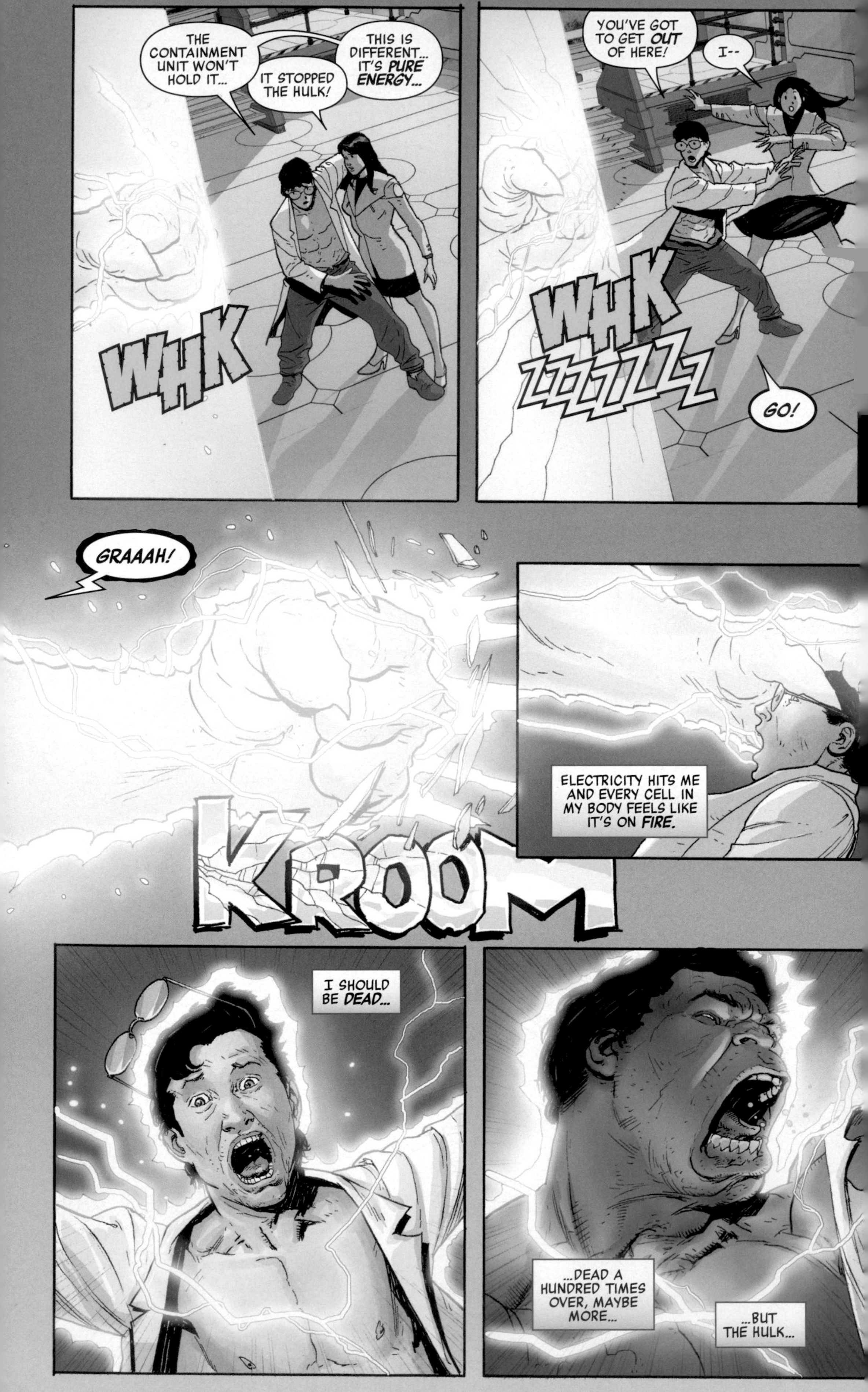
THE CONTAINMENT UNIT WON'T HOLD IT...
IT STOPPED THE HULK!
THIS IS DIFFERENT... IT'S PURE ENERGY...
WHK
YOU'VE GOT TO GET OUT OF HERE!
I--
WHK
ZZZZZZZZ
GO!
GRAAAH!
ELECTRICITY HITS ME AND EVERY CELL IN MY BODY FEELS LIKE IT'S ON FIRE.
KROOM
I SHOULD BE DEAD...
...DEAD A HUNDRED TIMES OVER, MAYBE MORE...
...BUT THE HULK...

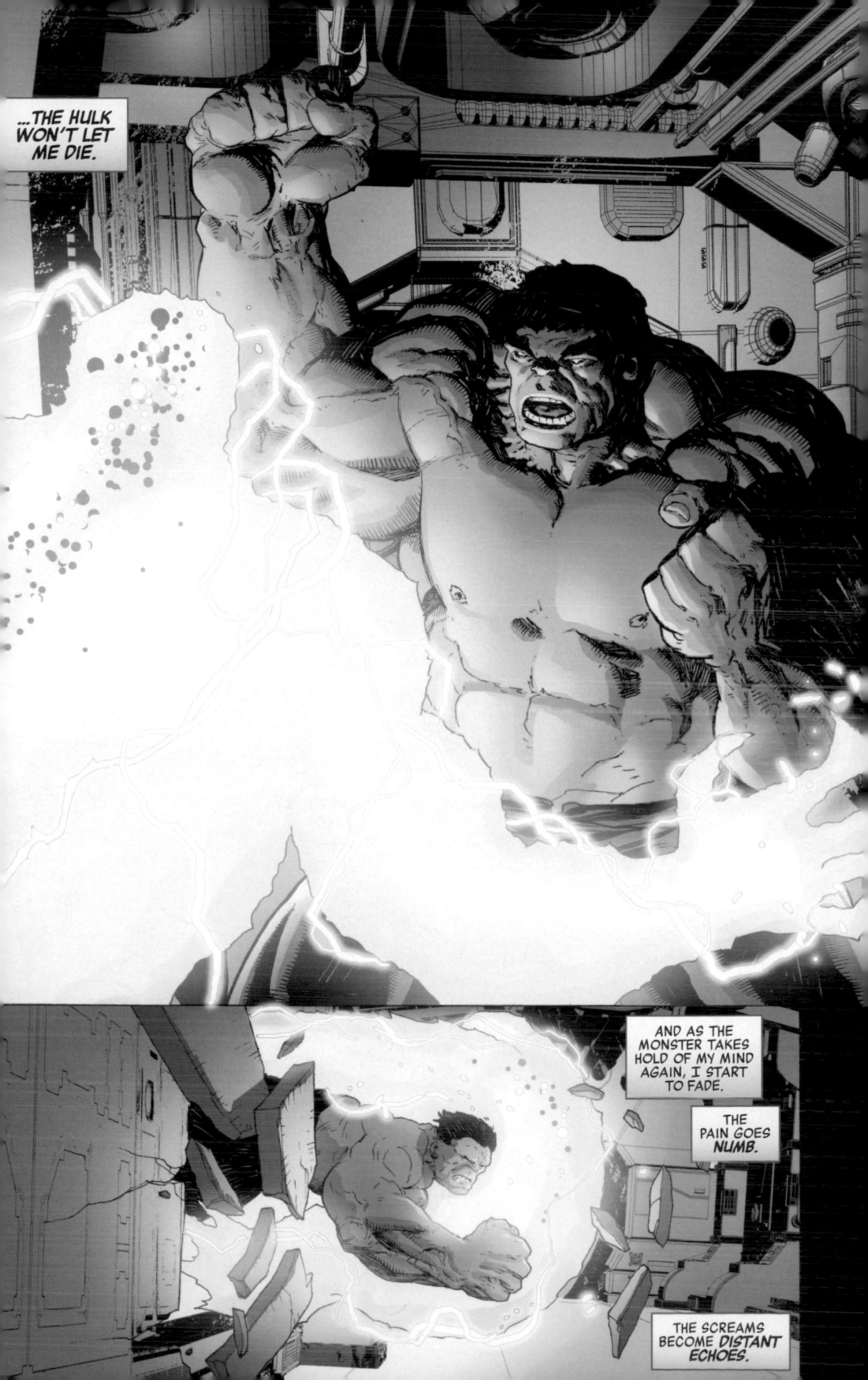
...THE HULK WON'T LET ME DIE.
AND AS THE MONSTER TAKES HOLD OF MY MIND AGAIN, I START TO FADE.
THE PAIN GOES NUMB.
THE SCREAMS BECOME DISTANT ECHOES.

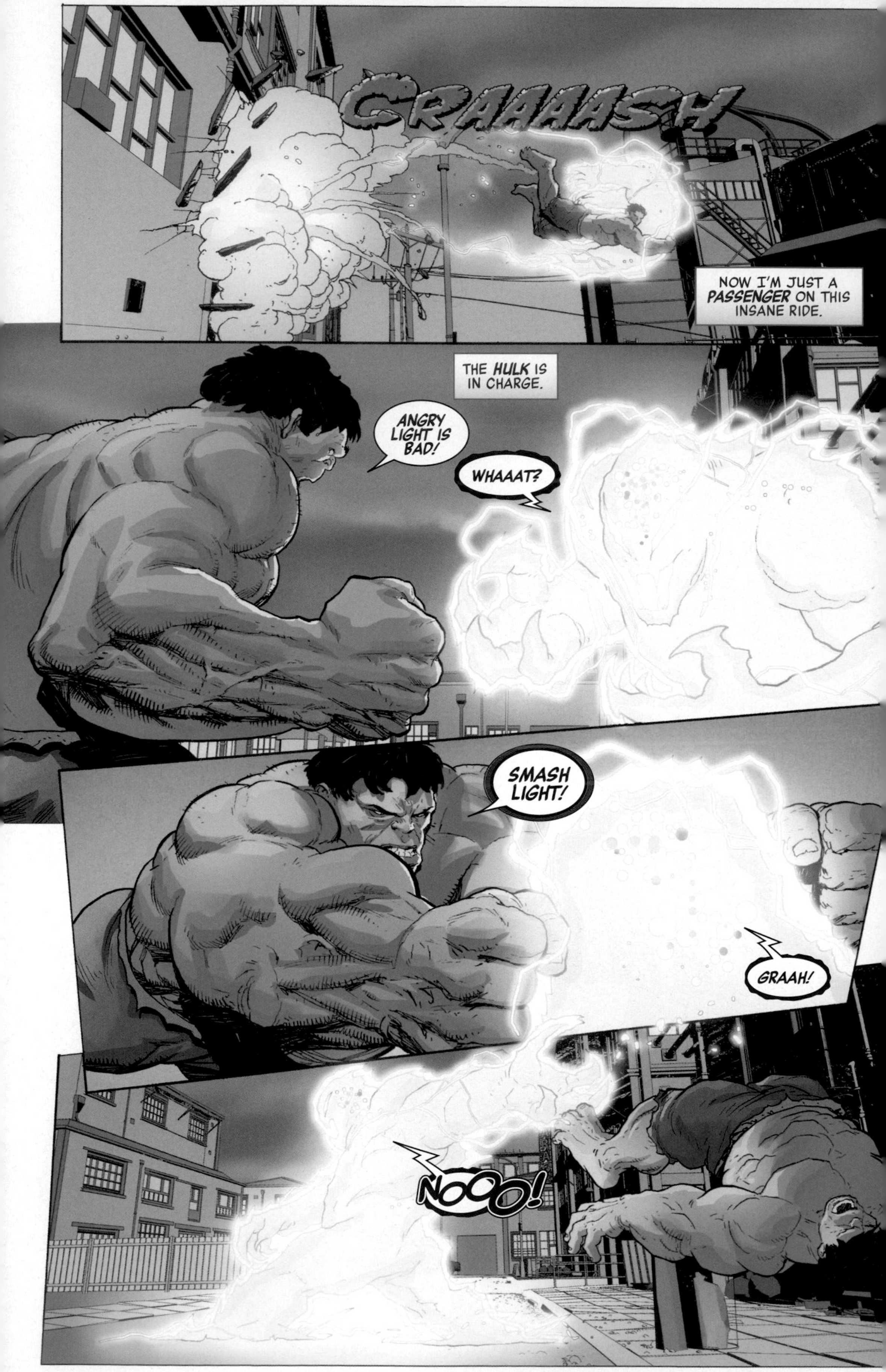
GRAAAASH
NOW I'M JUST A PASSENGER ON THIS INSANE RIDE.
THE HULK IS IN CHARGE.
ANGRY LIGHT IS BAD!
WHAAAT?
SMASH LIGHT!
GRAAH!
NOOO!

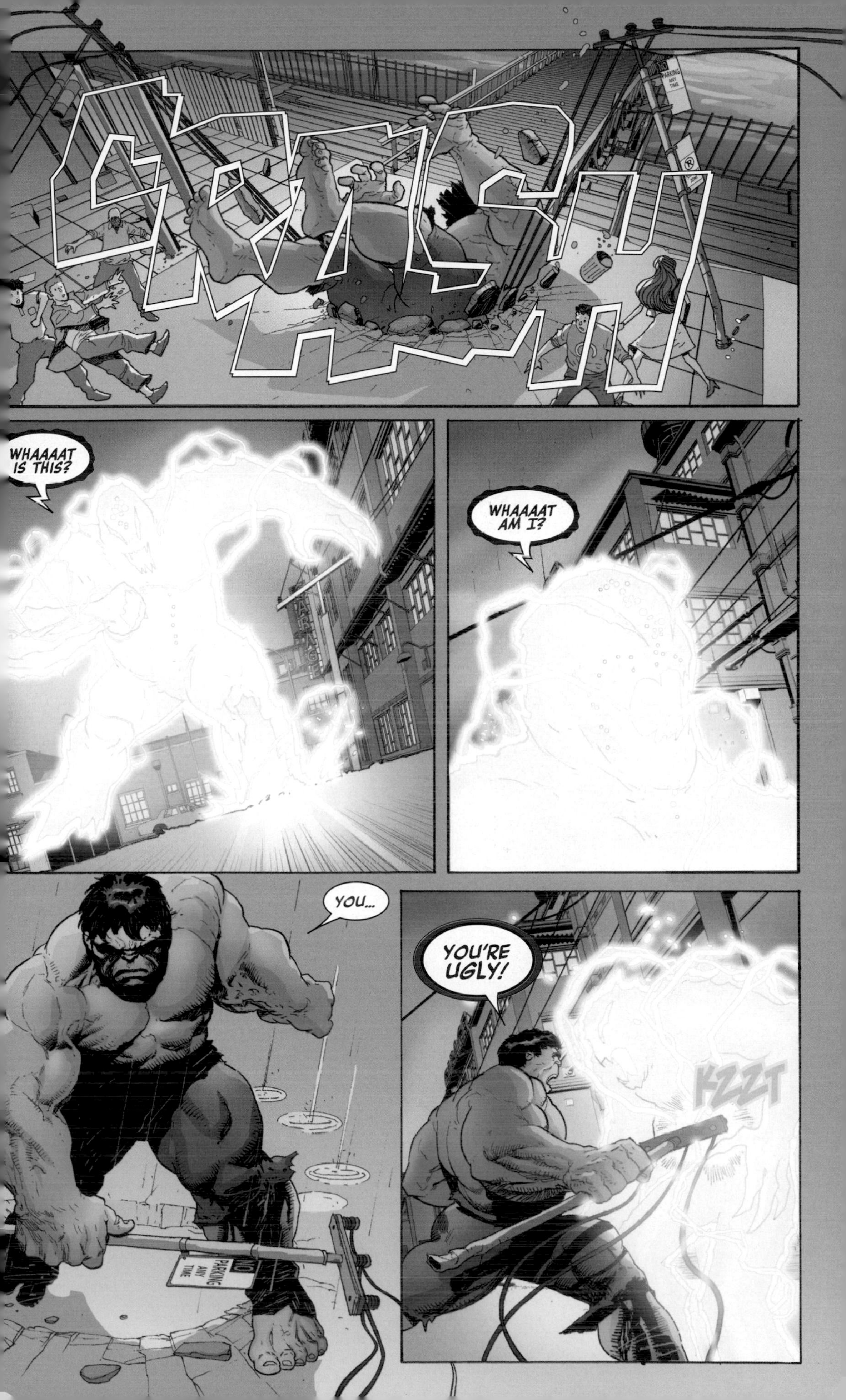
WHAAAAT IS THIS?
WHAAAAT AM I?
YOU...
NO PARKING ANY TIME
YOU'RE UGLY!
KZZT

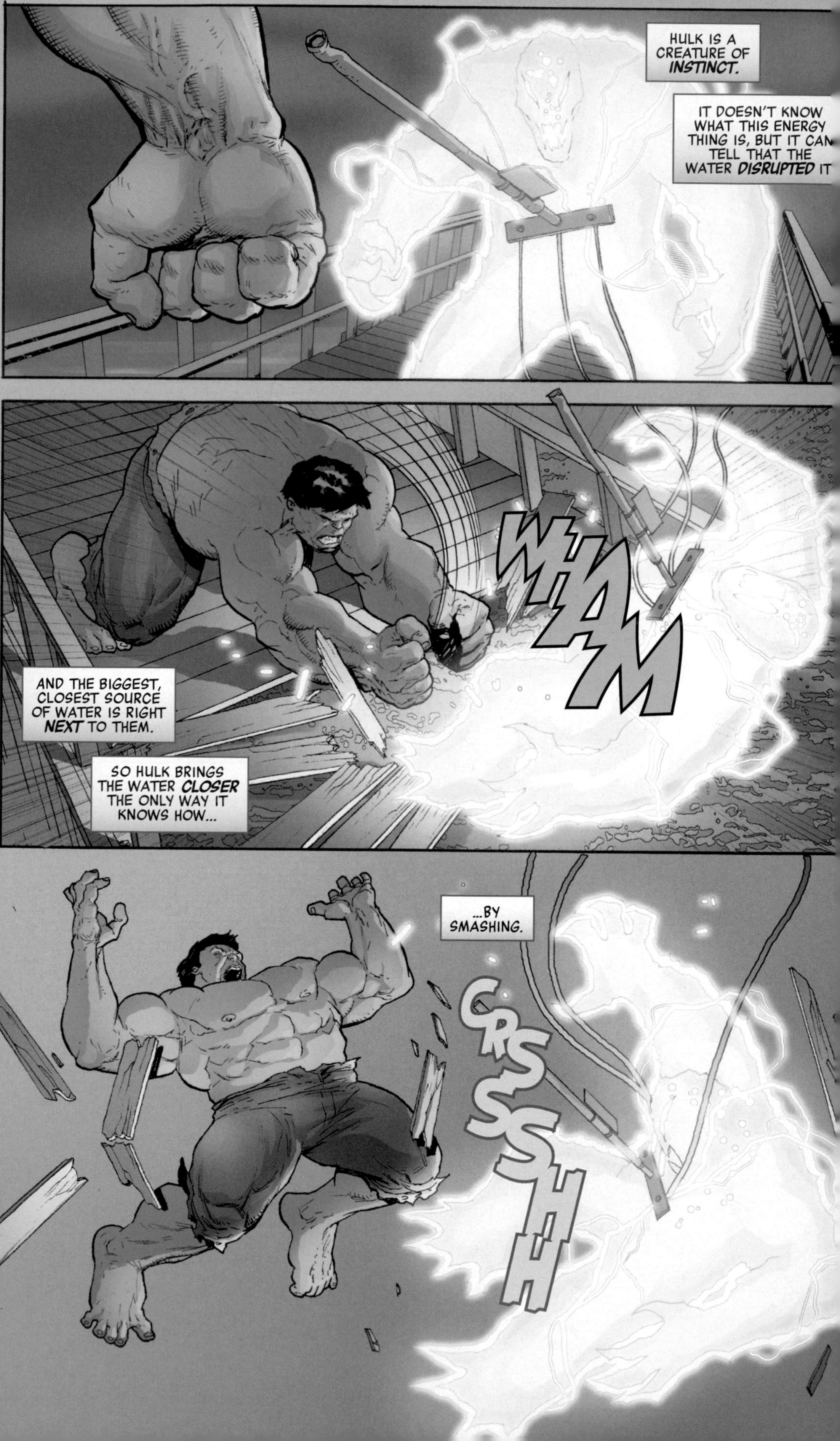

HULK IS A CREATURE OF INSTINCT.
IT DOESN'T KNOW WHAT THIS ENERGY THING IS, BUT IT CAN TELL THAT THE WATER DISRUPTED IT
WHAM
AND THE BIGGEST, CLOSEST SOURCE OF WATER IS RIGHT NEXT TO THEM.
SO HULK BRINGS THE WATER CLOSER THE ONLY WAY IT KNOWS HOW...
...BY SMASHING.
CRSSSHH

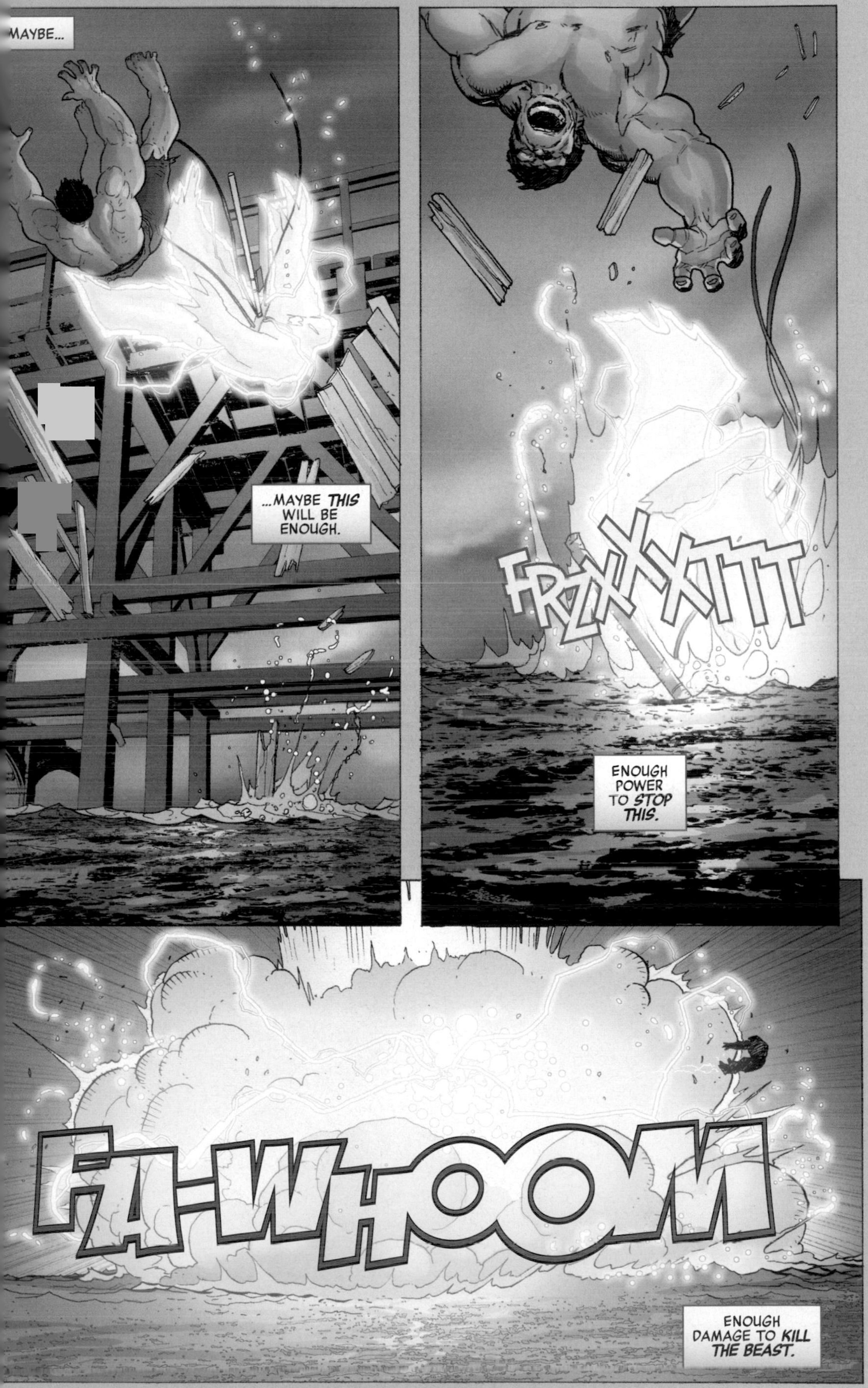

MAYBE...
...MAYBE THIS WILL BE ENOUGH.
FRZXXXTTT
ENOUGH POWER TO STOP THIS.
FA-WHOOM
ENOUGH DAMAGE TO KILL THE BEAST.

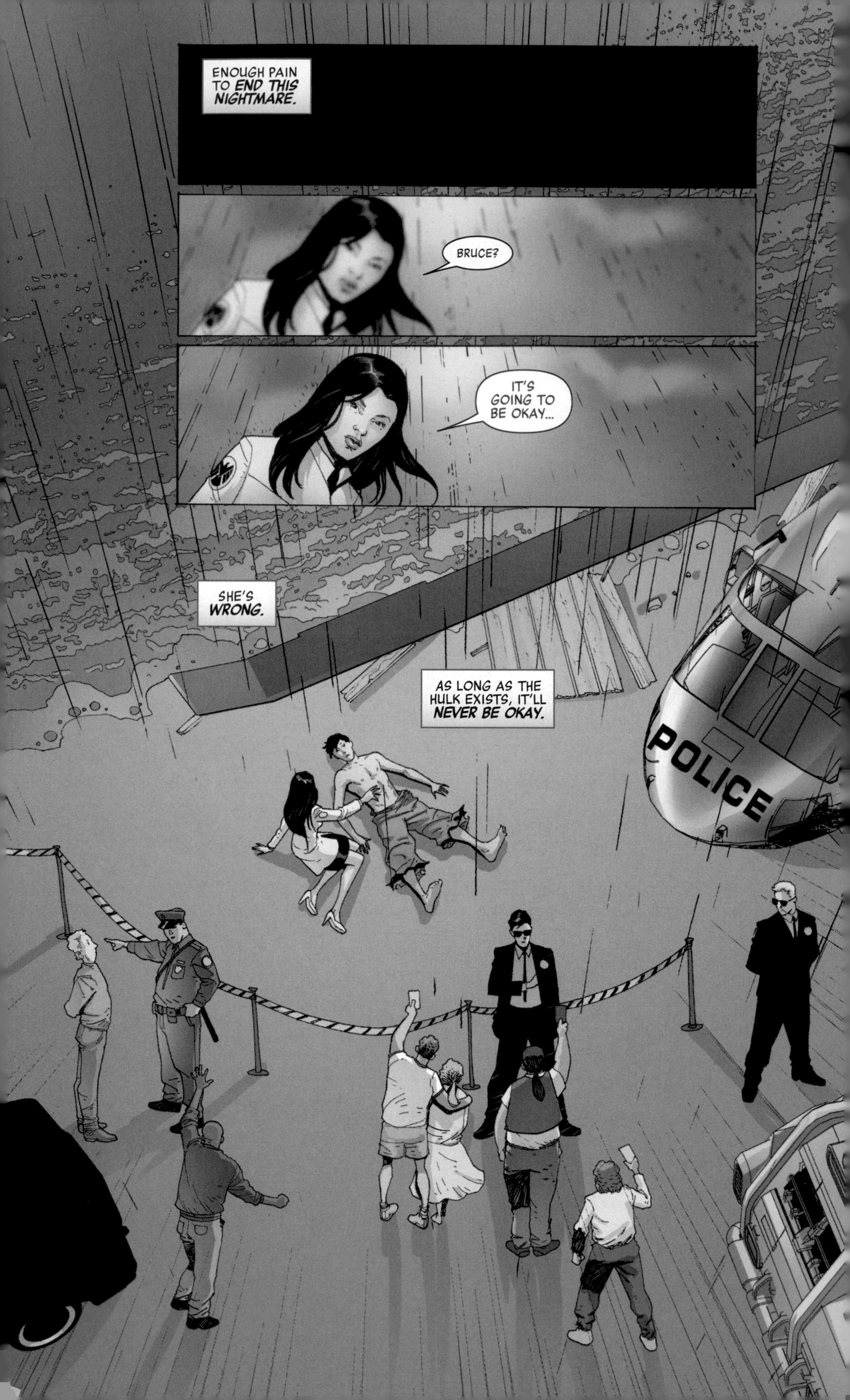
ENOUGH PAIN TO *END THIS NIGHTMARE.*
BRUCE?
IT'S GOING TO BE OKAY...
SHE'S *WRONG.*
AS LONG AS THE HULK EXISTS, IT'LL *NEVER BE OKAY.*
POLICE

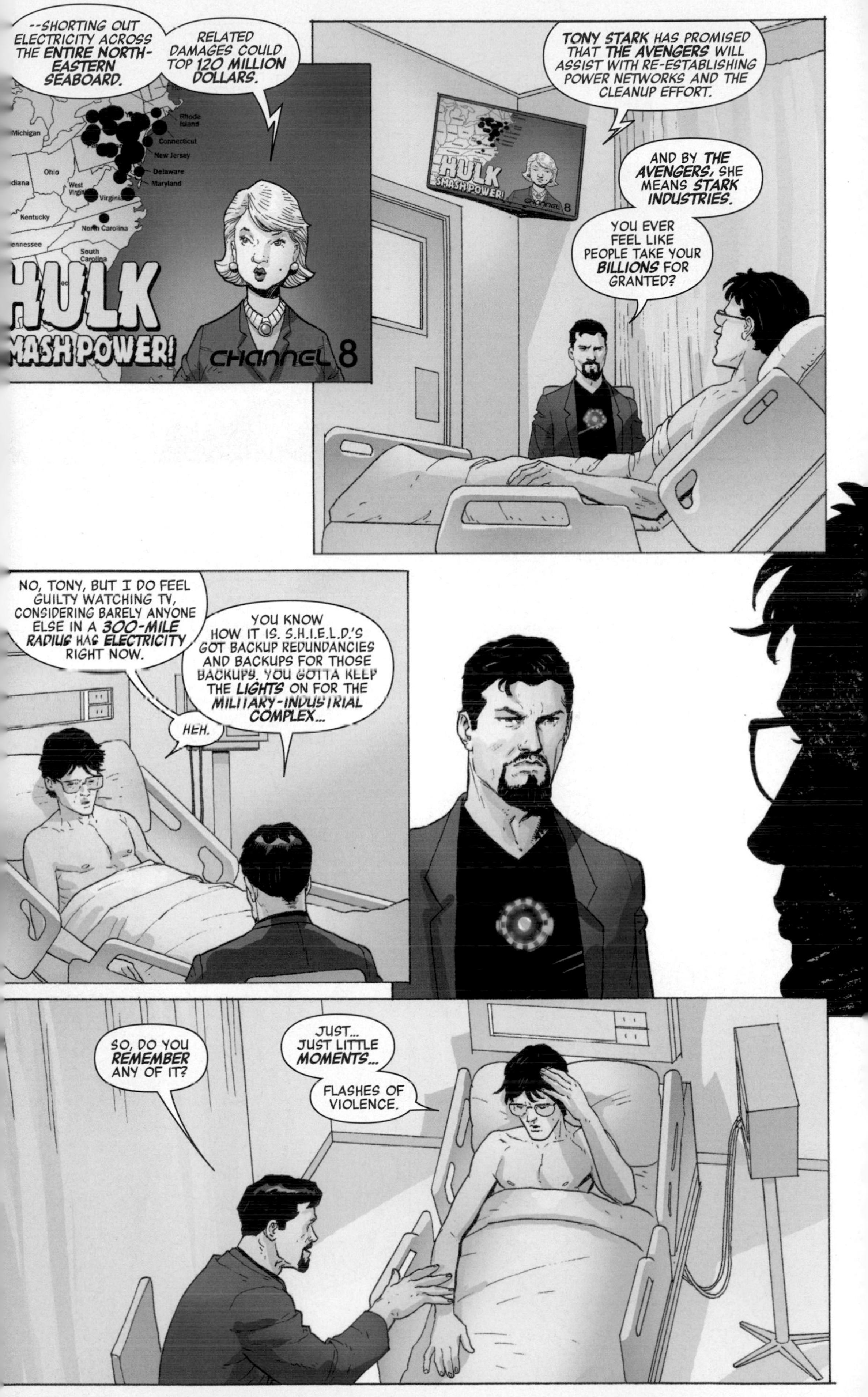
--SHORTING OUT ELECTRICITY ACROSS THE ENTIRE NORTH-EASTERN SEABOARD.
RELATED DAMAGES COULD TOP 120 MILLION DOLLARS.
Michigan
Rhode Island
Connecticut
New Jersey
Ohio
Delaware
Maryland
West Virginia
Virginia
Kentucky
North Carolina
South Carolina
HULK SMASH POWER!
CHANNEL 8
TONY STARK HAS PROMISED THAT THE AVENGERS WILL ASSIST WITH RE-ESTABLISHING POWER NETWORKS AND THE CLEANUP EFFORT.
AND BY THE AVENGERS, SHE MEANS STARK INDUSTRIES.
YOU EVER FEEL LIKE PEOPLE TAKE YOUR BILLIONS FOR GRANTED?
NO, TONY, BUT I DO FEEL GUILTY WATCHING TV, CONSIDERING BARELY ANYONE ELSE IN A 300-MILE RADIUS HAS ELECTRICITY RIGHT NOW.
HEH.
YOU KNOW HOW IT IS. S.H.I.E.L.D.'S GOT BACKUP REDUNDANCIES AND BACKUPS FOR THOSE BACKUPS. YOU GOTTA KEEP THE LIGHTS ON FOR THE MILITARY-INDUSTRIAL COMPLEX...
SO, DO YOU REMEMBER ANY OF IT?
JUST... JUST LITTLE MOMENTS...
FLASHES OF VIOLENCE.

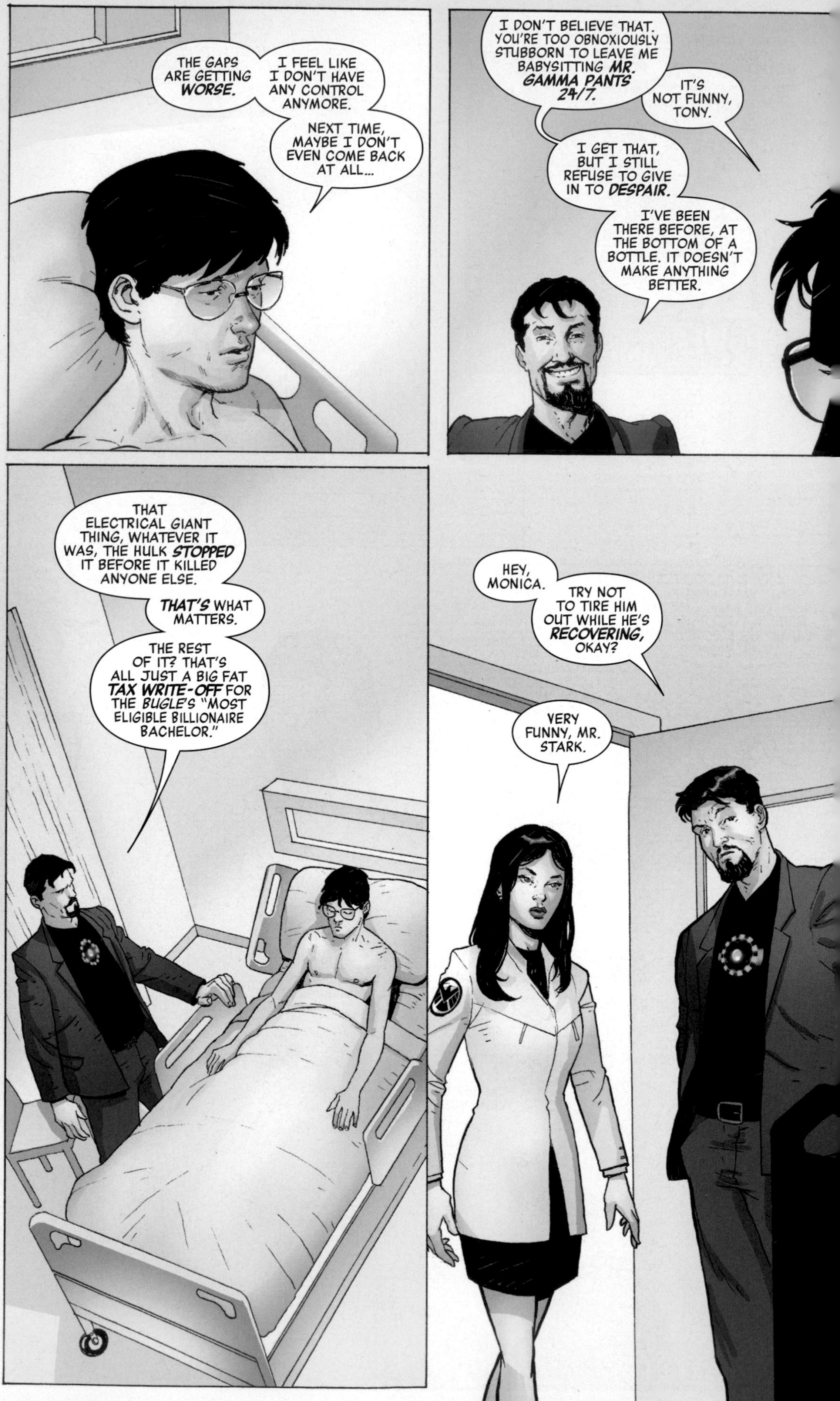
THE GAPS ARE GETTING WORSE.
I FEEL LIKE I DON'T HAVE ANY CONTROL ANYMORE.
NEXT TIME, MAYBE I DON'T EVEN COME BACK AT ALL...
I DON'T BELIEVE THAT. YOU'RE TOO OBNOXIOUSLY STUBBORN TO LEAVE ME BABYSITTING MR. GAMMA PANTS 24/7.
IT'S NOT FUNNY, TONY.
I GET THAT, BUT I STILL REFUSE TO GIVE IN TO DESPAIR.
I'VE BEEN THERE BEFORE, AT THE BOTTOM OF A BOTTLE. IT DOESN'T MAKE ANYTHING BETTER.
THAT ELECTRICAL GIANT THING, WHATEVER IT WAS, THE HULK STOPPED IT BEFORE IT KILLED ANYONE ELSE.
THAT'S WHAT MATTERS.
THE REST OF IT? THAT'S ALL JUST A BIG FAT TAX WRITE-OFF FOR THE BUGLE'S "MOST ELIGIBLE BILLIONAIRE BACHELOR."
HEY, MONICA.
TRY NOT TO TIRE HIM OUT WHILE HE'S RECOVERING, OKAY?
VERY FUNNY, MR. STARK.

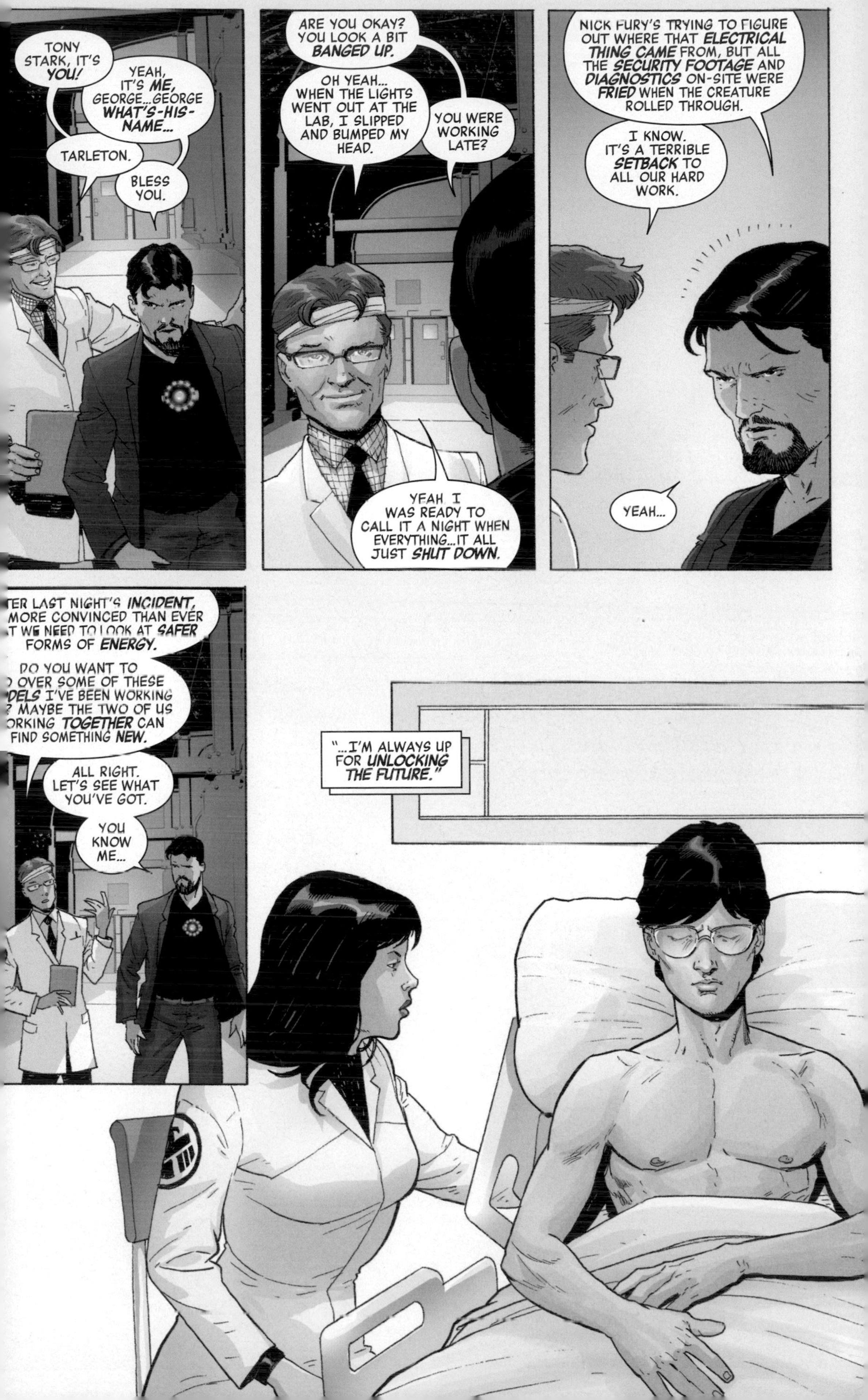
TONY STARK, IT'S YOU!
YEAH, IT'S ME, GEORGE...GEORGE WHAT'S-HIS-NAME...
TARLETON.
BLESS YOU.
ARE YOU OKAY? YOU LOOK A BIT BANGED UP.
OH YEAH... WHEN THE LIGHTS WENT OUT AT THE LAB, I SLIPPED AND BUMPED MY HEAD.
YOU WERE WORKING LATE?
YEAH I WAS READY TO CALL IT A NIGHT WHEN EVERYTHING...IT ALL JUST SHUT DOWN.
NICK FURY'S TRYING TO FIGURE OUT WHERE THAT ELECTRICAL THING CAME FROM, BUT ALL THE SECURITY FOOTAGE AND DIAGNOSTICS ON-SITE WERE FRIED WHEN THE CREATURE ROLLED THROUGH.
I KNOW. IT'S A TERRIBLE SETBACK TO ALL OUR HARD WORK.
YEAH...
TER LAST NIGHT'S INCIDENT, MORE CONVINCED THAN EVER T WE NEED TO LOOK AT SAFER FORMS OF ENERGY.
DO YOU WANT TO O OVER SOME OF THESE DELS I'VE BEEN WORKING ? MAYBE THE TWO OF US ORKING TOGETHER CAN FIND SOMETHING NEW.
ALL RIGHT. LET'S SEE WHAT YOU'VE GOT.
YOU KNOW ME...
"...I'M ALWAYS UP FOR UNLOCKING THE FUTURE."

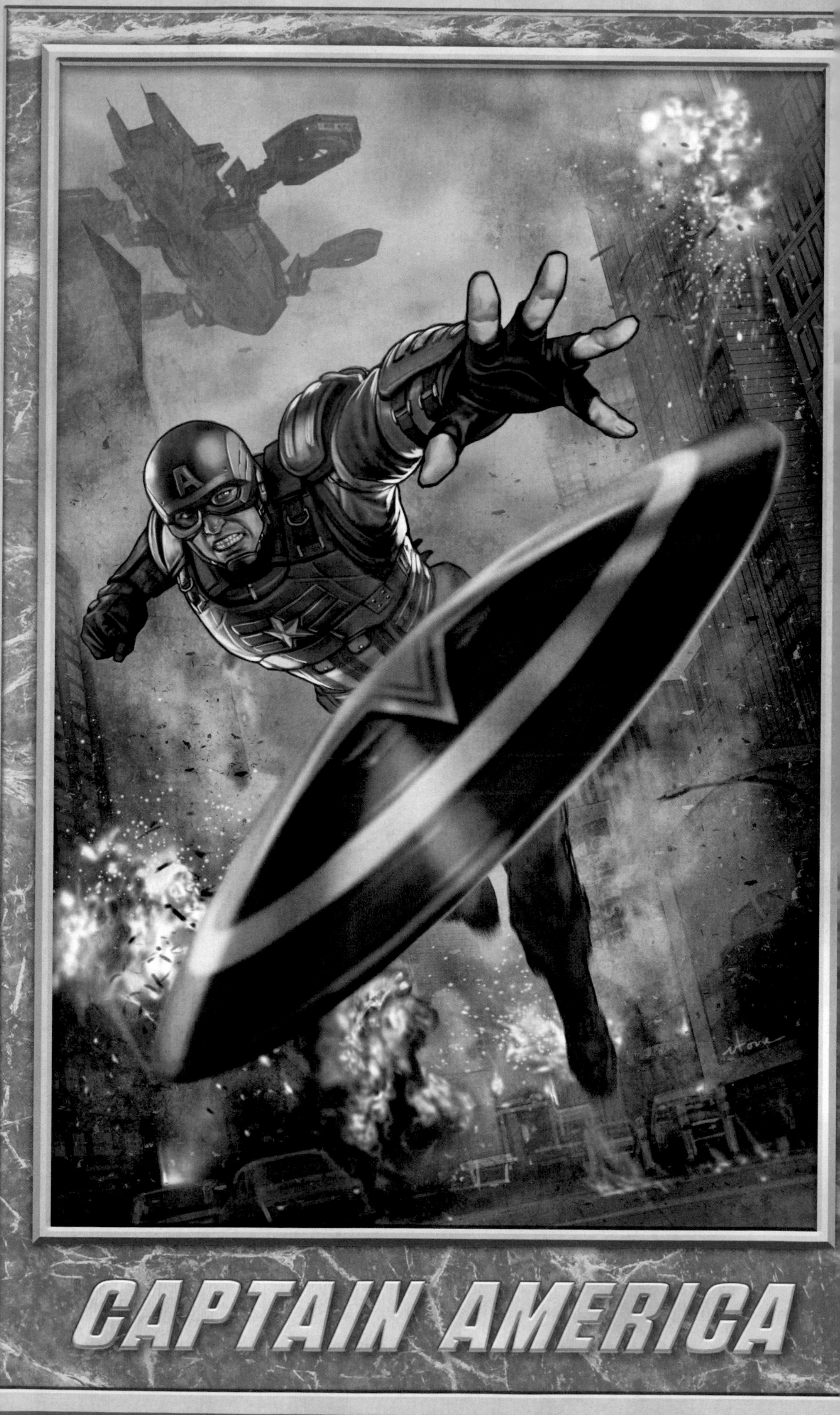
CAPTAIN AMERICA

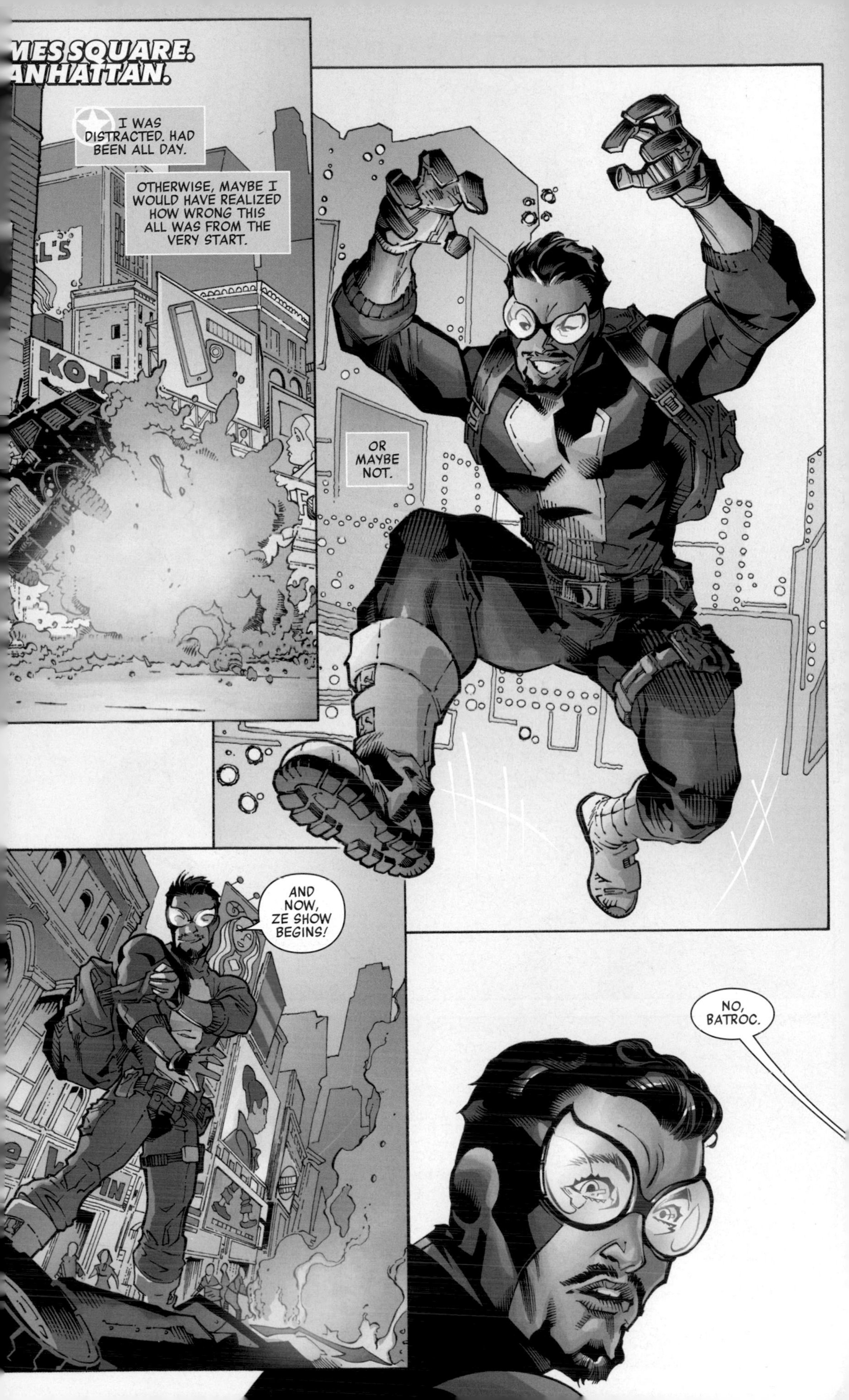
MES SQUARE.
ANHATTAN.
I WAS DISTRACTED. HAD BEEN ALL DAY.
OTHERWISE, MAYBE I WOULD HAVE REALIZED HOW WRONG THIS ALL WAS FROM THE VERY START.
OR MAYBE NOT.
AND NOW, ZE SHOW BEGINS!
NO, BATROC.

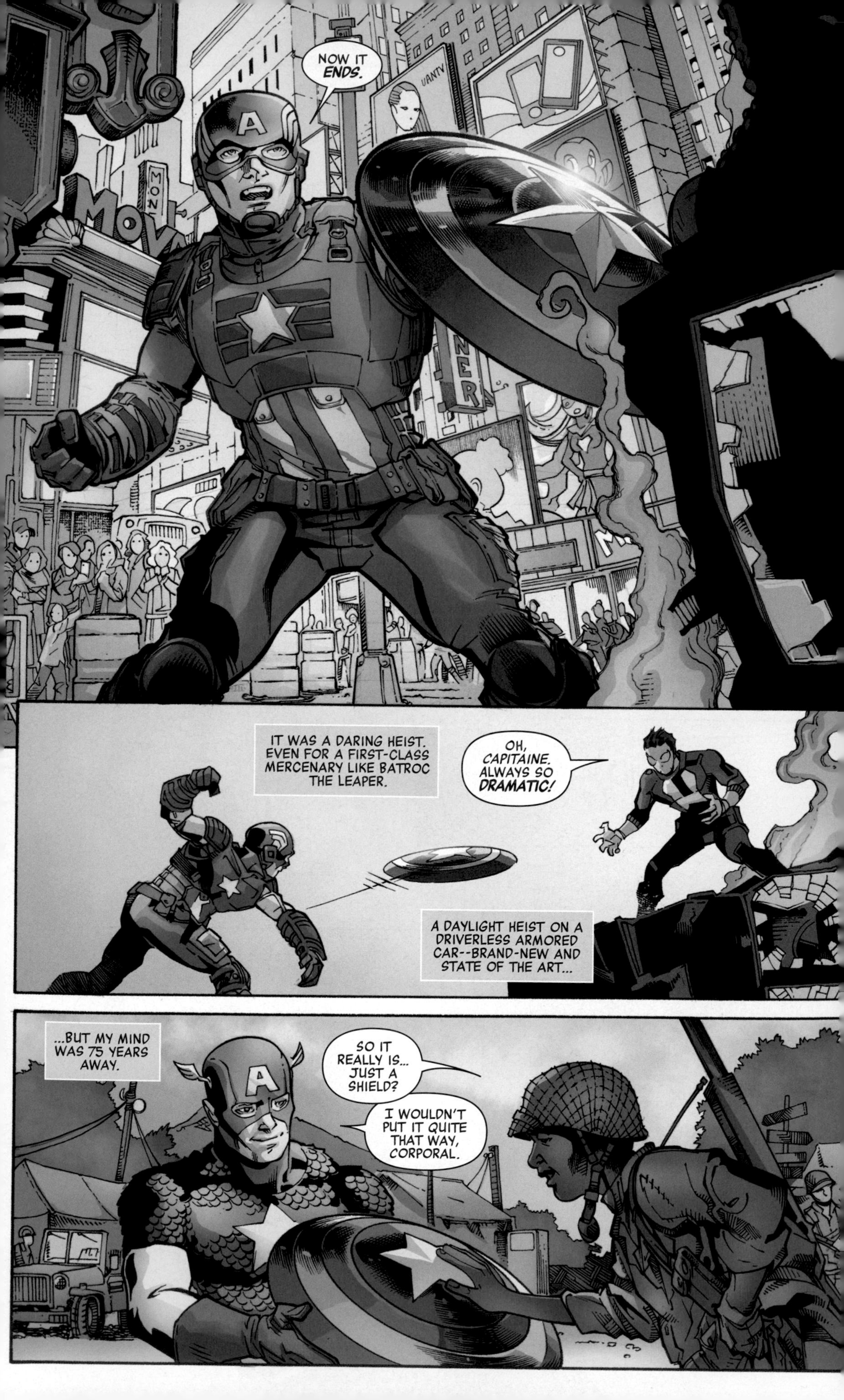

NOW IT ENDS.
IT WAS A DARING HEIST. EVEN FOR A FIRST-CLASS MERCENARY LIKE BATROC THE LEAPER.
OH, CAPITAINE. ALWAYS SO DRAMATIC!
A DAYLIGHT HEIST ON A DRIVERLESS ARMORED CAR--BRAND-NEW AND STATE OF THE ART...
...BUT MY MIND WAS 75 YEARS AWAY.
SO IT REALLY IS... JUST A SHIELD?
I WOULDN'T PUT IT QUITE THAT WAY, CORPORAL.

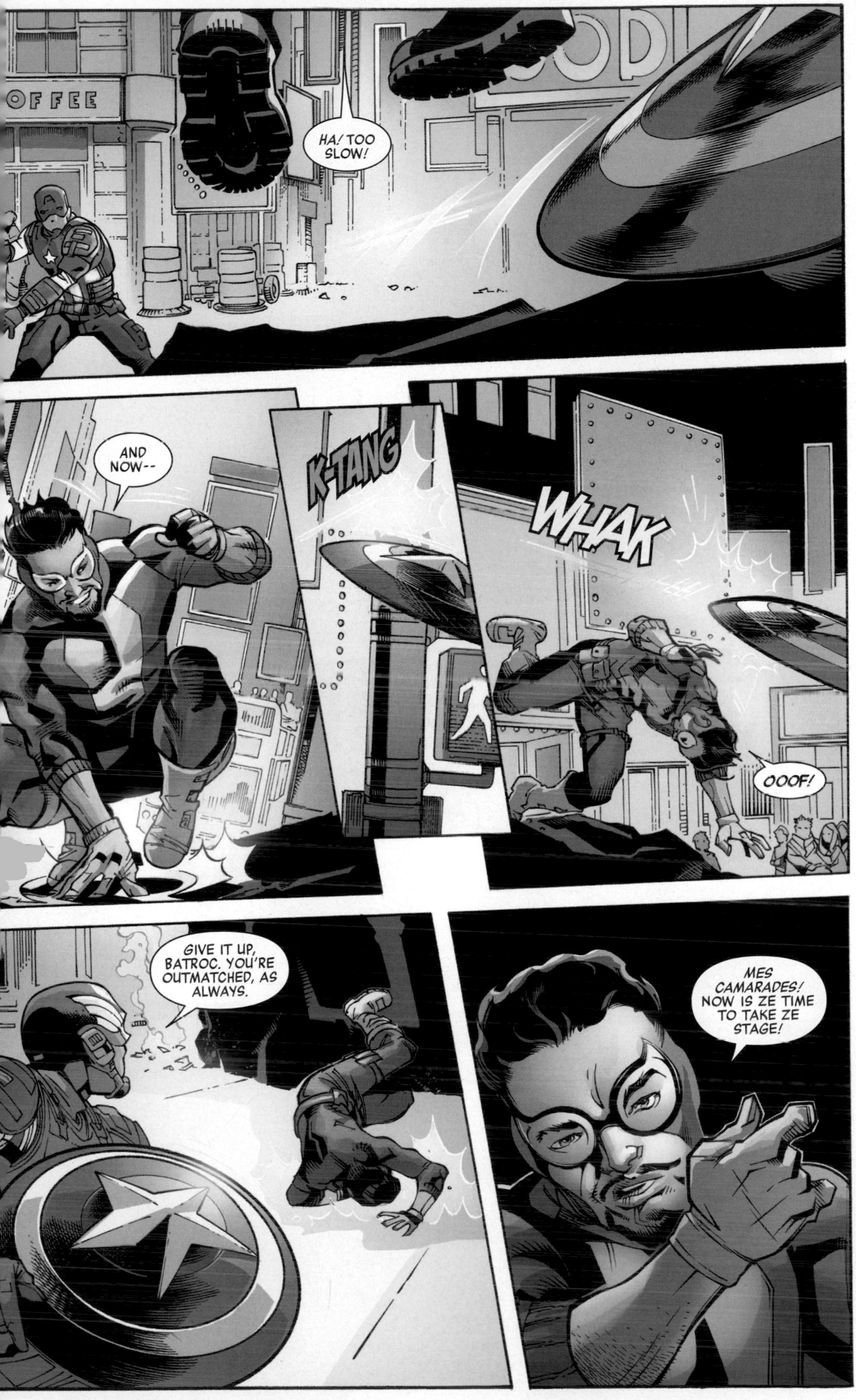
OFFEE
HA! TOO SLOW!
AND NOW--
K-TANG
WHAK
OOOF!
GIVE IT UP, BATROC. YOU'RE OUTMATCHED, AS ALWAYS.
MES CAMARADES! NOW IS ZE TIME TO TAKE ZE STAGE!

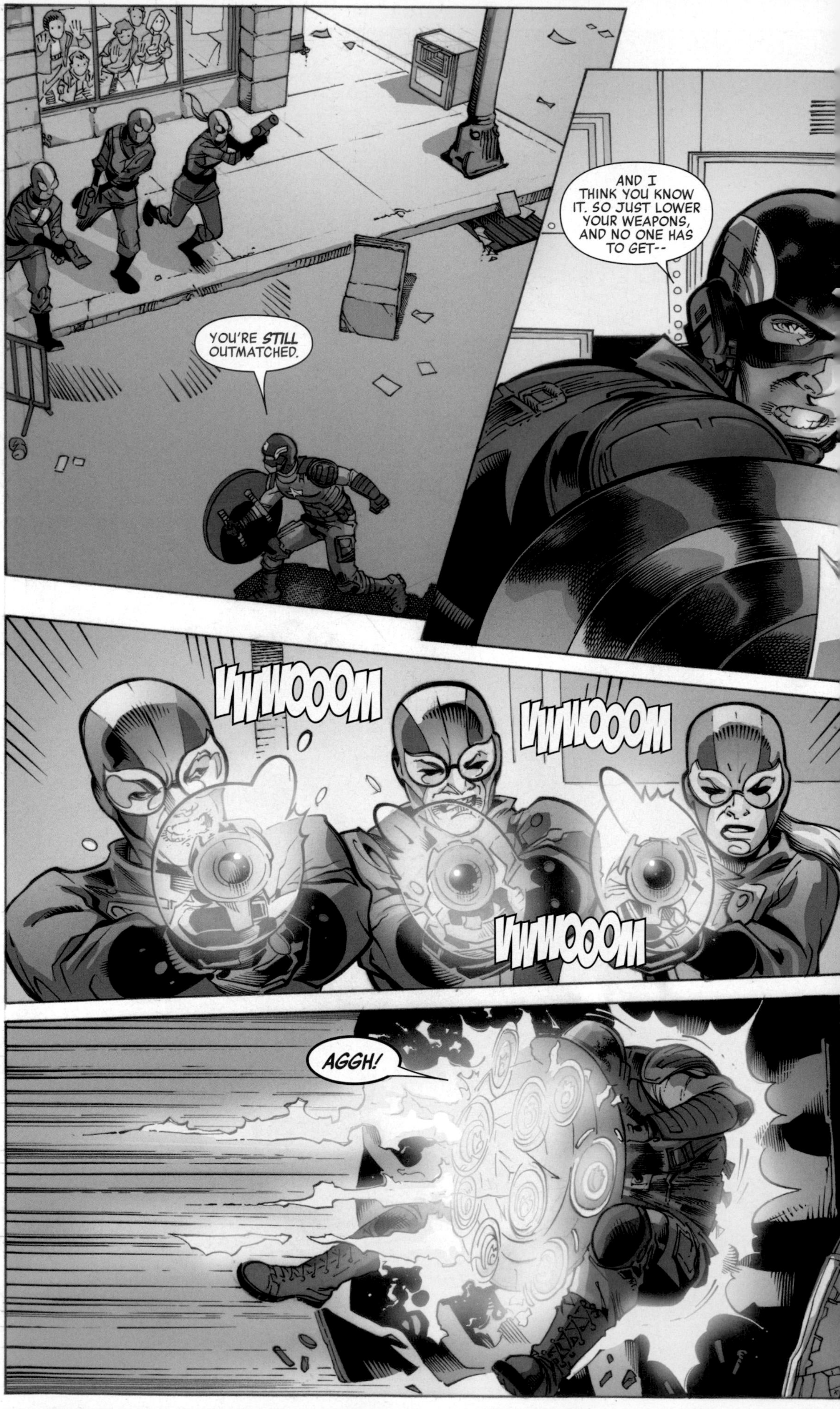
YOU'RE STILL OUTMATCHED.
AND I THINK YOU KNOW IT. SO JUST LOWER YOUR WEAPONS, AND NO ONE HAS TO GET--
VWWOOOM
VWWOOOM
VWWOOOM
AGGH!

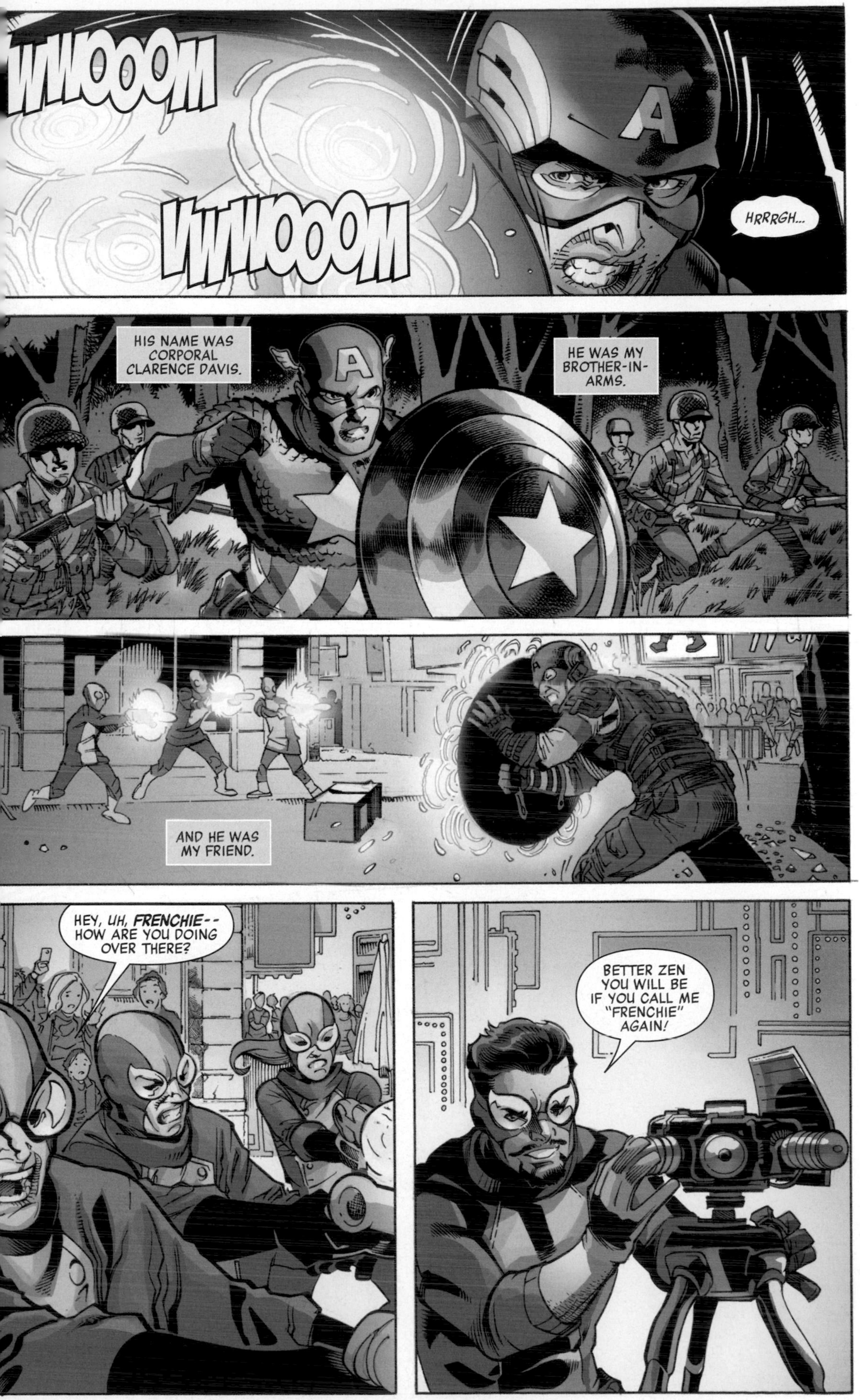
WWOOOM
VWWOOOM
HRRRGH...
HIS NAME WAS CORPORAL CLARENCE DAVIS.
HE WAS MY BROTHER-IN-ARMS.
AND HE WAS MY FRIEND.
HEY, UH, FRENCHIE-- HOW ARE YOU DOING OVER THERE?
BETTER ZEN YOU WILL BE IF YOU CALL ME "FRENCHIE" AGAIN!

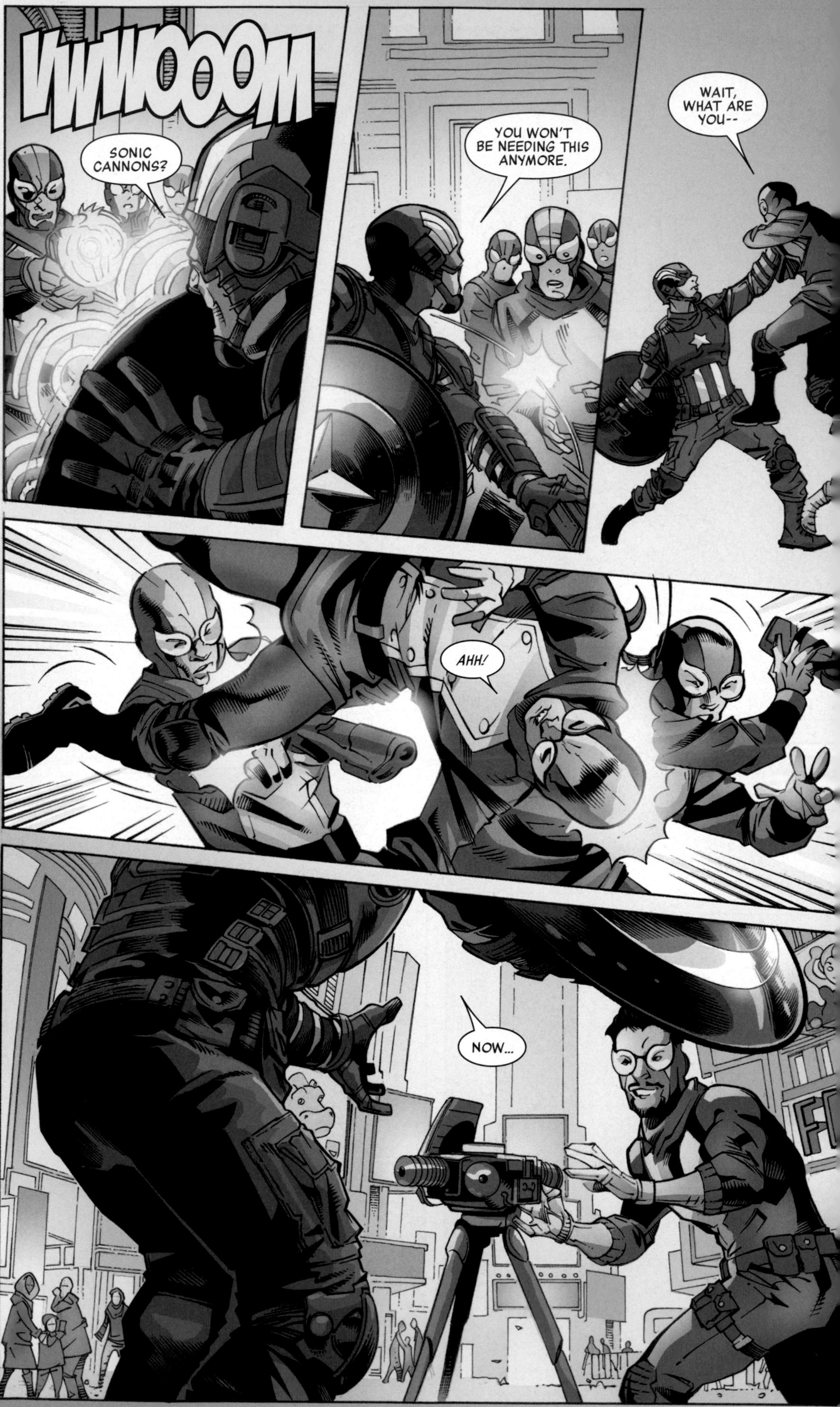
VWWOOOM
SONIC CANNONS?
YOU WON'T BE NEEDING THIS ANYMORE.
WAIT, WHAT ARE YOU--
AHH!
NOW...

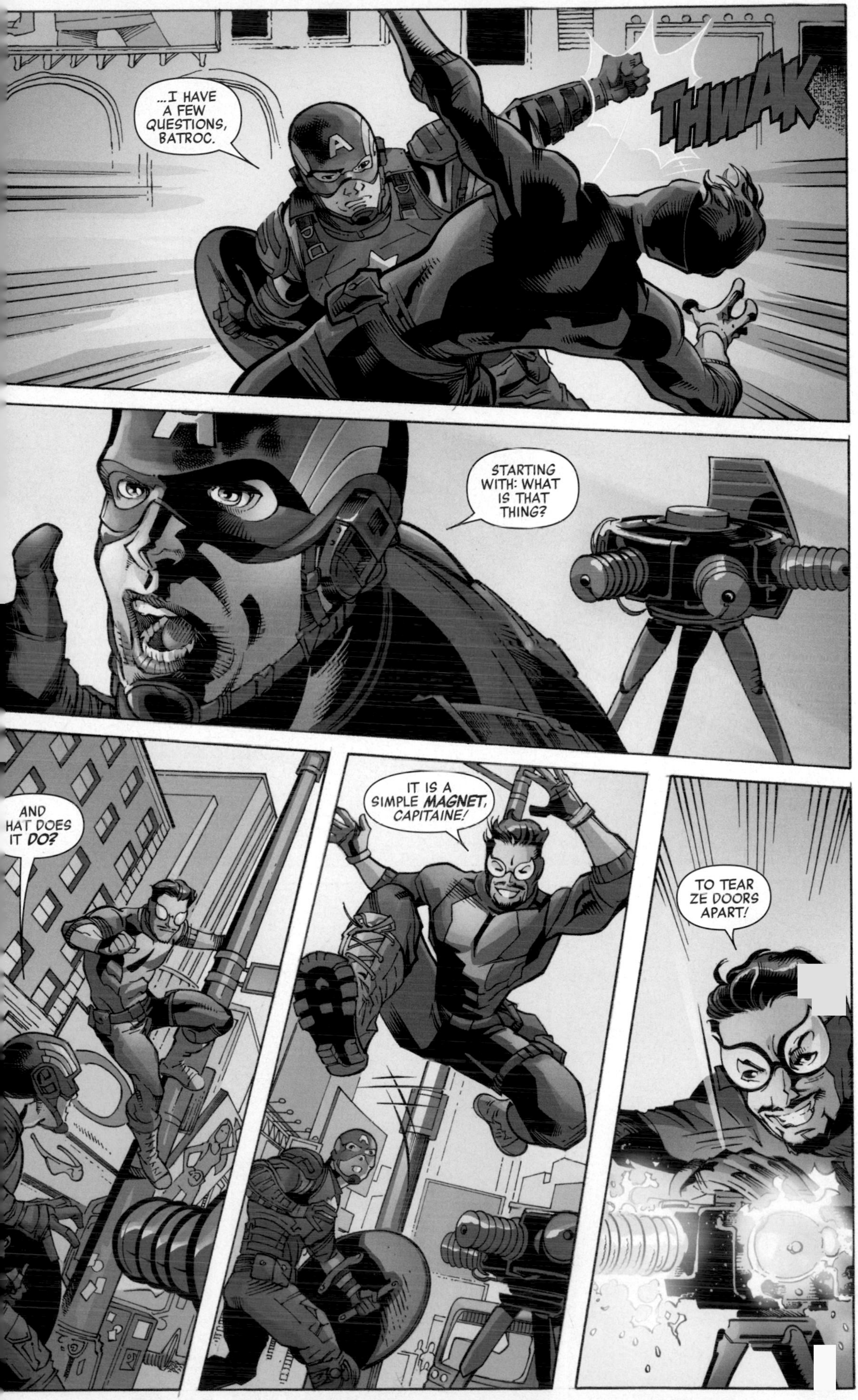

...I HAVE A FEW QUESTIONS, BATROC.
THWAK
STARTING WITH: WHAT IS THAT THING?
AND HAT DOES IT DO?
IT IS A SIMPLE MAGNET, CAPITAINE!
TO TEAR ZE DOORS APART!

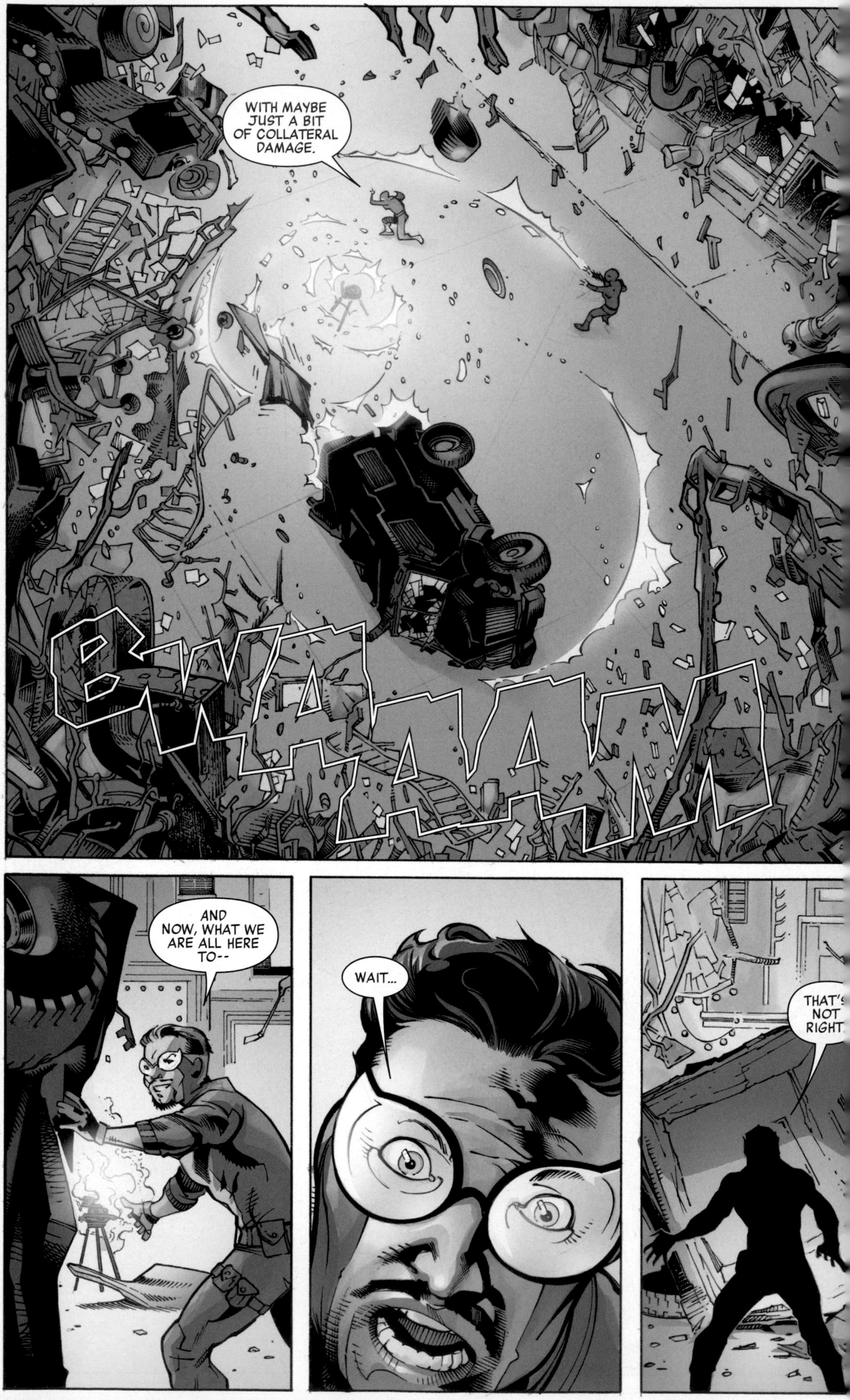
WITH MAYBE JUST A BIT OF COLLATERAL DAMAGE.
BWAAAM
AND NOW, WHAT WE ARE ALL HERE TO--
WAIT...
THAT'S NOT RIGHT.

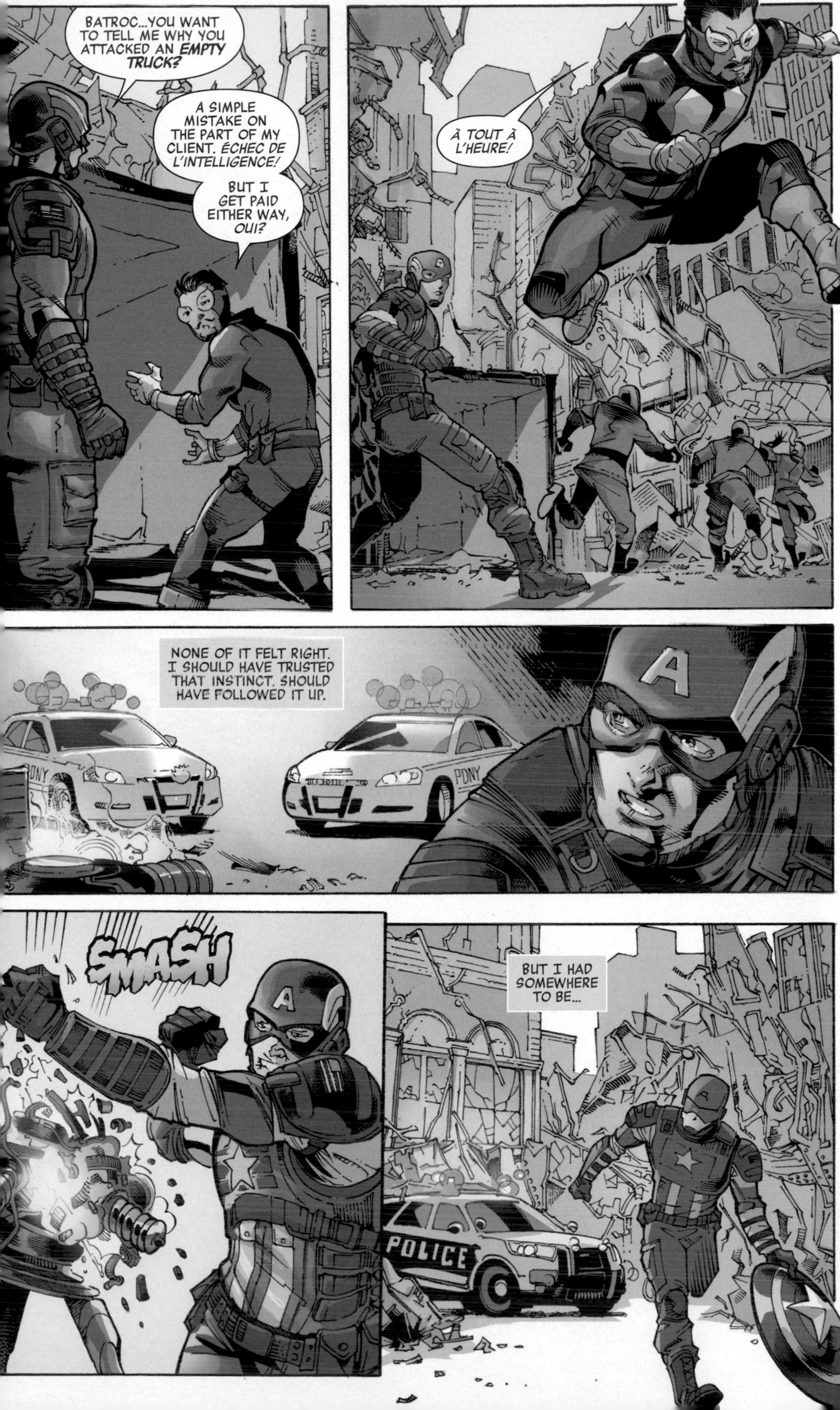
BATROC...YOU WANT TO TELL ME WHY YOU ATTACKED AN *EMPTY TRUCK?*
A SIMPLE MISTAKE ON THE PART OF MY CLIENT. *ÉCHEC DE L'INTELLIGENCE!*
BUT I GET PAID EITHER WAY, *OUI?*
À TOUT À L'HEURE!
NONE OF IT FELT RIGHT. I SHOULD HAVE TRUSTED THAT INSTINCT. SHOULD HAVE FOLLOWED IT UP.
PDNY
PDNY
SMASH
BUT I HAD SOMEWHERE TO BE...
POLICE

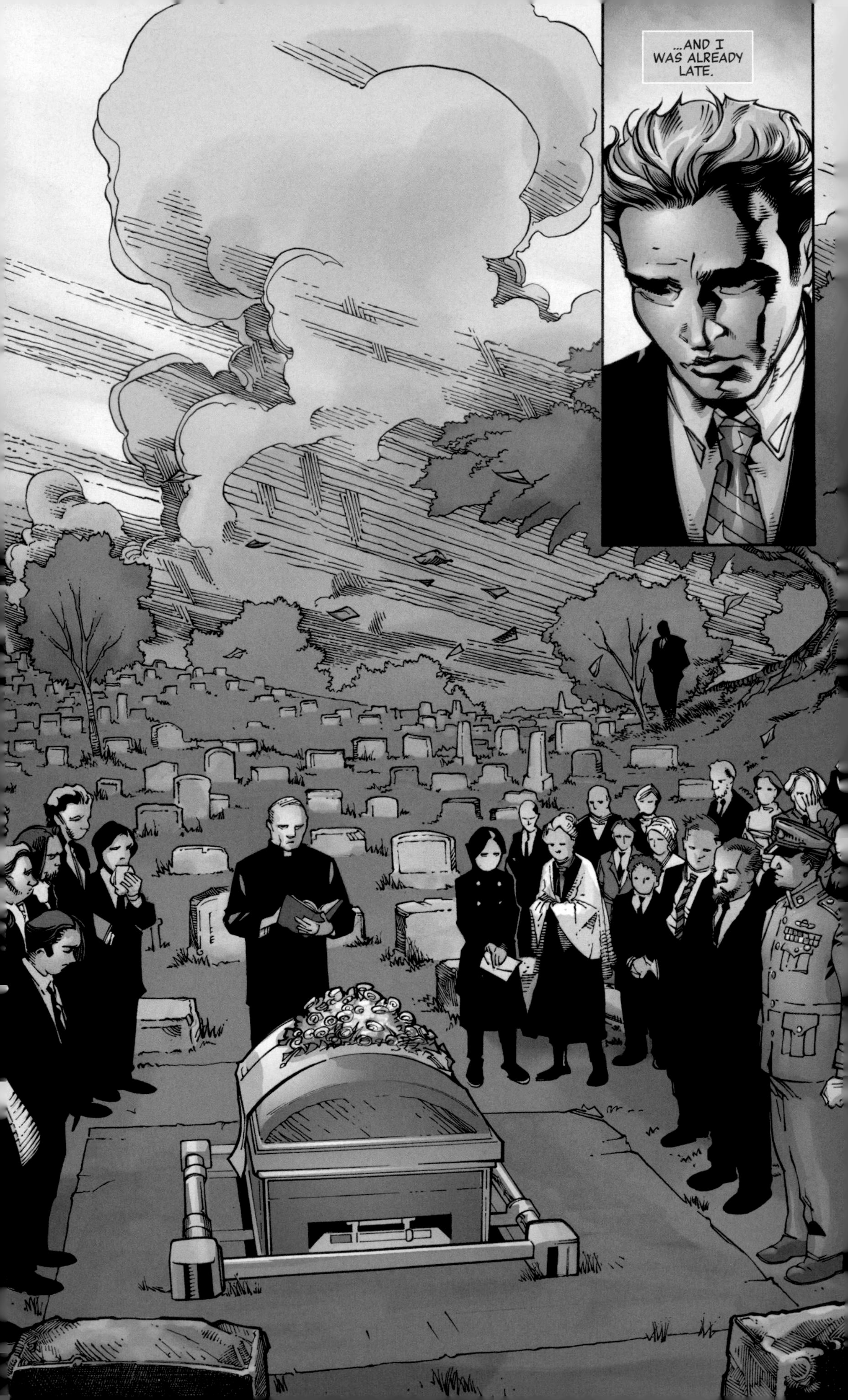
...AND I WAS ALREADY LATE.

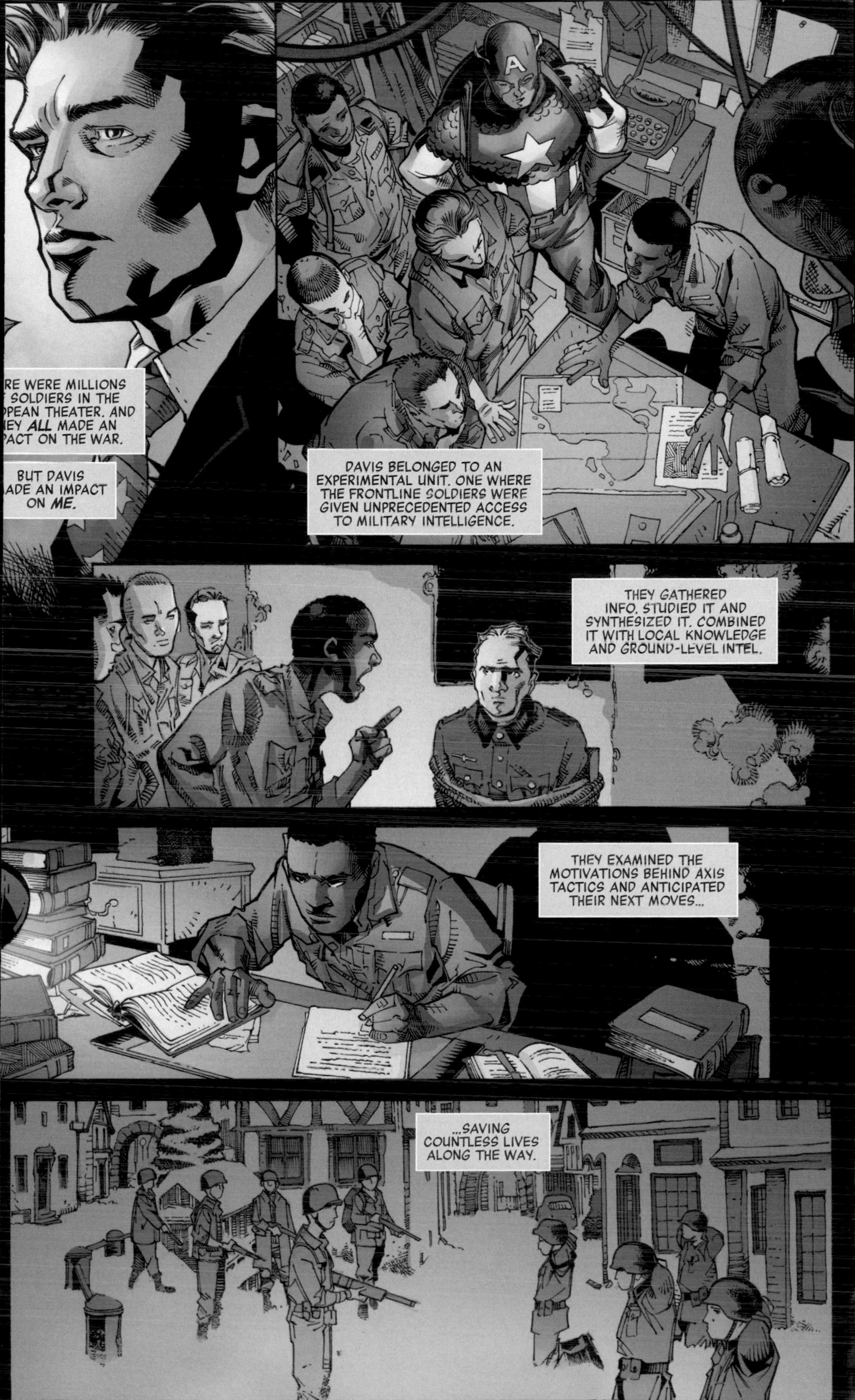

RE WERE MILLIONS
SOLDIERS IN THE
OPEAN THEATER. AND
EY ALL MADE AN
PACT ON THE WAR.
BUT DAVIS
ADE AN IMPACT
ON ME.
DAVIS BELONGED TO AN EXPERIMENTAL UNIT. ONE WHERE THE FRONTLINE SOLDIERS WERE GIVEN UNPRECEDENTED ACCESS TO MILITARY INTELLIGENCE.
THEY GATHERED INFO. STUDIED IT AND SYNTHESIZED IT. COMBINED IT WITH LOCAL KNOWLEDGE AND GROUND-LEVEL INTEL.
THEY EXAMINED THE MOTIVATIONS BEHIND AXIS TACTICS AND ANTICIPATED THEIR NEXT MOVES...
...SAVING COUNTLESS LIVES ALONG THE WAY.

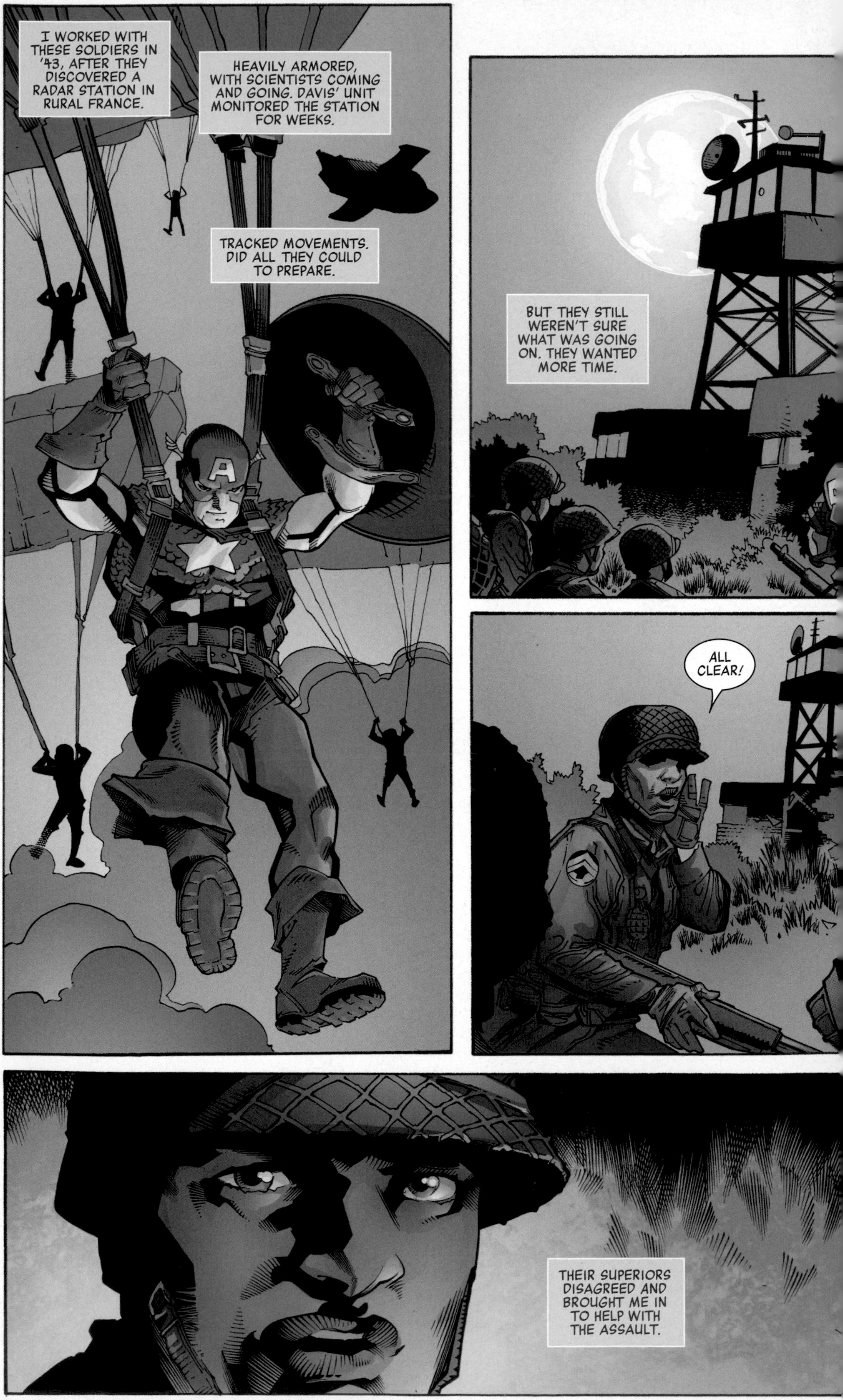
I WORKED WITH THESE SOLDIERS IN '43, AFTER THEY DISCOVERED A RADAR STATION IN RURAL FRANCE.
HEAVILY ARMORED, WITH SCIENTISTS COMING AND GOING. DAVIS' UNIT MONITORED THE STATION FOR WEEKS.
TRACKED MOVEMENTS. DID ALL THEY COULD TO PREPARE.
BUT THEY STILL WEREN'T SURE WHAT WAS GOING ON. THEY WANTED MORE TIME.
ALL CLEAR!
THEIR SUPERIORS DISAGREED AND BROUGHT ME IN TO HELP WITH THE ASSAULT.

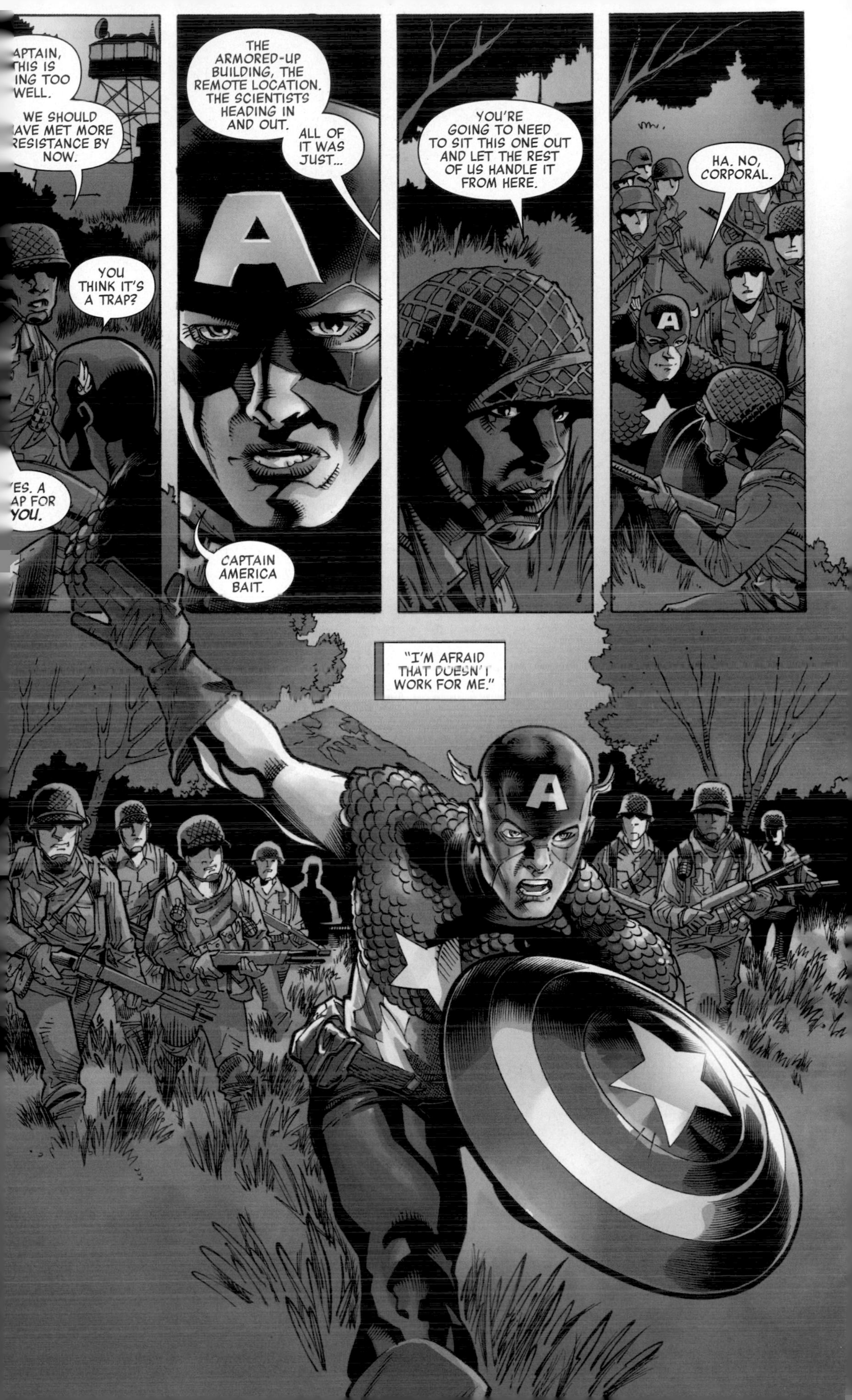
APTAIN, THIS IS ING TOO WELL.
WE SHOULD AVE MET MORE RESISTANCE BY NOW.
YOU THINK IT'S A TRAP?
ES. A AP FOR *YOU.*
THE ARMORED-UP BUILDING, THE REMOTE LOCATION. THE SCIENTISTS HEADING IN AND OUT.
ALL OF IT WAS JUST...
CAPTAIN AMERICA BAIT.
YOU'RE GOING TO NEED TO SIT THIS ONE OUT AND LET THE REST OF US HANDLE IT FROM HERE.
HA. NO, CORPORAL.
"I'M AFRAID THAT DOESN'T WORK FOR ME."

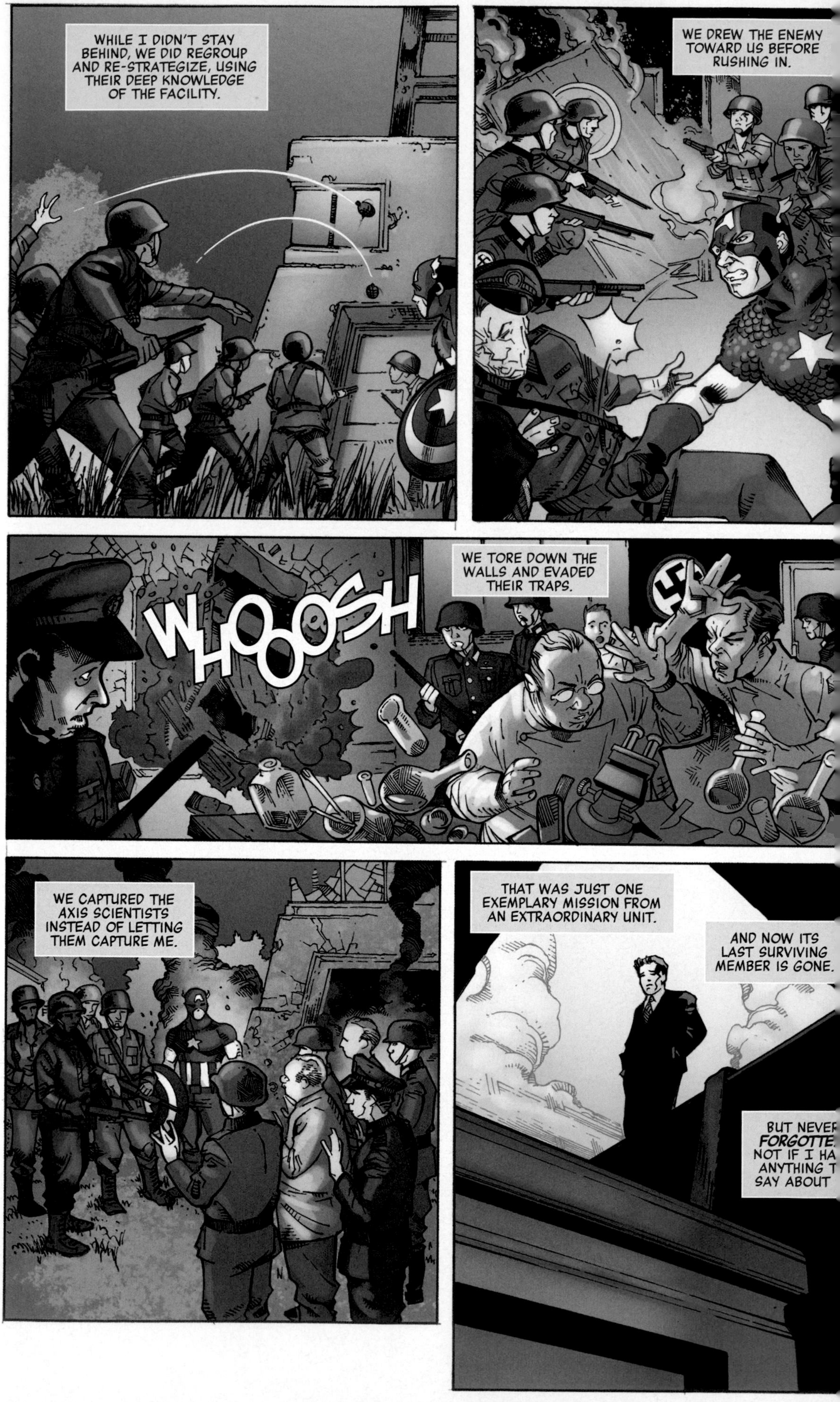
WHILE I DIDN'T STAY BEHIND, WE DID REGROUP AND RE-STRATEGIZE, USING THEIR DEEP KNOWLEDGE OF THE FACILITY.
WE DREW THE ENEMY TOWARD US BEFORE RUSHING IN.
WHOOOSH
WE TORE DOWN THE WALLS AND EVADED THEIR TRAPS.
WE CAPTURED THE AXIS SCIENTISTS INSTEAD OF LETTING THEM CAPTURE ME.
THAT WAS JUST ONE EXEMPLARY MISSION FROM AN EXTRAORDINARY UNIT.
AND NOW ITS LAST SURVIVING MEMBER IS GONE.
BUT NEVER

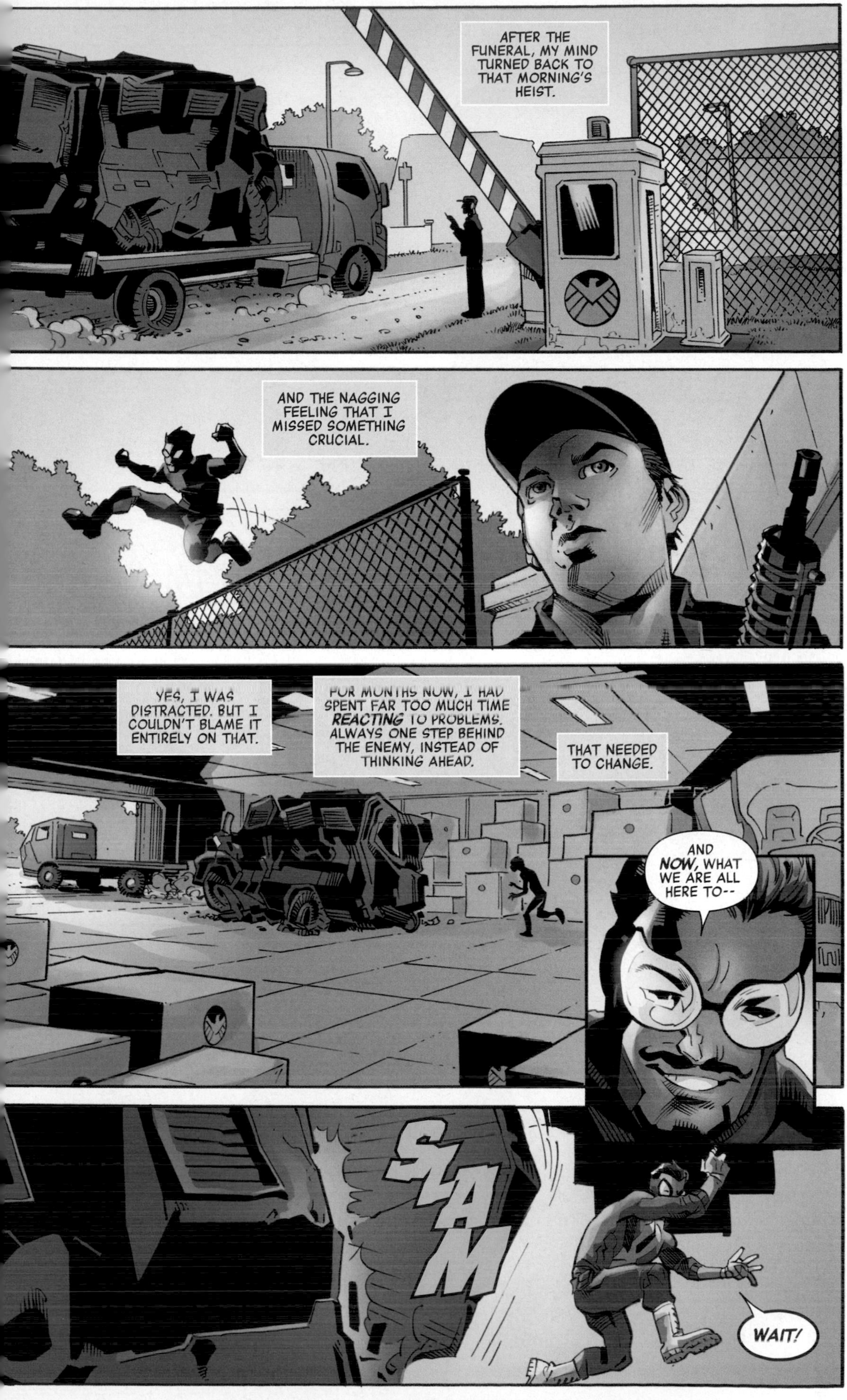
AFTER THE FUNERAL, MY MIND TURNED BACK TO THAT MORNING'S HEIST.
AND THE NAGGING FEELING THAT I MISSED SOMETHING CRUCIAL.
YES, I WAS DISTRACTED. BUT I COULDN'T BLAME IT ENTIRELY ON THAT.
FOR MONTHS NOW, I HAD SPENT FAR TOO MUCH TIME REACTING TO PROBLEMS. ALWAYS ONE STEP BEHIND THE ENEMY, INSTEAD OF THINKING AHEAD.
THAT NEEDED TO CHANGE.
AND NOW, WHAT WE ARE ALL HERE TO--
SLAM
WAIT!

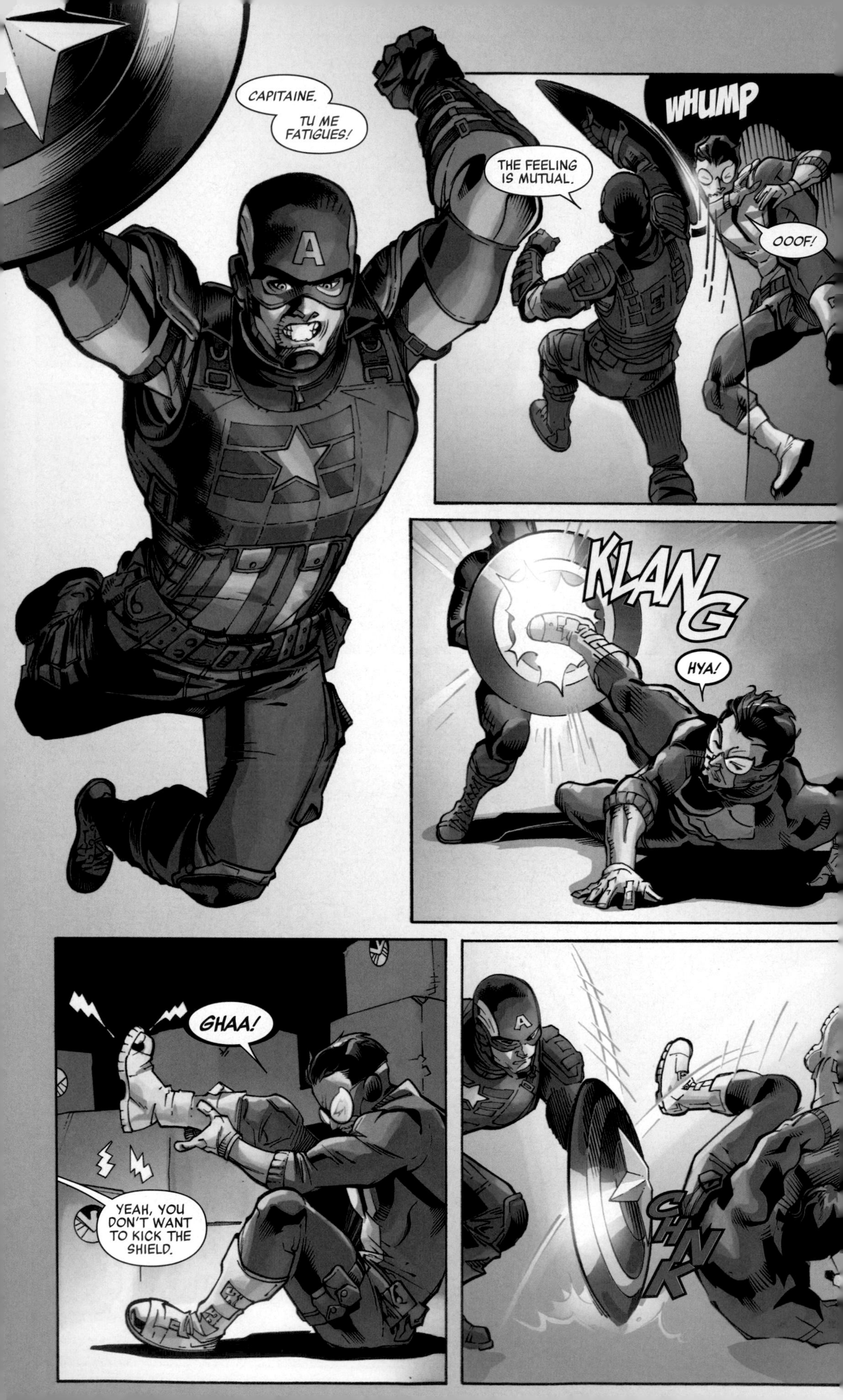
CAPITAINE.
TU ME FATIGUES!
THE FEELING IS MUTUAL.
WHUMP
OOOF!
KLANG
HYA!
GHAA!
YEAH, YOU DON'T WANT TO KICK THE SHIELD.
CHNK

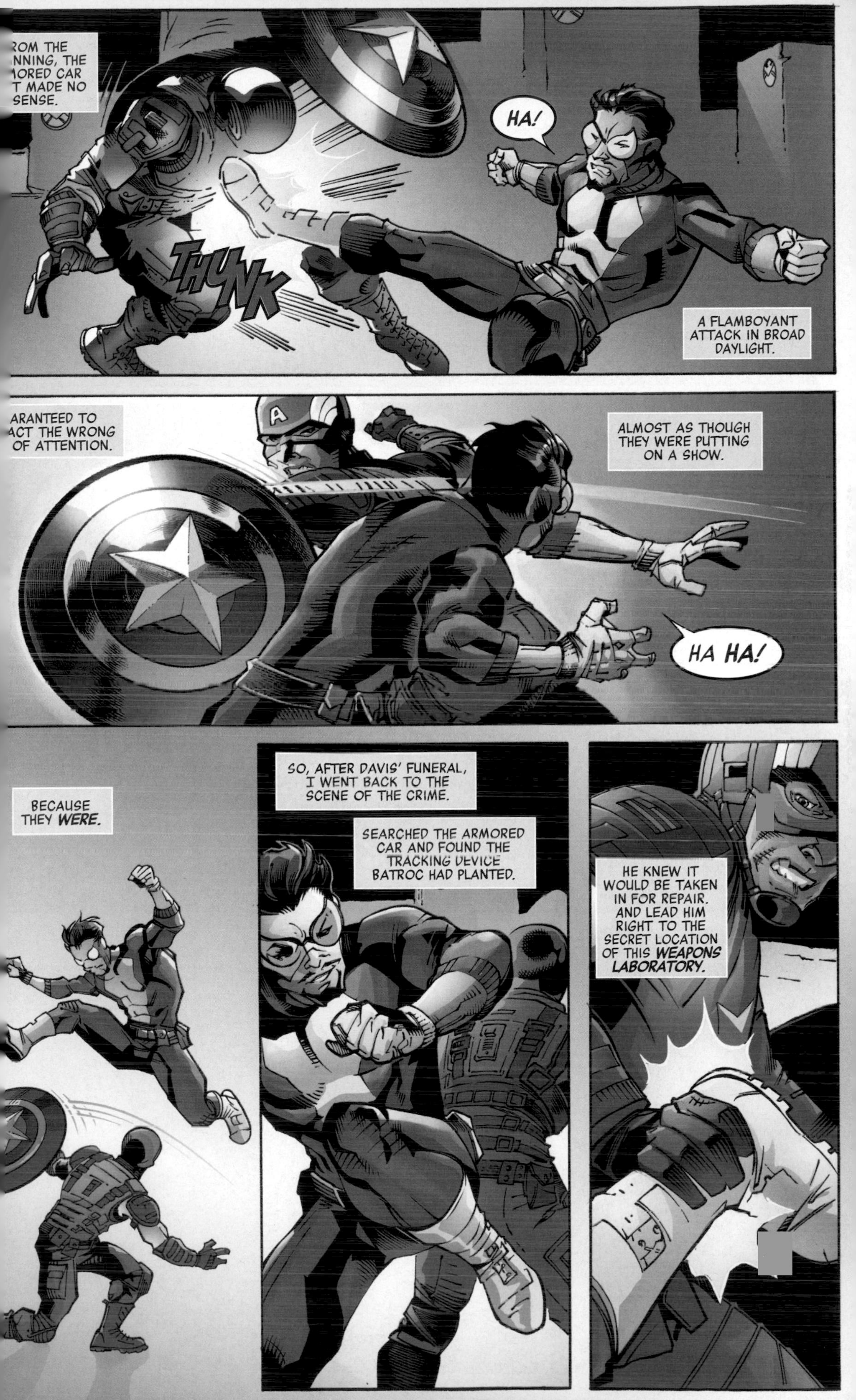
ROM THE NNING, THE MORED CAR T MADE NO SENSE.
HA!
THUNK
A FLAMBOYANT ATTACK IN BROAD DAYLIGHT.
ARANTEED TO ACT THE WRONG OF ATTENTION.
ALMOST AS THOUGH THEY WERE PUTTING ON A SHOW.
HA HA!
BECAUSE THEY *WERE.*
SO, AFTER DAVIS' FUNERAL, I WENT BACK TO THE SCENE OF THE CRIME.
SEARCHED THE ARMORED CAR AND FOUND THE TRACKING DEVICE BATROC HAD PLANTED.
HE KNEW IT WOULD BE TAKEN IN FOR REPAIR. AND LEAD HIM RIGHT TO THE SECRET LOCATION OF THIS *WEAPONS LABORATORY.*

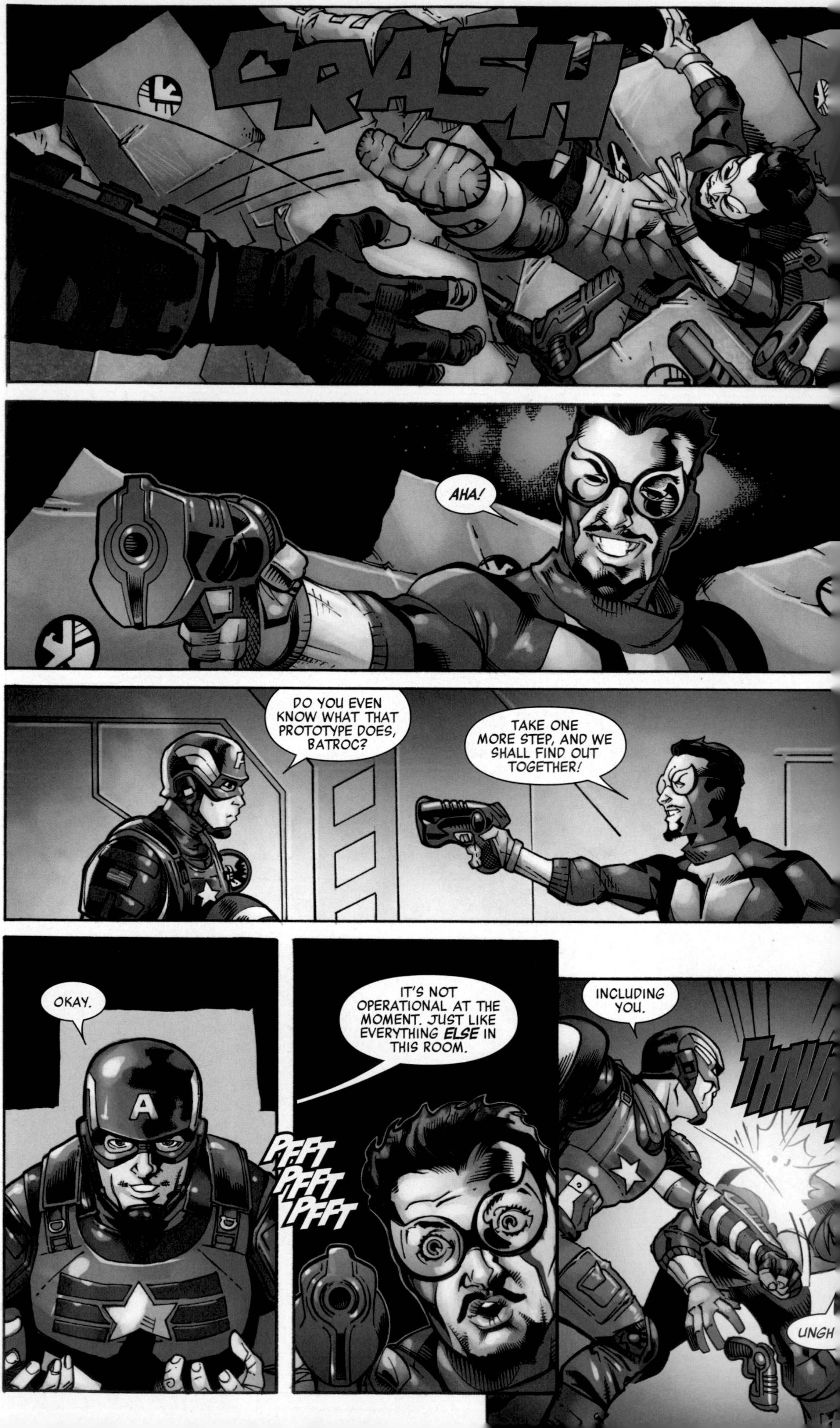
CRASH
AHA!
DO YOU EVEN KNOW WHAT THAT PROTOTYPE DOES, BATROC?
TAKE ONE MORE STEP, AND WE SHALL FIND OUT TOGETHER!
OKAY.
PFFT PFFT PFFT
IT'S NOT OPERATIONAL AT THE MOMENT. JUST LIKE EVERYTHING ELSE IN THIS ROOM.
INCLUDING YOU.
UNGH

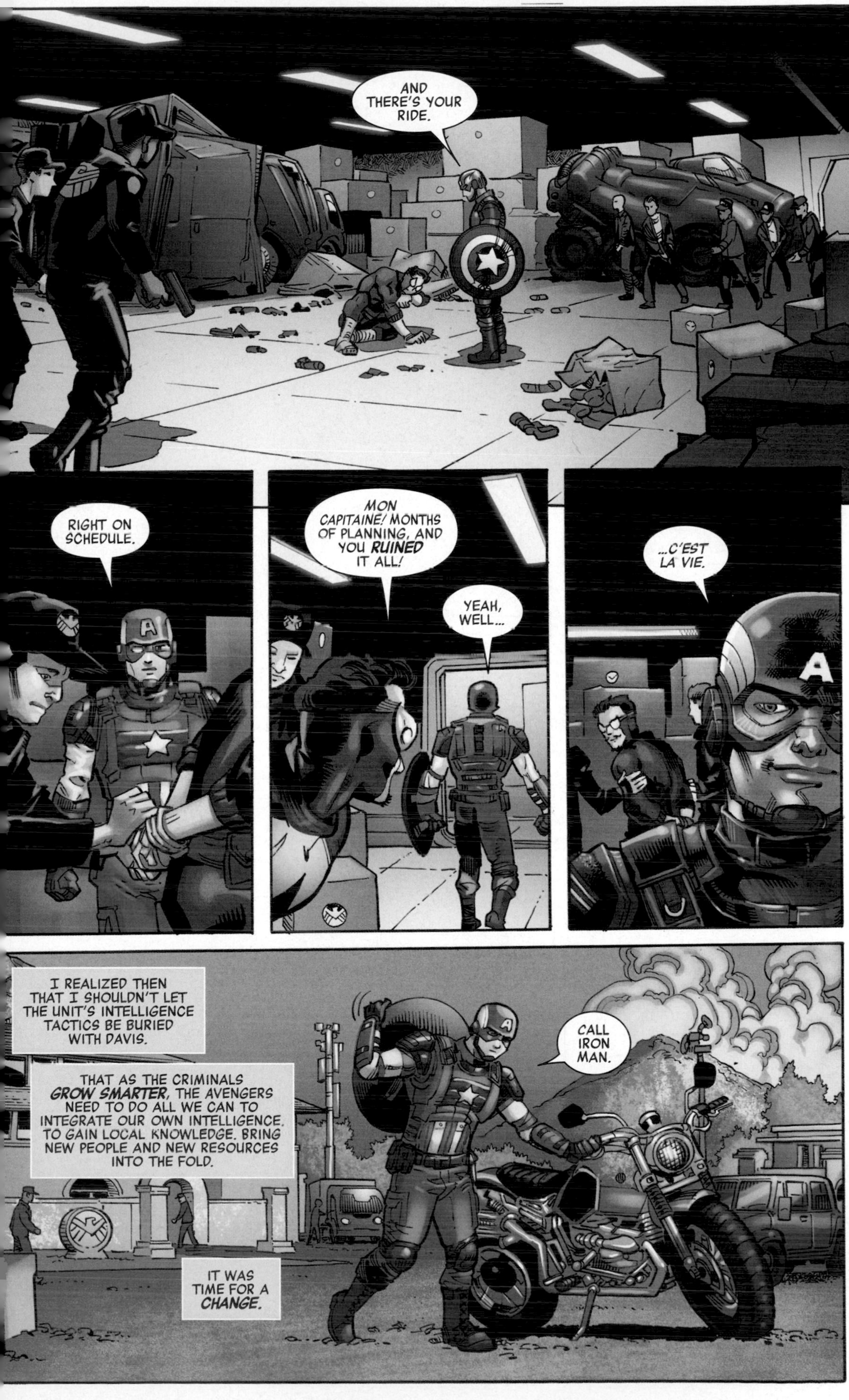
AND THERE'S YOUR RIDE.
RIGHT ON SCHEDULE.
MON CAPITAINE! MONTHS OF PLANNING, AND YOU RUINED IT ALL!
YEAH, WELL...
...C'EST LA VIE.
I REALIZED THEN THAT I SHOULDN'T LET THE UNIT'S INTELLIGENCE TACTICS BE BURIED WITH DAVIS.
THAT AS THE CRIMINALS GROW SMARTER, THE AVENGERS NEED TO DO ALL WE CAN TO INTEGRATE OUR OWN INTELLIGENCE. TO GAIN LOCAL KNOWLEDGE. BRING NEW PEOPLE AND NEW RESOURCES INTO THE FOLD.
CALL IRON MAN.
IT WAS TIME FOR A CHANGE.

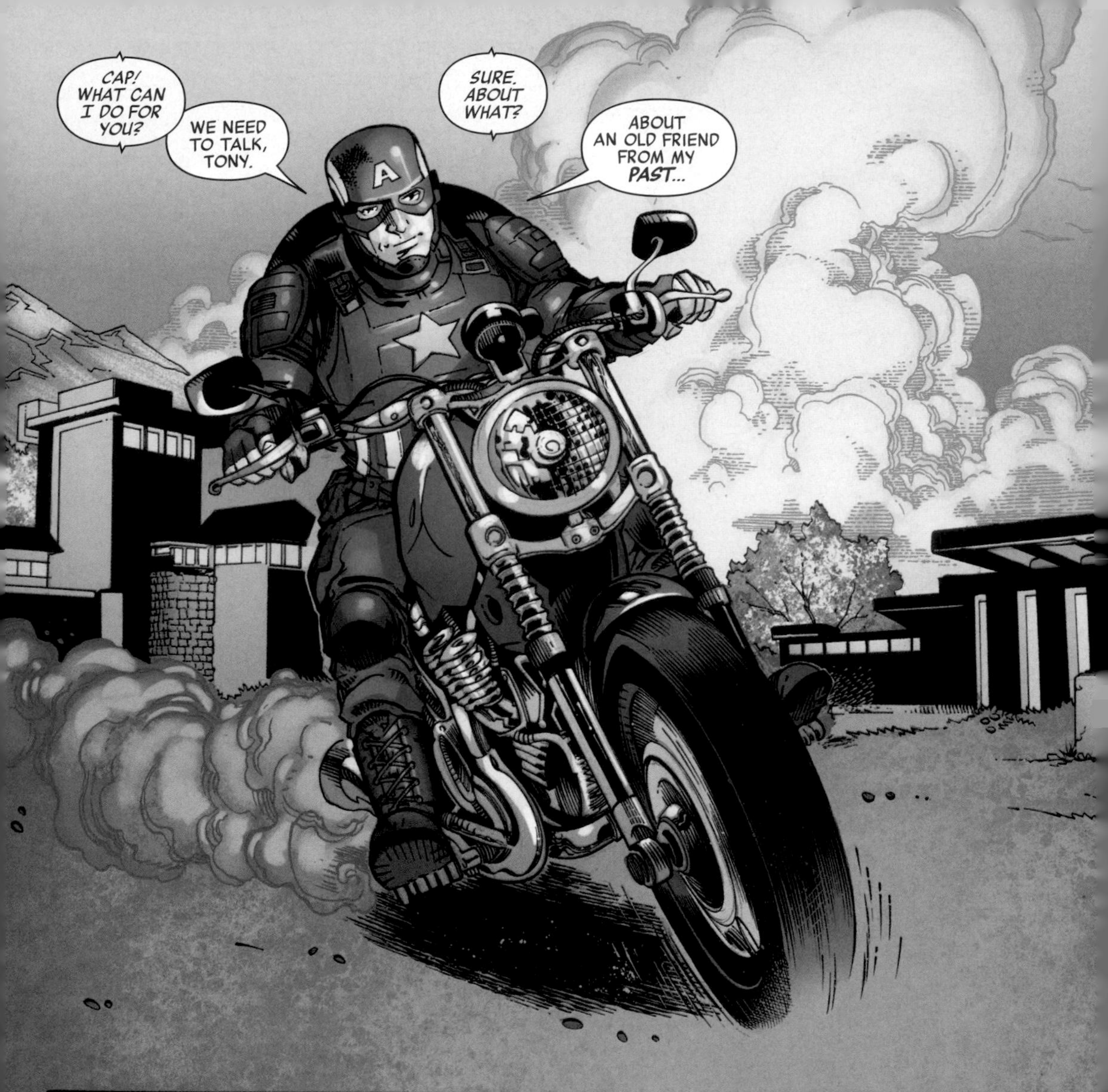
CAP! WHAT CAN I DO FOR YOU?
WE NEED TO TALK, TONY.
SURE. ABOUT WHAT?
ABOUT AN OLD FRIEND FROM MY PAST...

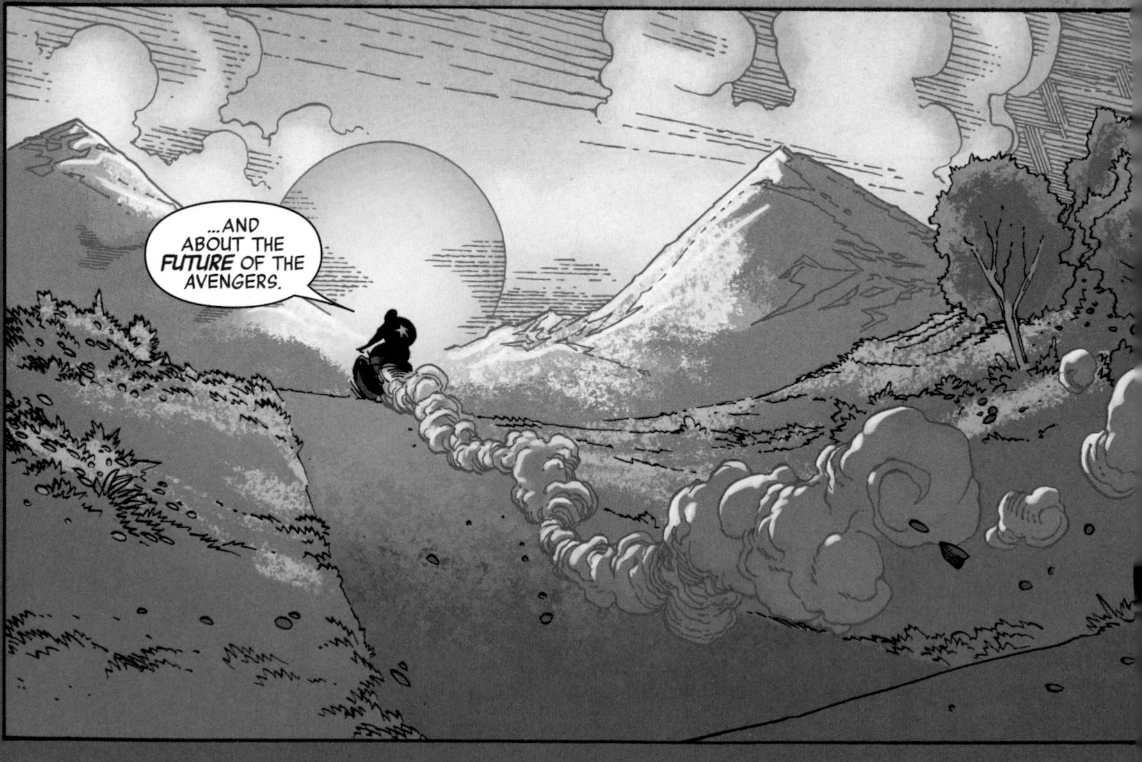
...AND ABOUT THE FUTURE OF THE AVENGERS.

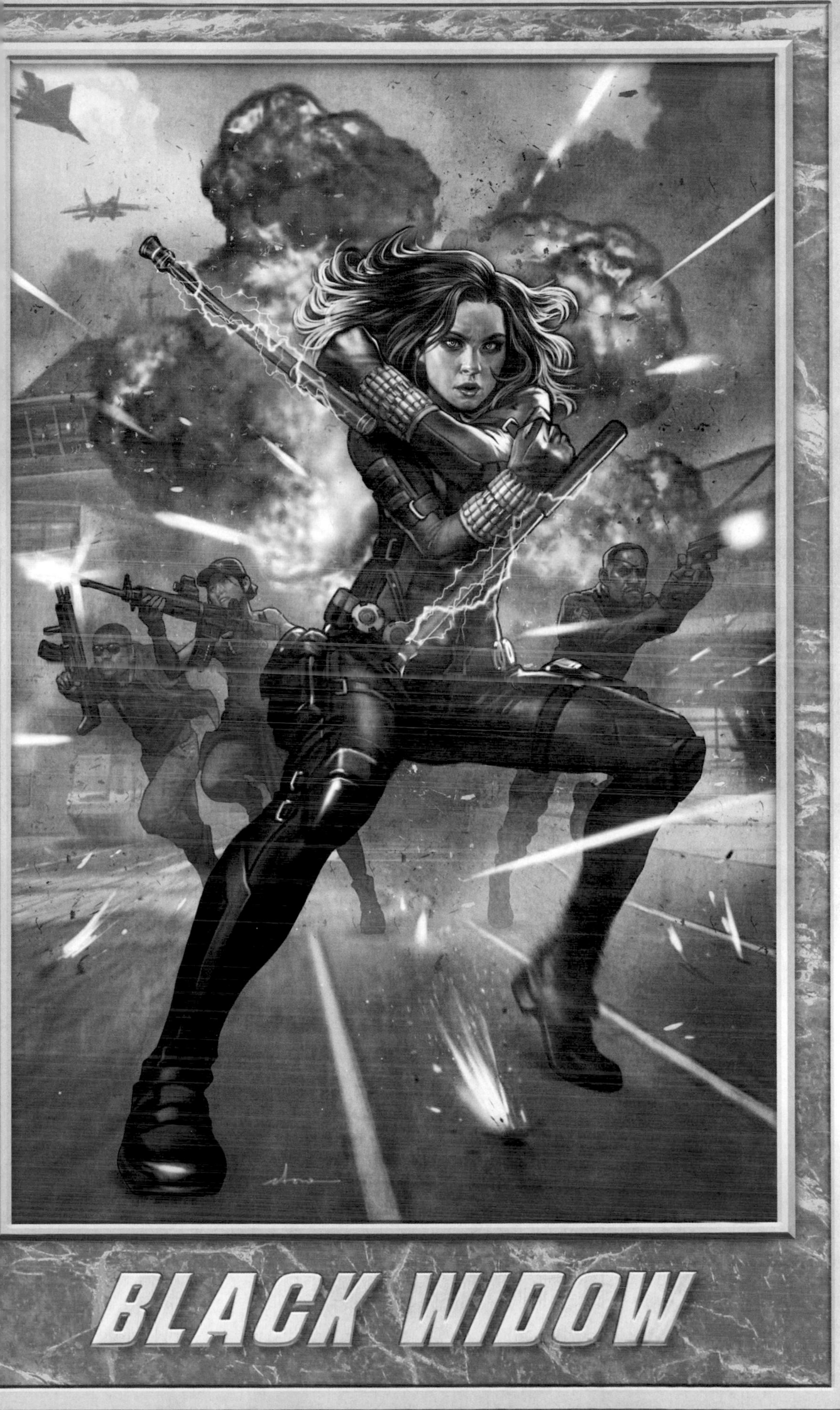
BLACK WIDOW

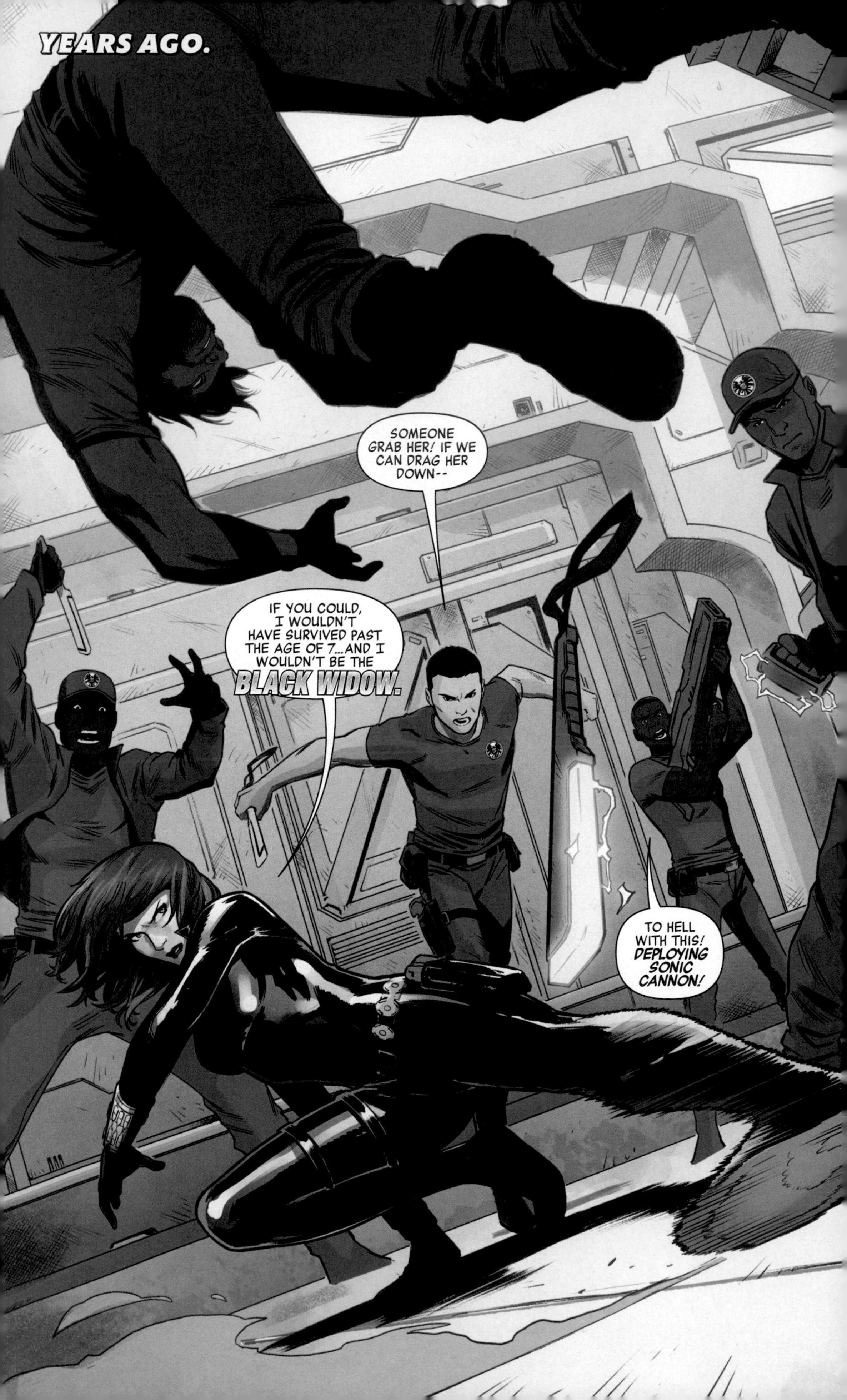

YEARS AGO.
SOMEONE GRAB HER! IF WE CAN DRAG HER DOWN--
IF YOU COULD, I WOULDN'T HAVE SURVIVED PAST THE AGE OF 7...AND I WOULDN'T BE THE BLACK WIDOW.
TO HELL WITH THIS! DEPLOYING SONIC CANNON!

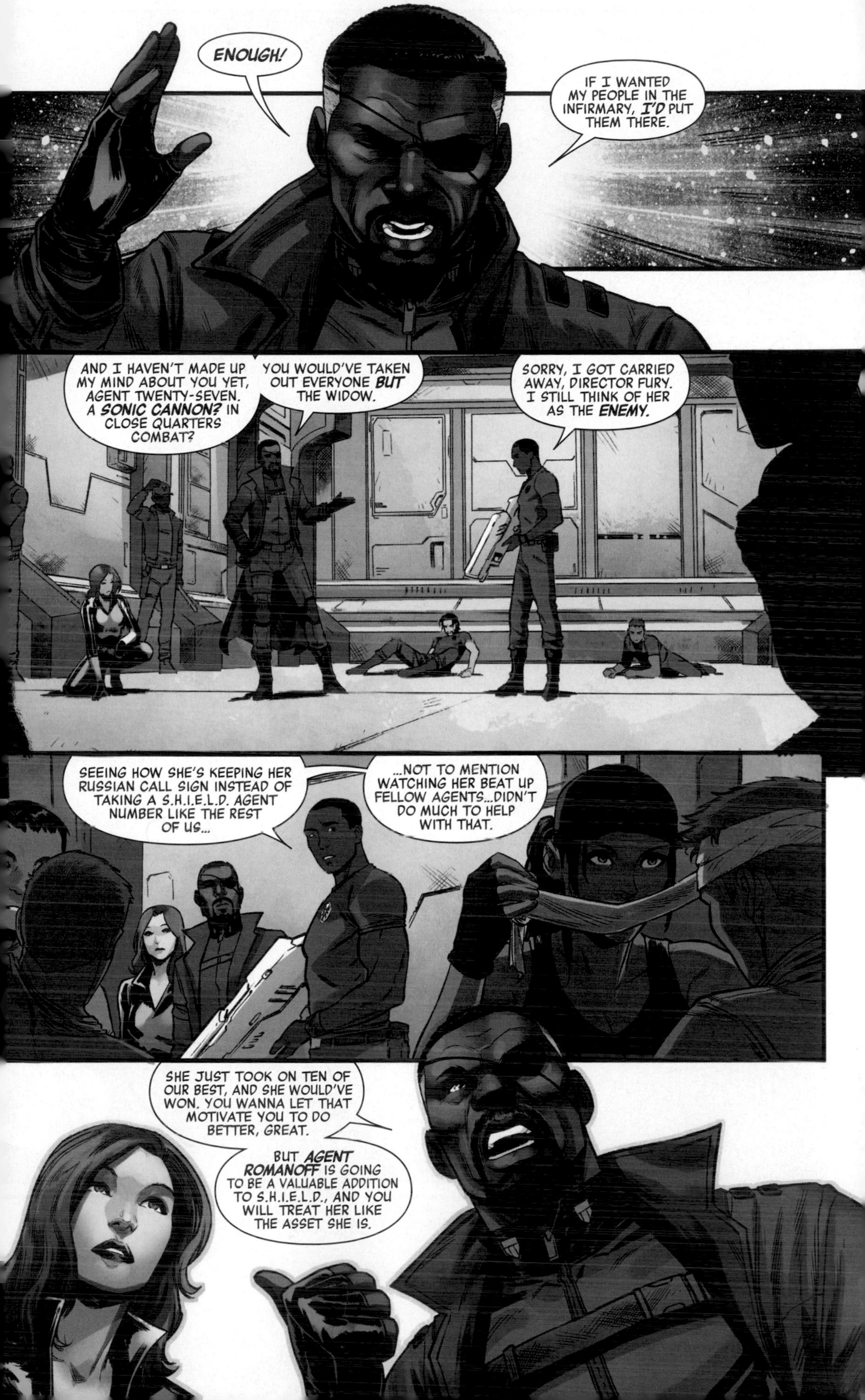
ENOUGH!
IF I WANTED MY PEOPLE IN THE INFIRMARY, I'D PUT THEM THERE.
AND I HAVEN'T MADE UP MY MIND ABOUT YOU YET, AGENT TWENTY-SEVEN. A SONIC CANNON? IN CLOSE QUARTERS COMBAT?
YOU WOULD'VE TAKEN OUT EVERYONE BUT THE WIDOW.
SORRY, I GOT CARRIED AWAY, DIRECTOR FURY. I STILL THINK OF HER AS THE ENEMY.
SEEING HOW SHE'S KEEPING HER RUSSIAN CALL SIGN INSTEAD OF TAKING A S.H.I.E.L.D. AGENT NUMBER LIKE THE REST OF US...
...NOT TO MENTION WATCHING HER BEAT UP FELLOW AGENTS...DIDN'T DO MUCH TO HELP WITH THAT.
SHE JUST TOOK ON TEN OF OUR BEST, AND SHE WOULD'VE WON. YOU WANNA LET THAT MOTIVATE YOU TO DO BETTER, GREAT.
BUT AGENT ROMANOFF IS GOING TO BE A VALUABLE ADDITION TO S.H.I.E.L.D., AND YOU WILL TREAT HER LIKE THE ASSET SHE IS.

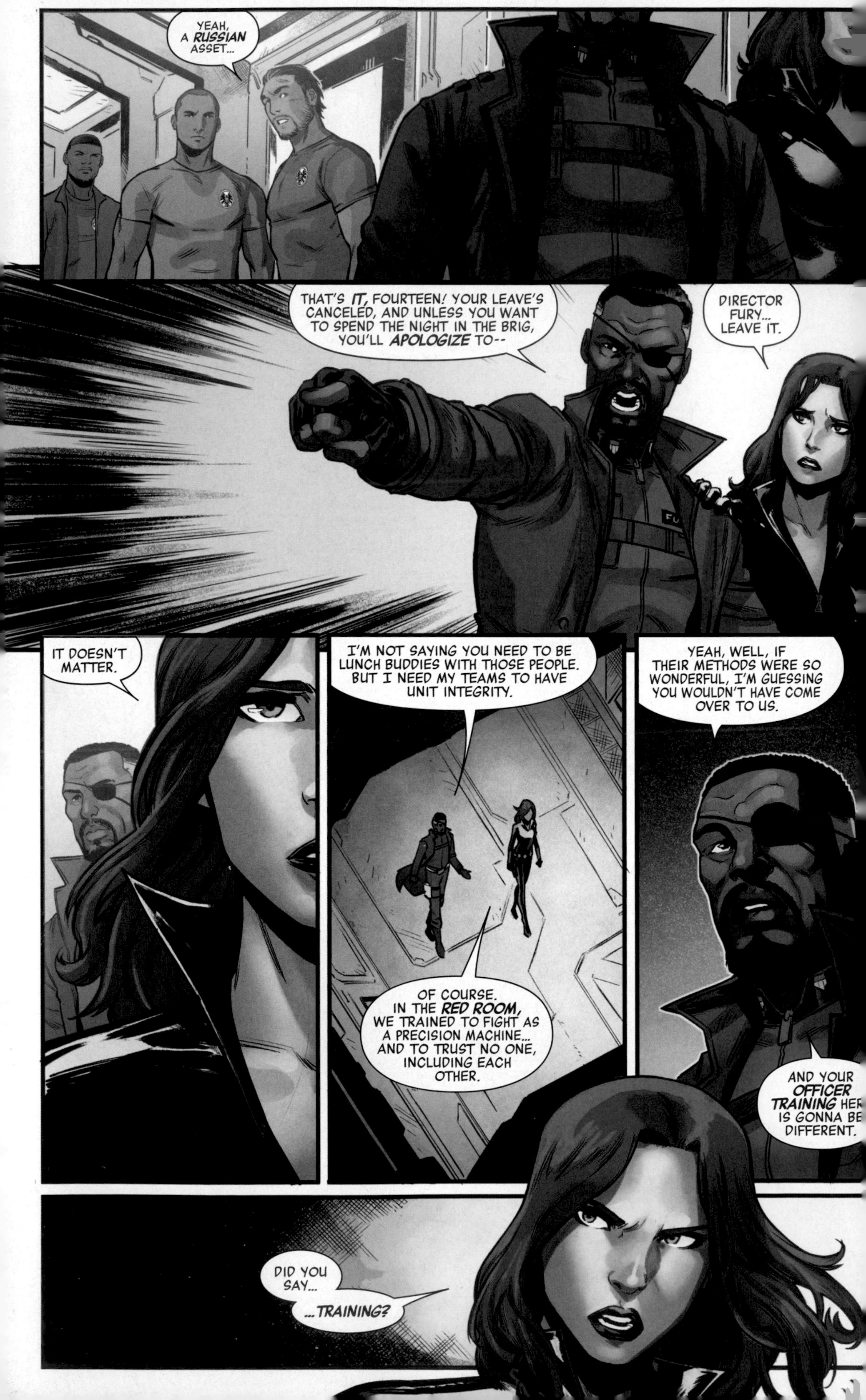
YEAH, A RUSSIAN ASSET...
THAT'S IT, FOURTEEN! YOUR LEAVE'S CANCELED, AND UNLESS YOU WANT TO SPEND THE NIGHT IN THE BRIG, YOU'LL APOLOGIZE TO--
DIRECTOR FURY... LEAVE IT.
IT DOESN'T MATTER.
I'M NOT SAYING YOU NEED TO BE LUNCH BUDDIES WITH THOSE PEOPLE. BUT I NEED MY TEAMS TO HAVE UNIT INTEGRITY.
OF COURSE. IN THE RED ROOM, WE TRAINED TO FIGHT AS A PRECISION MACHINE... AND TO TRUST NO ONE, INCLUDING EACH OTHER.
YEAH, WELL, IF THEIR METHODS WERE SO WONDERFUL, I'M GUESSING YOU WOULDN'T HAVE COME OVER TO US.
AND YOUR OFFICER TRAINING HER IS GONNA BE DIFFERENT.
DID YOU SAY...
...TRAINING?

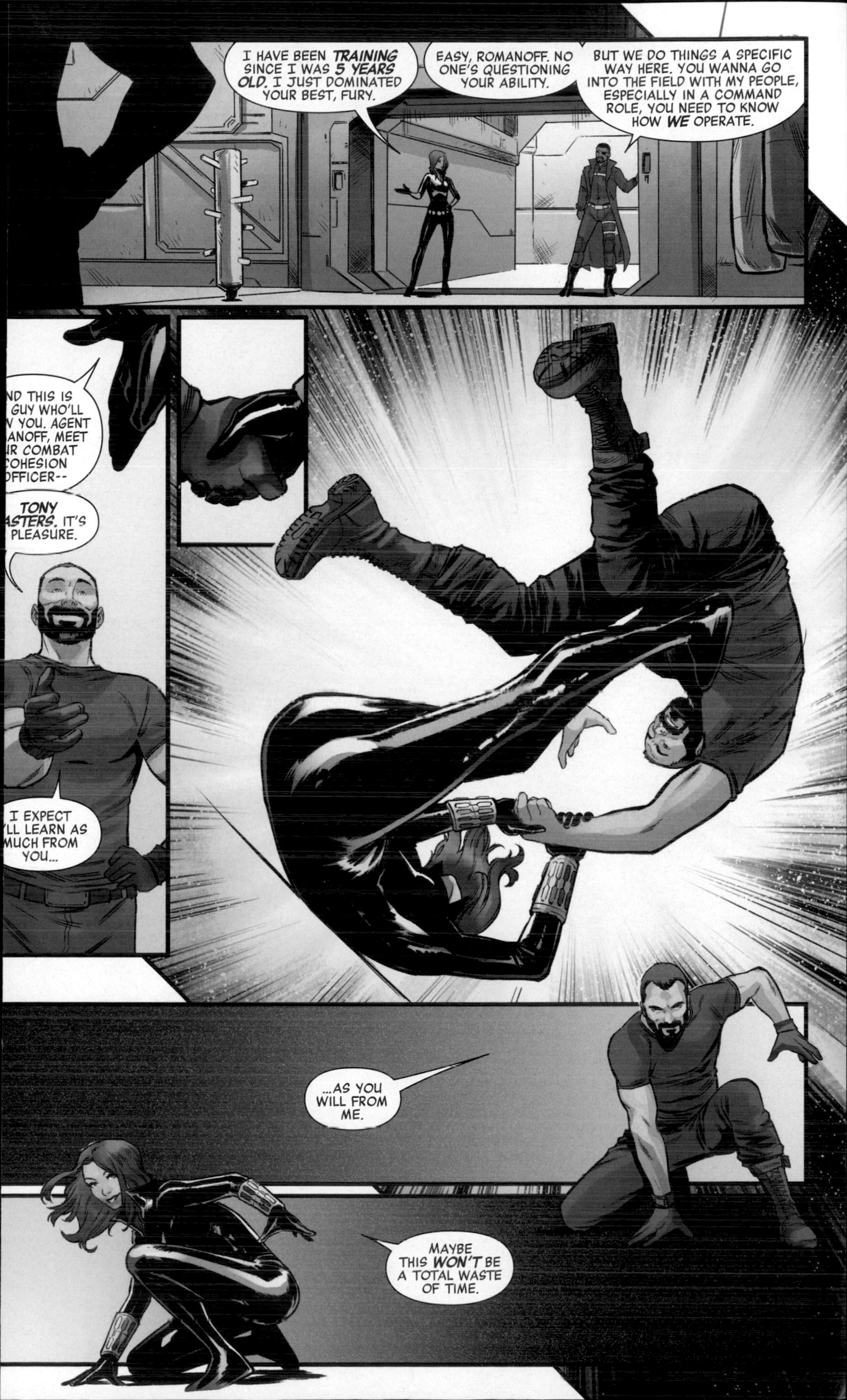
I HAVE BEEN TRAINING SINCE I WAS 5 YEARS OLD. I JUST DOMINATED YOUR BEST, FURY.
EASY, ROMANOFF. NO ONE'S QUESTIONING YOUR ABILITY.
BUT WE DO THINGS A SPECIFIC WAY HERE. YOU WANNA GO INTO THE FIELD WITH MY PEOPLE, ESPECIALLY IN A COMMAND ROLE, YOU NEED TO KNOW HOW WE OPERATE.
ND THIS IS GUY WHO'LL W YOU. AGENT ANOFF, MEET R COMBAT COHESION OFFICER--
TONY ASTERS. IT'S PLEASURE.
I EXPECT 'LL LEARN AS MUCH FROM YOU...
...AS YOU WILL FROM ME.
MAYBE THIS WON'T BE A TOTAL WASTE OF TIME.

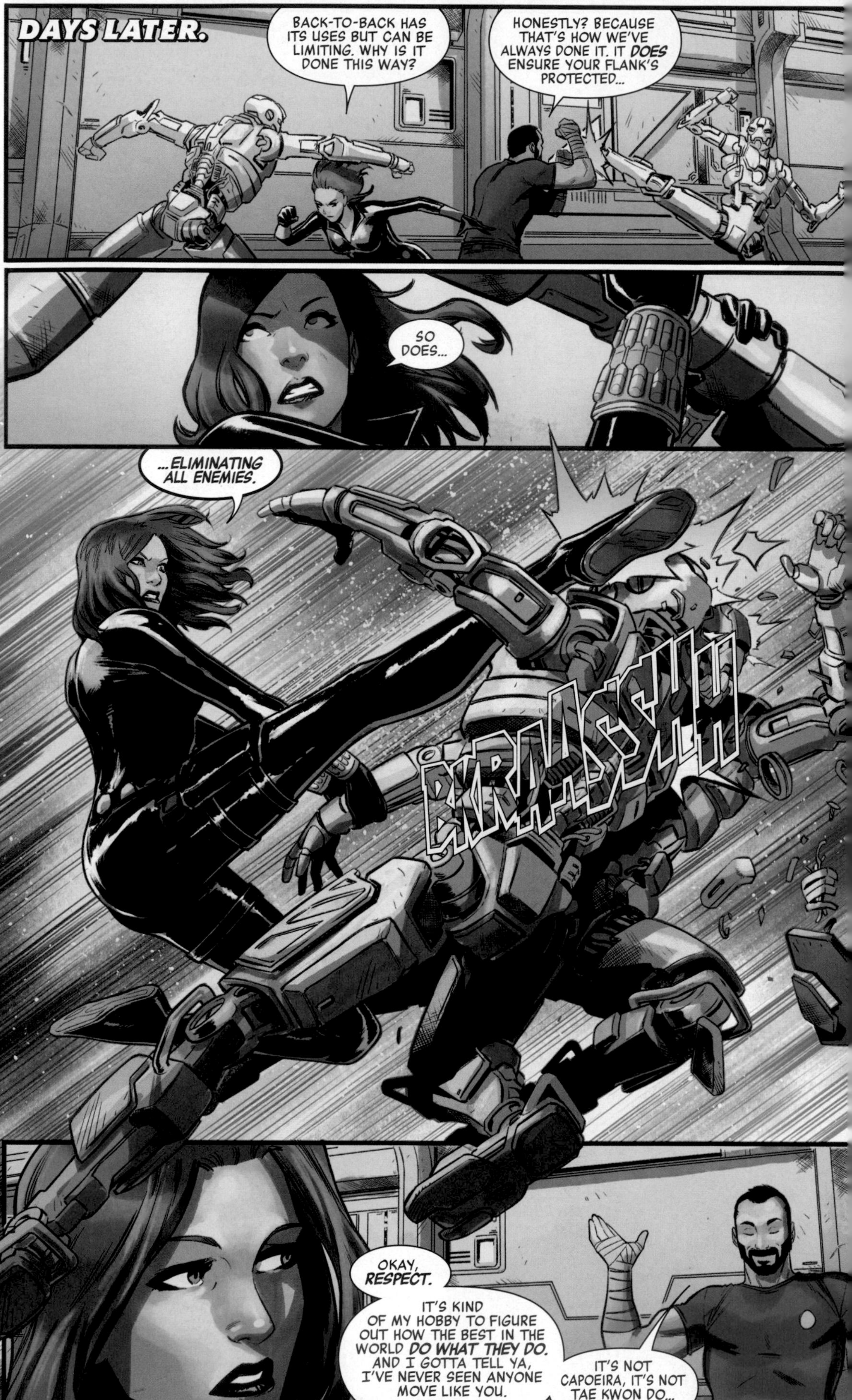

DAYS LATER.
BACK-TO-BACK HAS ITS USES BUT CAN BE LIMITING. WHY IS IT DONE THIS WAY?
HONESTLY? BECAUSE THAT'S HOW WE'VE ALWAYS DONE IT. IT *DOES* ENSURE YOUR FLANK'S PROTECTED...
SO DOES...
...ELIMINATING ALL ENEMIES.
KRRASSHH
OKAY, *RESPECT.*
IT'S KIND OF MY HOBBY TO FIGURE OUT HOW THE BEST IN THE WORLD *DO WHAT THEY DO.* AND I GOTTA TELL YA, I'VE NEVER SEEN ANYONE MOVE LIKE YOU.
IT'S NOT CAPOEIRA, IT'S NOT TAE KWON DO...

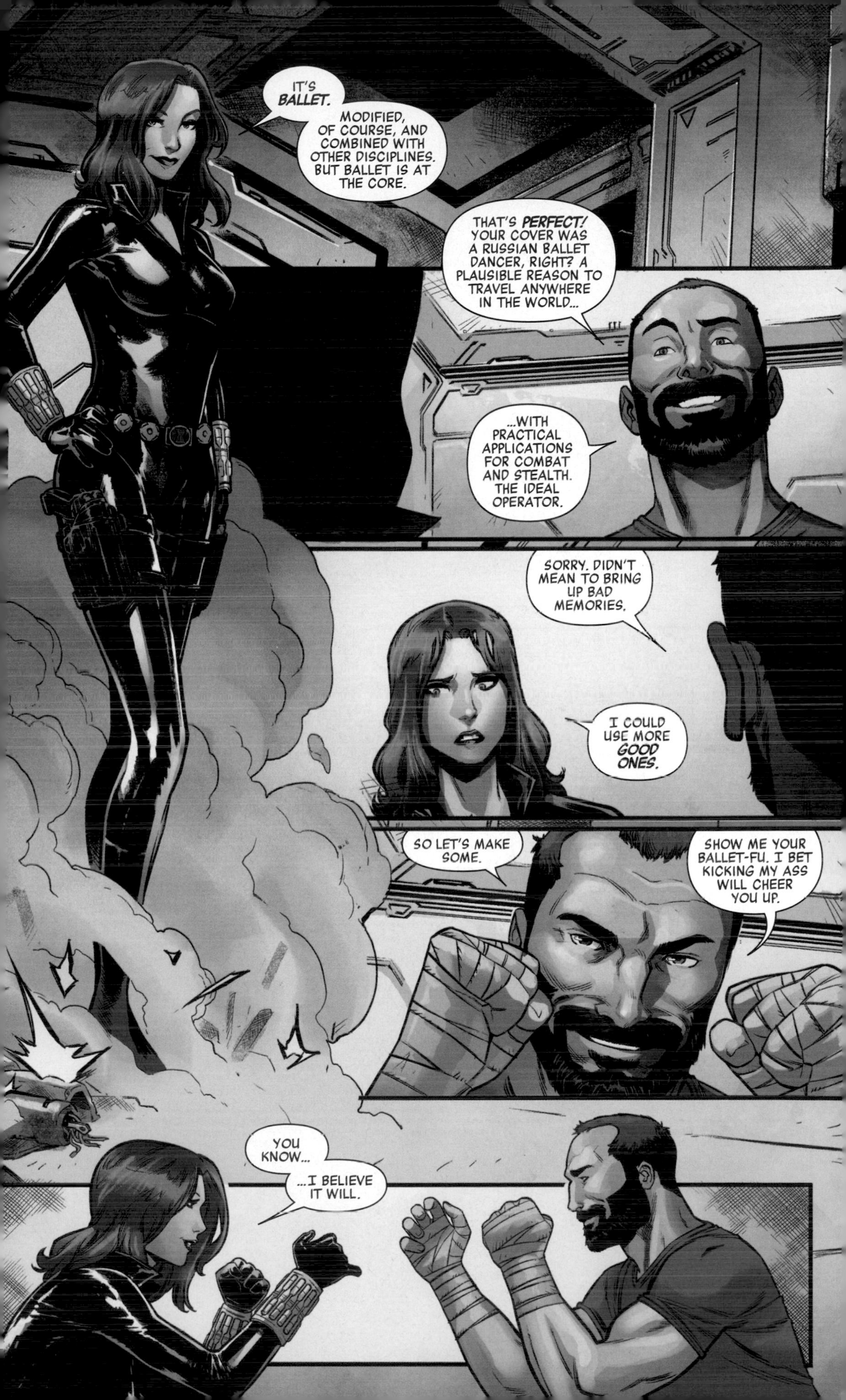
IT'S BALLET.
MODIFIED, OF COURSE, AND COMBINED WITH OTHER DISCIPLINES. BUT BALLET IS AT THE CORE.
THAT'S PERFECT! YOUR COVER WAS A RUSSIAN BALLET DANCER, RIGHT? A PLAUSIBLE REASON TO TRAVEL ANYWHERE IN THE WORLD...
...WITH PRACTICAL APPLICATIONS FOR COMBAT AND STEALTH. THE IDEAL OPERATOR.
SORRY. DIDN'T MEAN TO BRING UP BAD MEMORIES.
I COULD USE MORE GOOD ONES.
SO LET'S MAKE SOME.
SHOW ME YOUR BALLET-FU. I BET KICKING MY ASS WILL CHEER YOU UP.
YOU KNOW...
...I BELIEVE IT WILL.

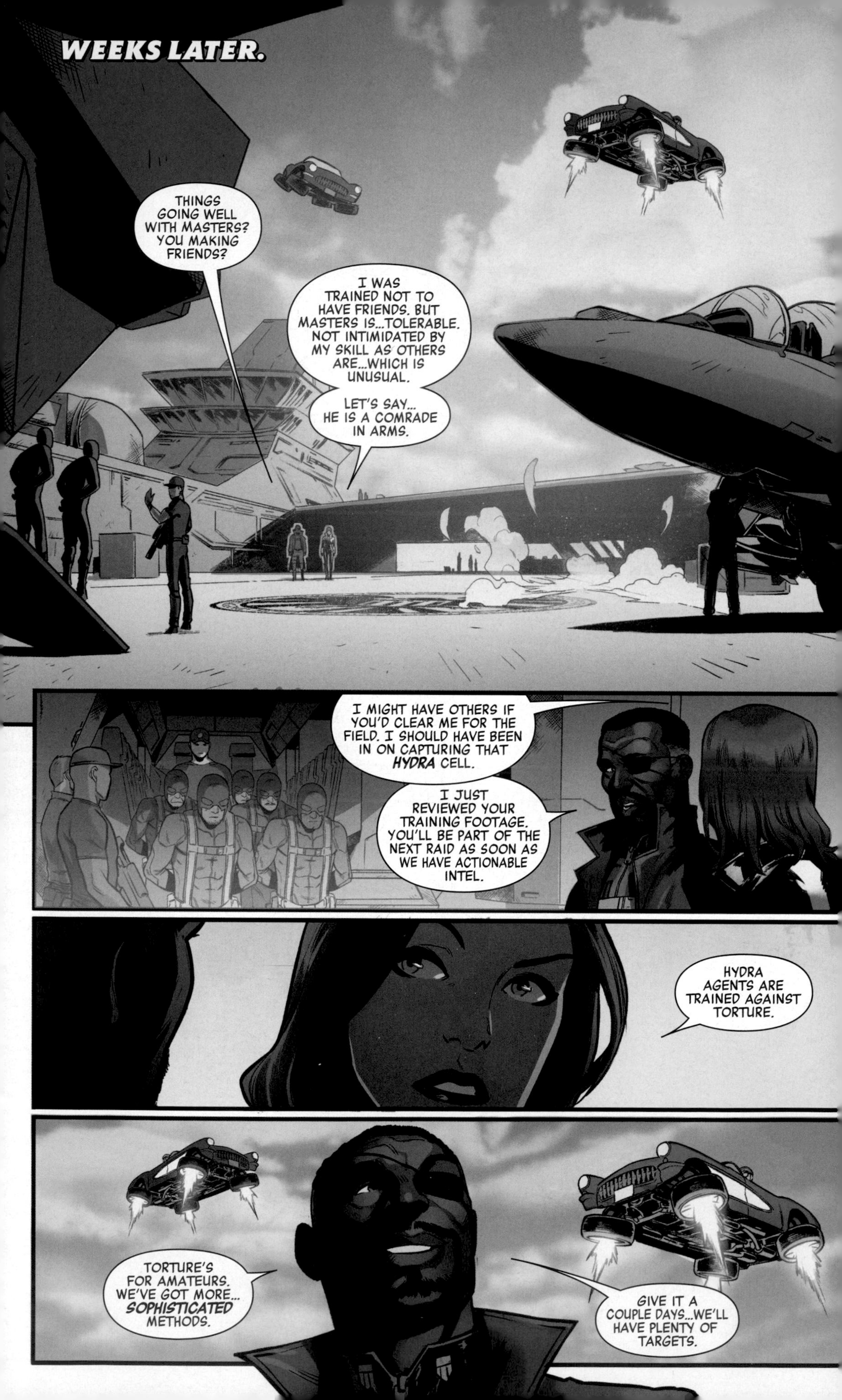
WEEKS LATER.
THINGS GOING WELL WITH MASTERS? YOU MAKING FRIENDS?
I WAS TRAINED NOT TO HAVE FRIENDS. BUT MASTERS IS...TOLERABLE. NOT INTIMIDATED BY MY SKILL AS OTHERS ARE...WHICH IS UNUSUAL.
LET'S SAY... HE IS A COMRADE IN ARMS.
I MIGHT HAVE OTHERS IF YOU'D CLEAR ME FOR THE FIELD. I SHOULD HAVE BEEN IN ON CAPTURING THAT HYDRA CELL.
I JUST REVIEWED YOUR TRAINING FOOTAGE. YOU'LL BE PART OF THE NEXT RAID AS SOON AS WE HAVE ACTIONABLE INTEL.
HYDRA AGENTS ARE TRAINED AGAINST TORTURE.
TORTURE'S FOR AMATEURS. WE'VE GOT MORE... SOPHISTICATED METHODS.
GIVE IT A COUPLE DAYS...WE'LL HAVE PLENTY OF TARGETS.

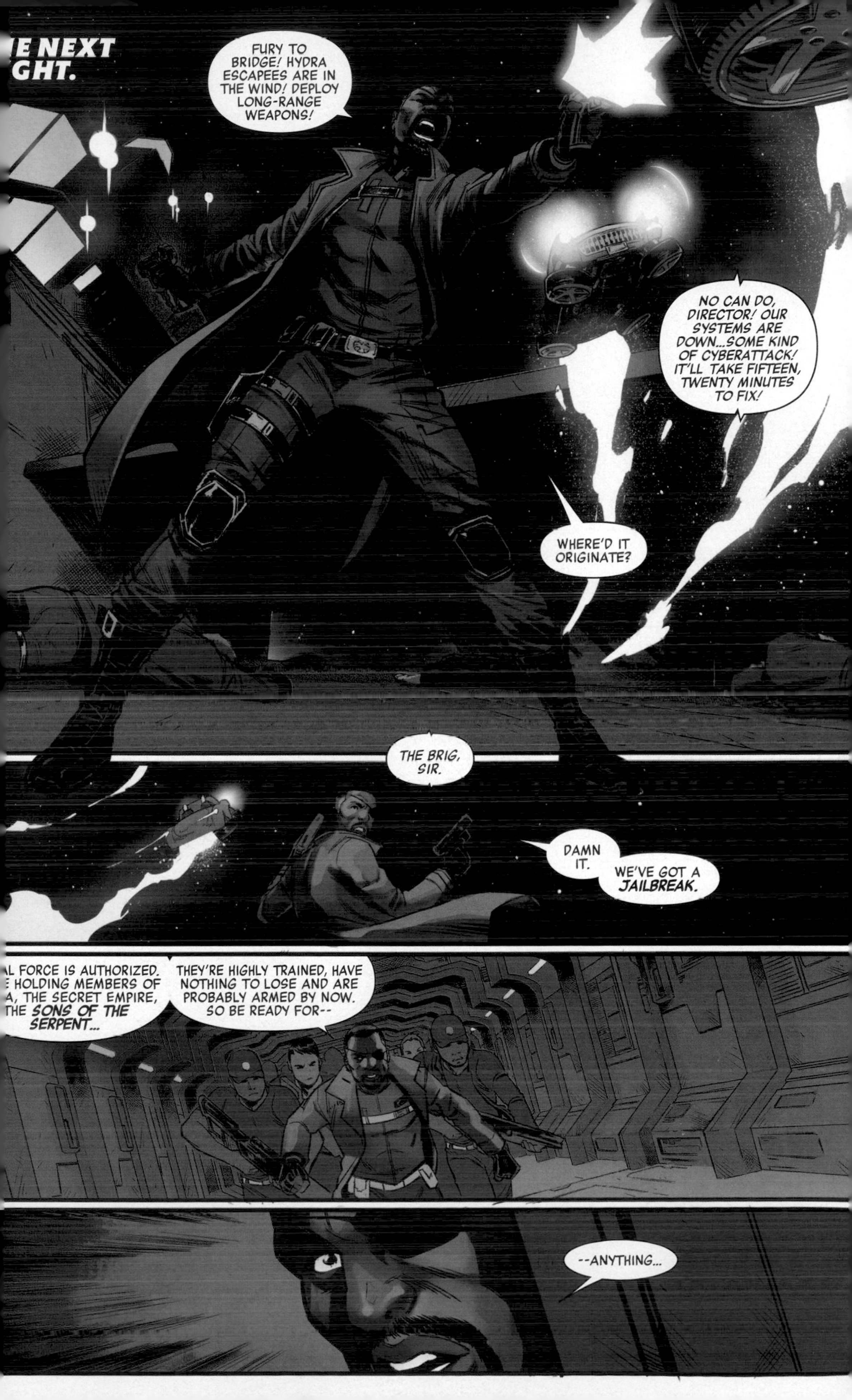
E NEXT
GHT.
FURY TO BRIDGE! HYDRA ESCAPEES ARE IN THE WIND! DEPLOY LONG-RANGE WEAPONS!
NO CAN DO, DIRECTOR! OUR SYSTEMS ARE DOWN...SOME KIND OF CYBERATTACK! IT'LL TAKE FIFTEEN, TWENTY MINUTES TO FIX!
WHERE'D IT ORIGINATE?
THE BRIG, SIR.
DAMN IT.
WE'VE GOT A JAILBREAK.
L FORCE IS AUTHORIZED.
E HOLDING MEMBERS OF
A, THE SECRET EMPIRE,
THE SONS OF THE SERPENT...
THEY'RE HIGHLY TRAINED, HAVE NOTHING TO LOSE AND ARE PROBABLY ARMED BY NOW. SO BE READY FOR--
--ANYTHING...

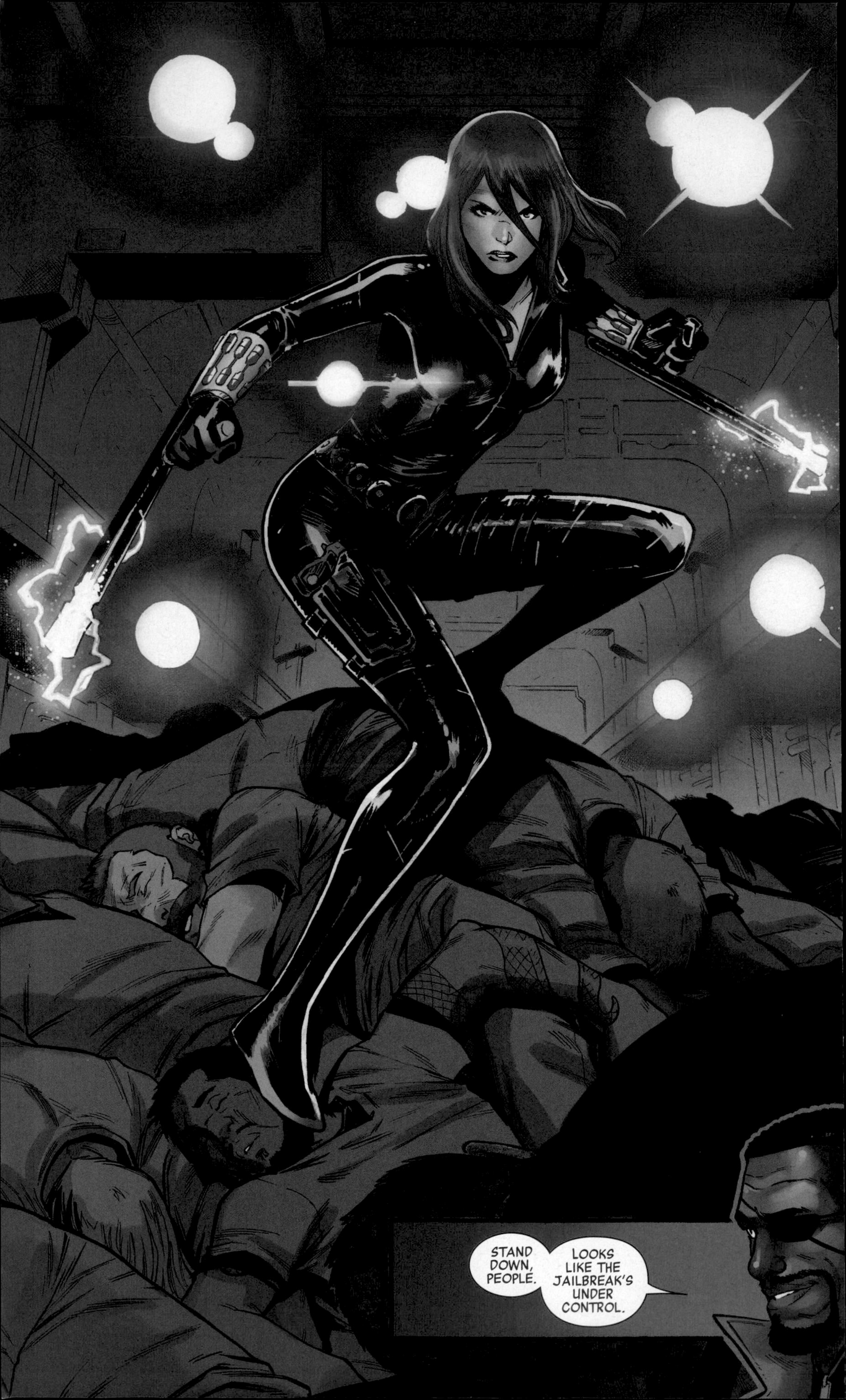
STAND DOWN, PEOPLE.
LOOKS LIKE THE JAILBREAK'S UNDER CONTROL.

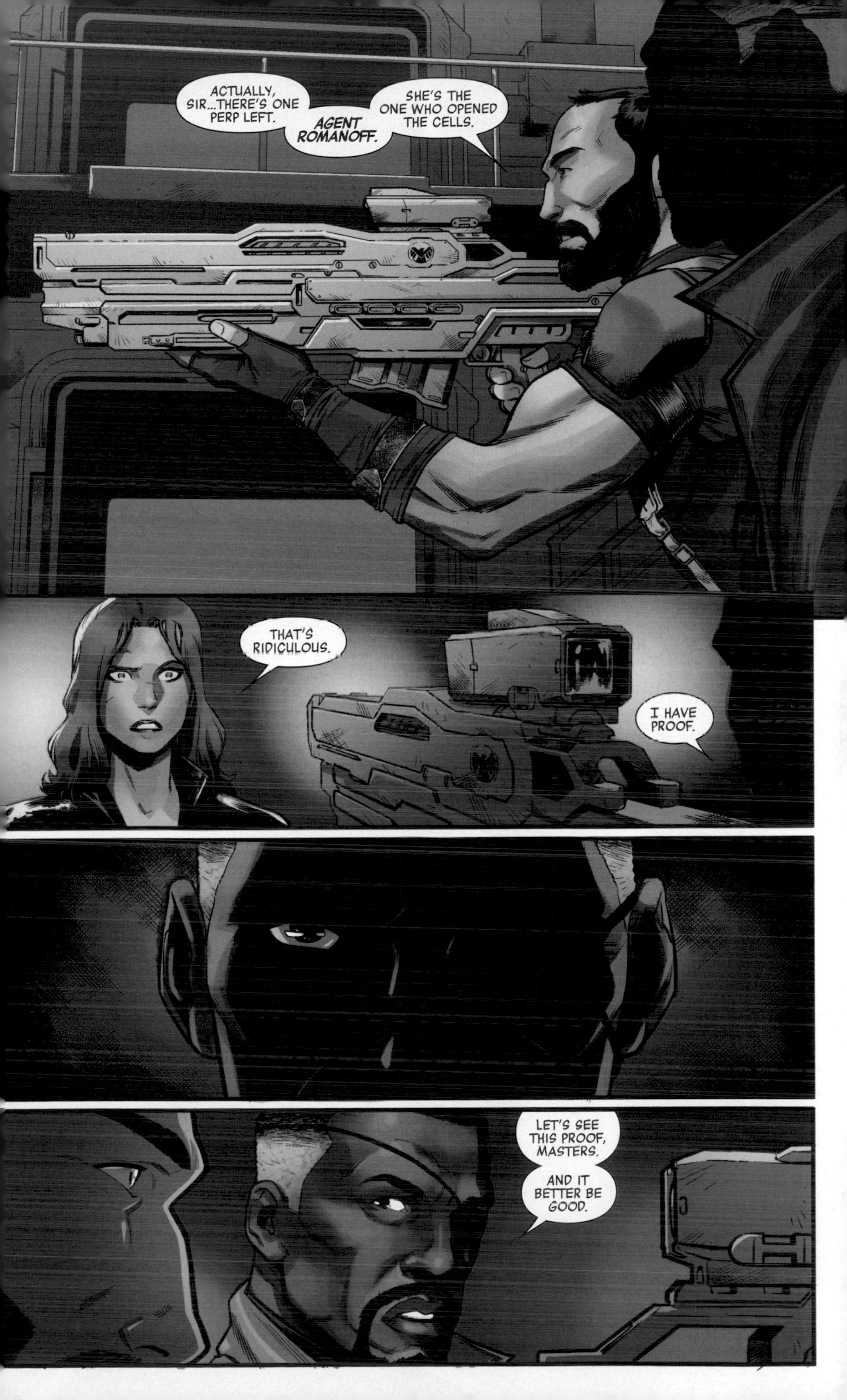
ACTUALLY, SIR...THERE'S ONE PERP LEFT.
AGENT ROMANOFF.
SHE'S THE ONE WHO OPENED THE CELLS.
THAT'S RIDICULOUS.
I HAVE PROOF.
LET'S SEE THIS PROOF, MASTERS.
AND IT BETTER BE GOOD.

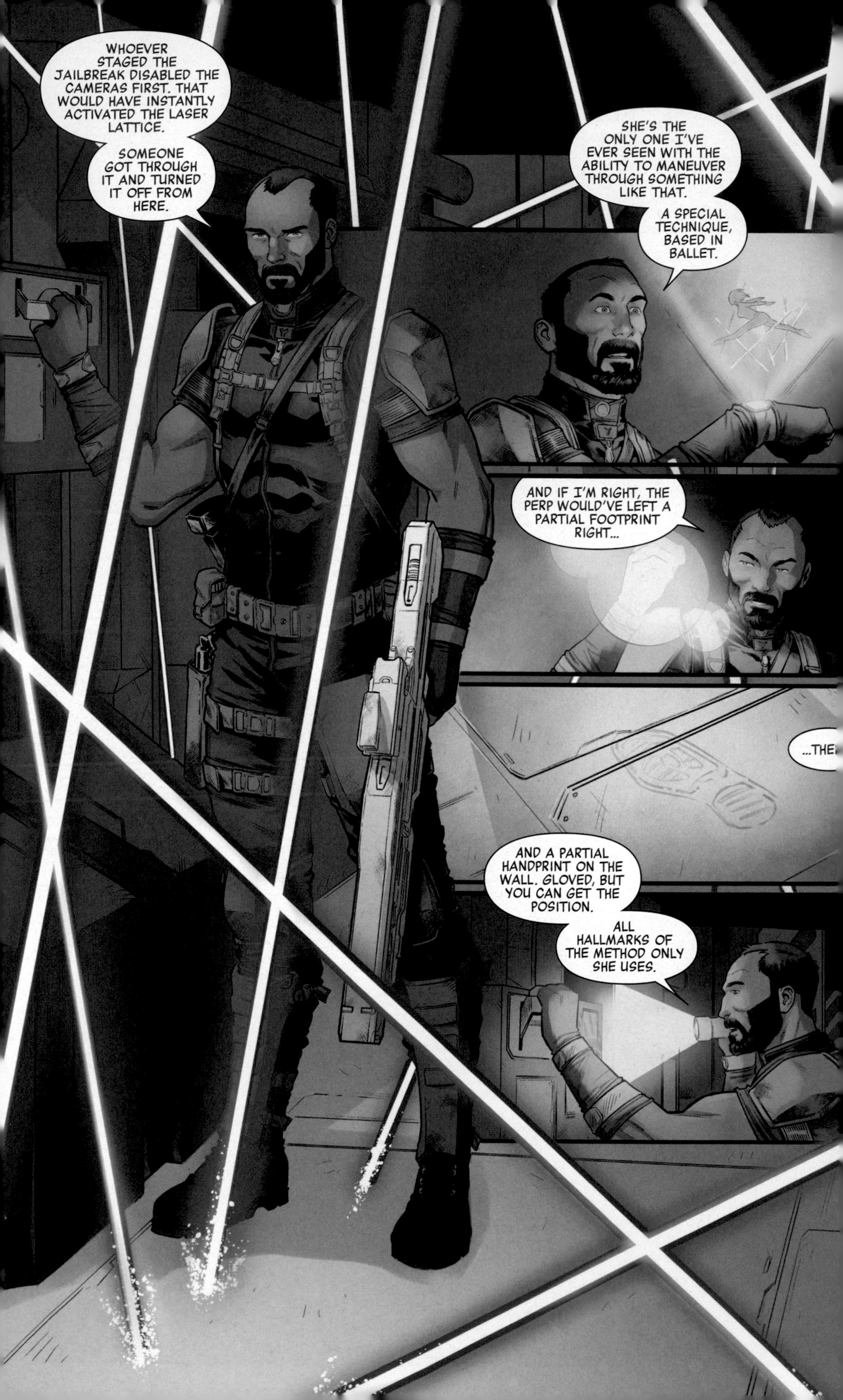
WHOEVER STAGED THE JAILBREAK DISABLED THE CAMERAS FIRST. THAT WOULD HAVE INSTANTLY ACTIVATED THE LASER LATTICE.
SOMEONE GOT THROUGH IT AND TURNED IT OFF FROM HERE.
SHE'S THE ONLY ONE I'VE EVER SEEN WITH THE ABILITY TO MANEUVER THROUGH SOMETHING LIKE THAT.
A SPECIAL TECHNIQUE, BASED IN BALLET.
AND IF I'M RIGHT, THE PERP WOULD'VE LEFT A PARTIAL FOOTPRINT RIGHT...
...THE
AND A PARTIAL HANDPRINT ON THE WALL. GLOVED, BUT YOU CAN GET THE POSITION.
ALL HALLMARKS OF THE METHOD ONLY SHE USES.

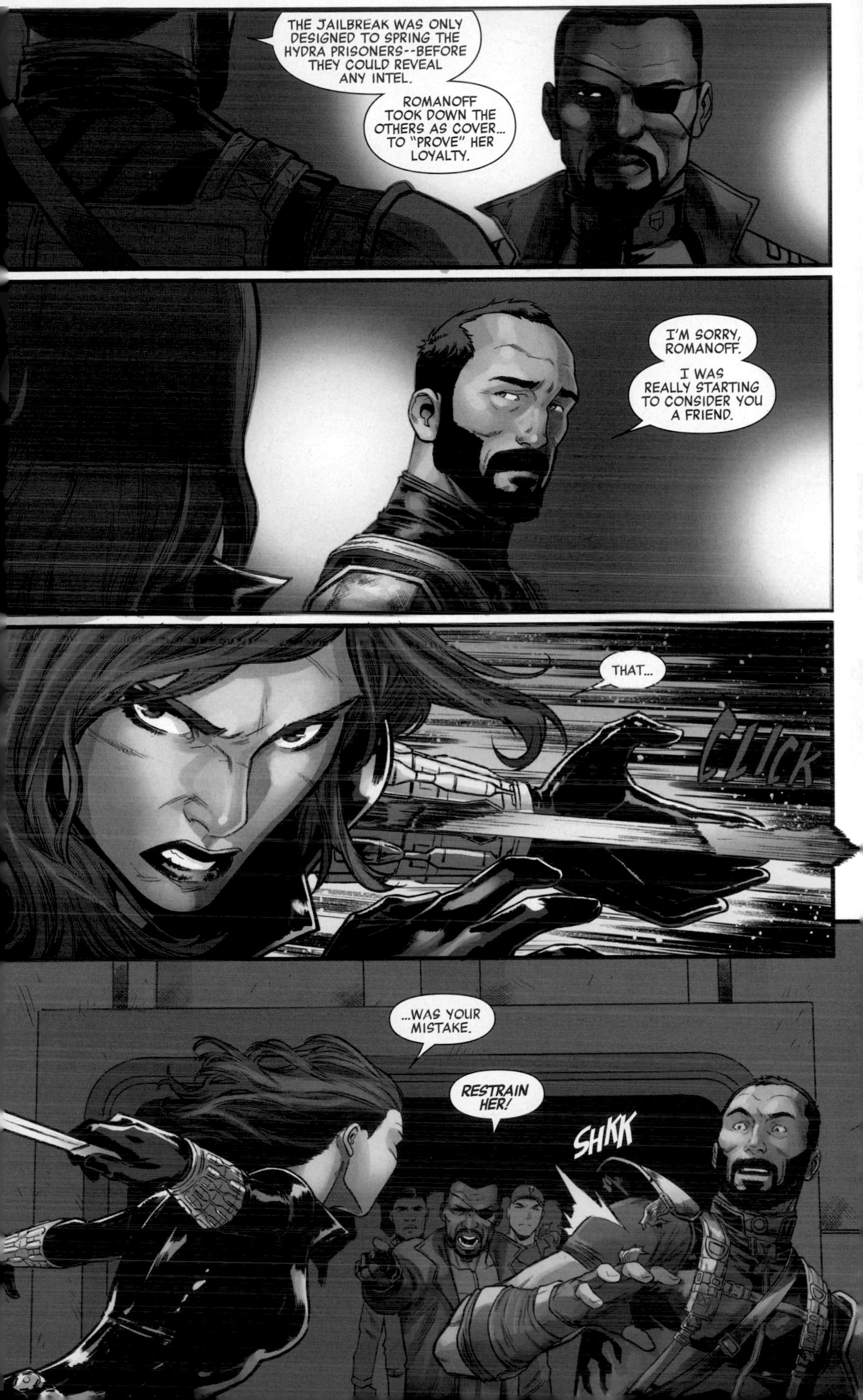
THE JAILBREAK WAS ONLY DESIGNED TO SPRING THE HYDRA PRISONERS--BEFORE THEY COULD REVEAL ANY INTEL.
ROMANOFF TOOK DOWN THE OTHERS AS COVER... TO "PROVE" HER LOYALTY.
I'M SORRY, ROMANOFF.
I WAS REALLY STARTING TO CONSIDER YOU A FRIEND.
THAT...
CLICK
...WAS YOUR MISTAKE.
RESTRAIN HER!
SHKK

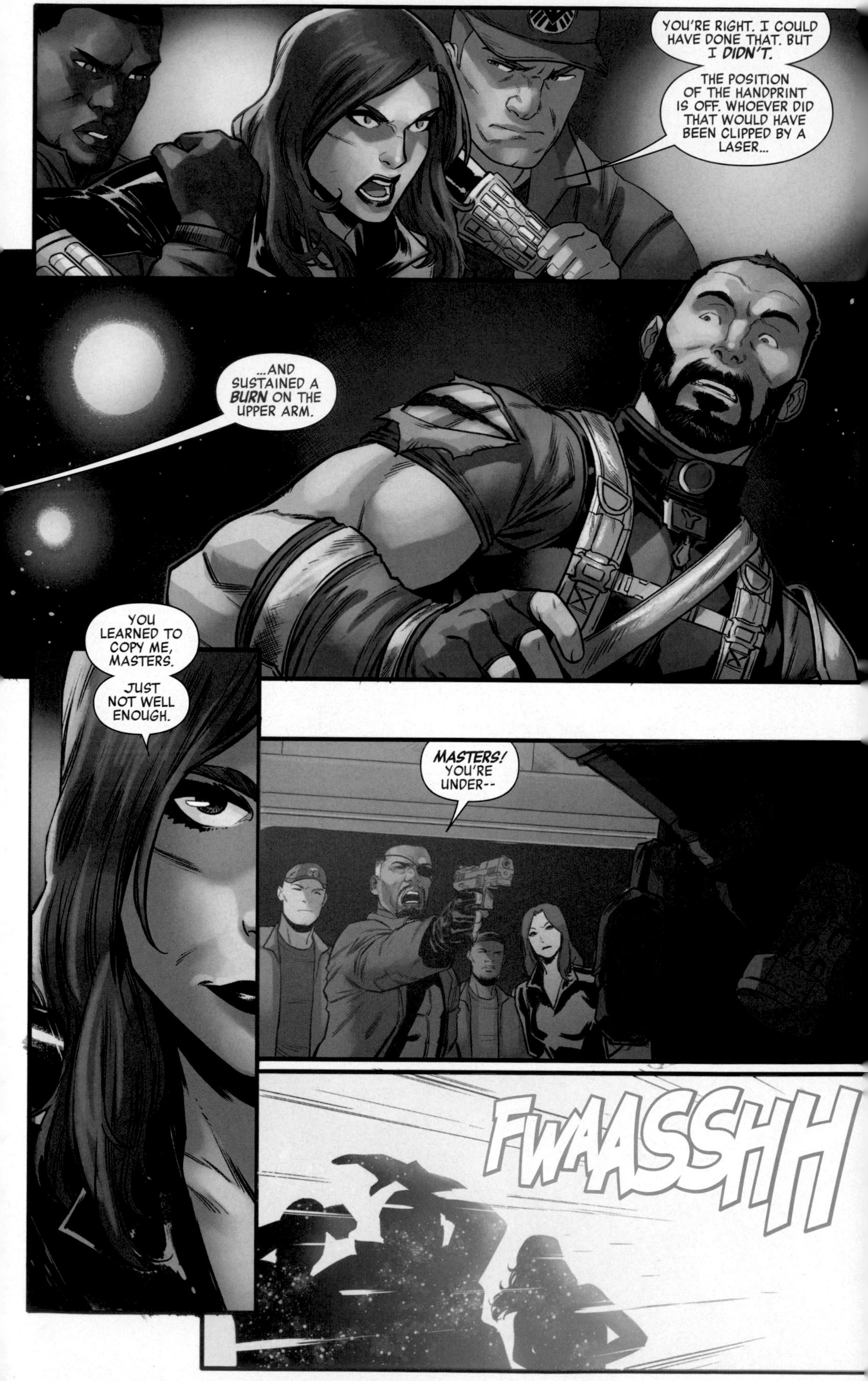
YOU'RE RIGHT. I COULD HAVE DONE THAT. BUT I DIDN'T.
THE POSITION OF THE HANDPRINT IS OFF. WHOEVER DID THAT WOULD HAVE BEEN CLIPPED BY A LASER...
...AND SUSTAINED A BURN ON THE UPPER ARM.
YOU LEARNED TO COPY ME, MASTERS.
JUST NOT WELL ENOUGH.
MASTERS! YOU'RE UNDER--
FWAASSHH

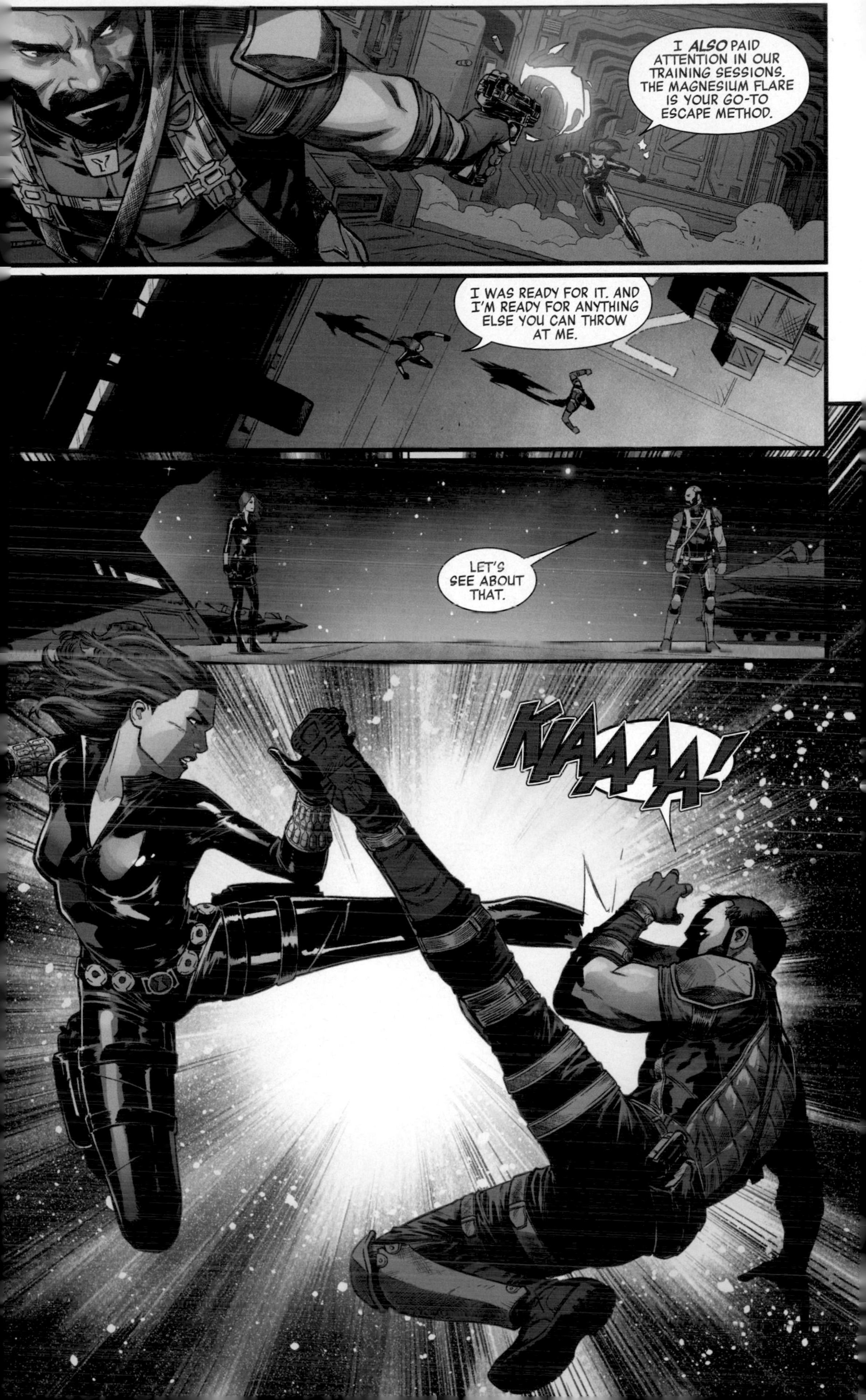
I ALSO PAID ATTENTION IN OUR TRAINING SESSIONS. THE MAGNESIUM FLARE IS YOUR GO-TO ESCAPE METHOD.
I WAS READY FOR IT. AND I'M READY FOR ANYTHING ELSE YOU CAN THROW AT ME.
LET'S SEE ABOUT THAT.
KIAAAA!

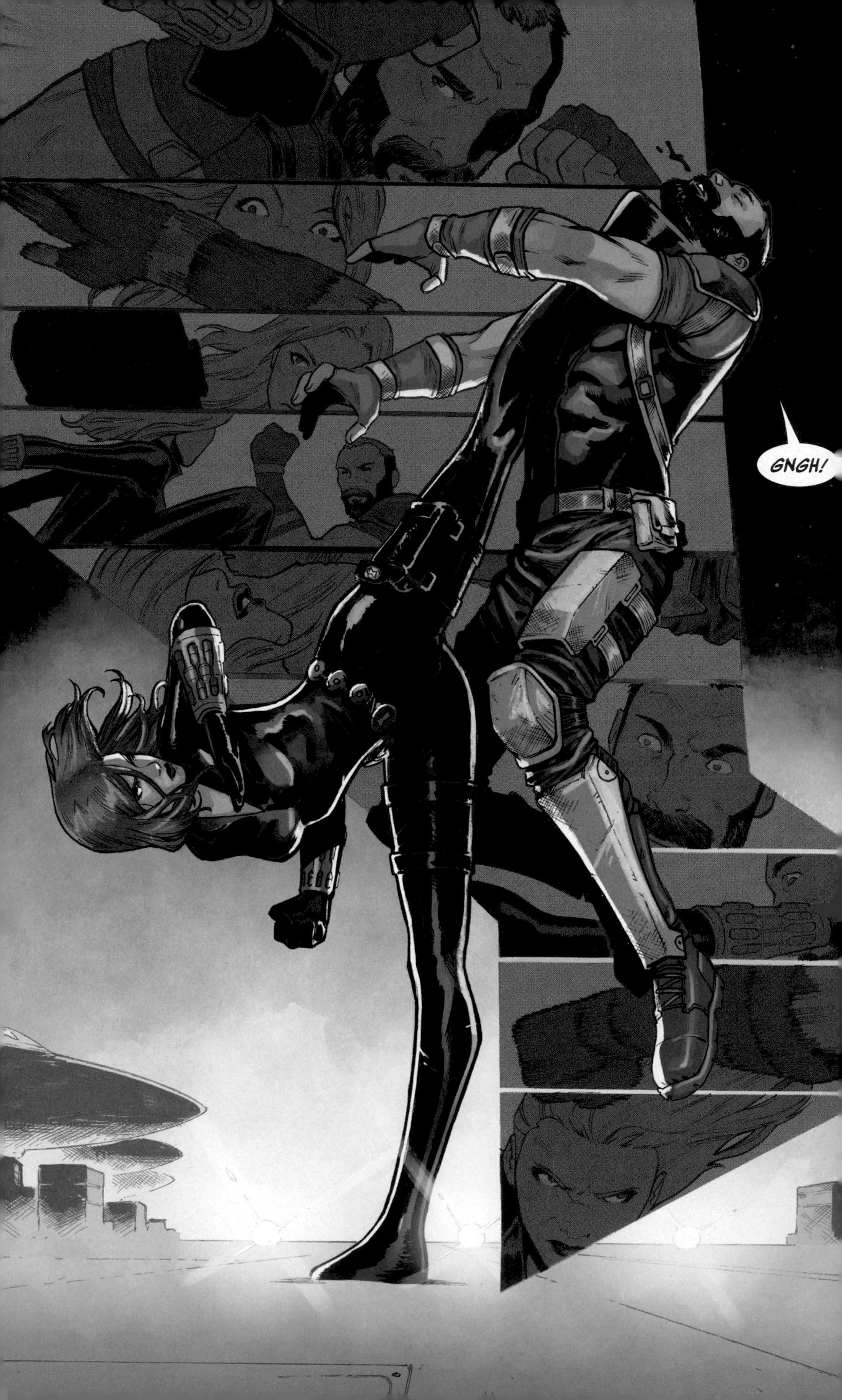
GNGH!

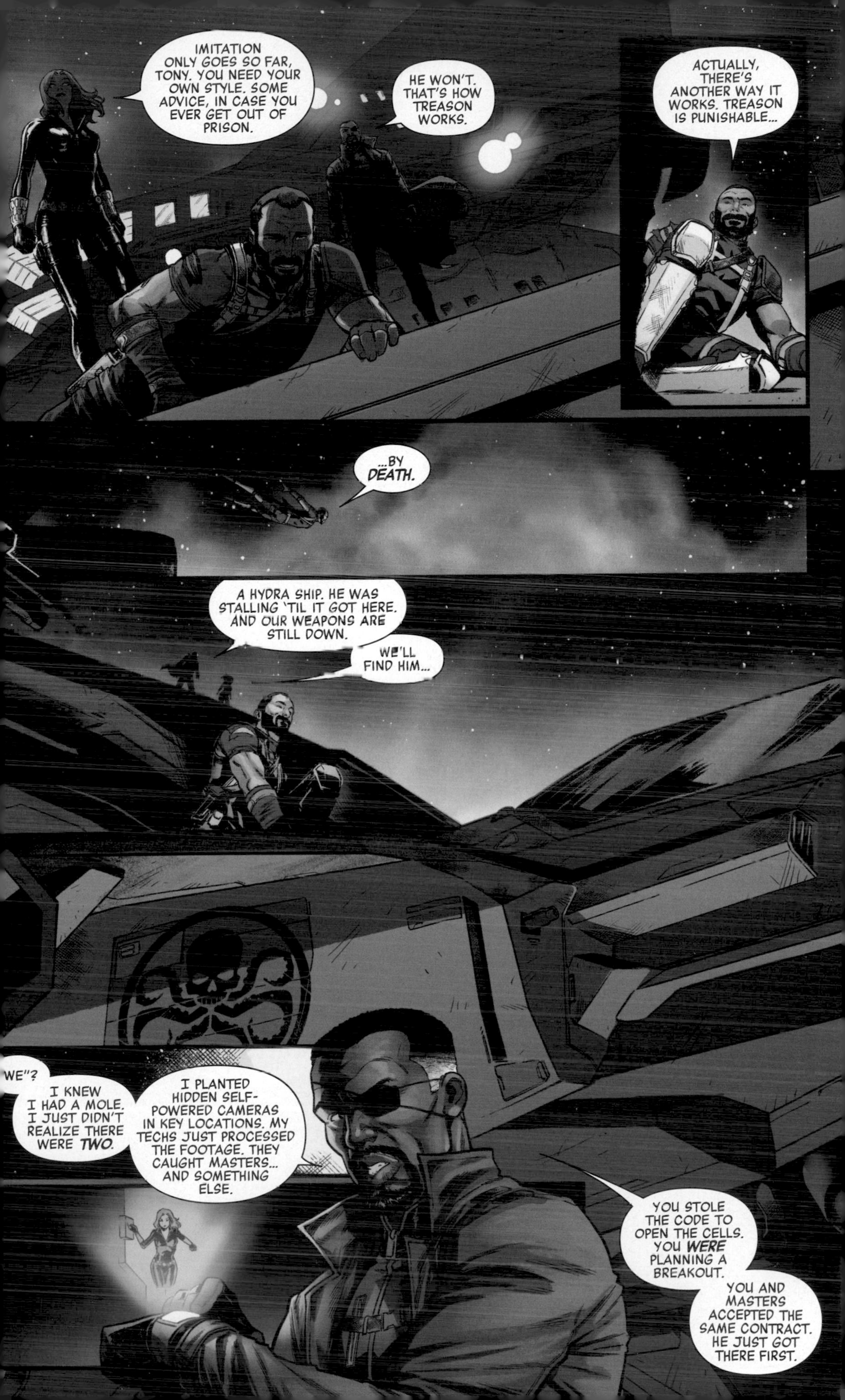
IMITATION ONLY GOES SO FAR, TONY. YOU NEED YOUR OWN STYLE. SOME ADVICE, IN CASE YOU EVER GET OUT OF PRISON.
HE WON'T. THAT'S HOW TREASON WORKS.
ACTUALLY, THERE'S ANOTHER WAY IT WORKS. TREASON IS PUNISHABLE...
...BY DEATH.
A HYDRA SHIP. HE WAS STALLING 'TIL IT GOT HERE. AND OUR WEAPONS ARE STILL DOWN.
WE'LL FIND HIM...
WE"?
I KNEW I HAD A MOLE. I JUST DIDN'T REALIZE THERE WERE TWO.
I PLANTED HIDDEN SELF-POWERED CAMERAS IN KEY LOCATIONS. MY TECHS JUST PROCESSED THE FOOTAGE. THEY CAUGHT MASTERS... AND SOMETHING ELSE.
YOU STOLE THE CODE TO OPEN THE CELLS. YOU WERE PLANNING A BREAKOUT.
YOU AND MASTERS ACCEPTED THE SAME CONTRACT. HE JUST GOT THERE FIRST.

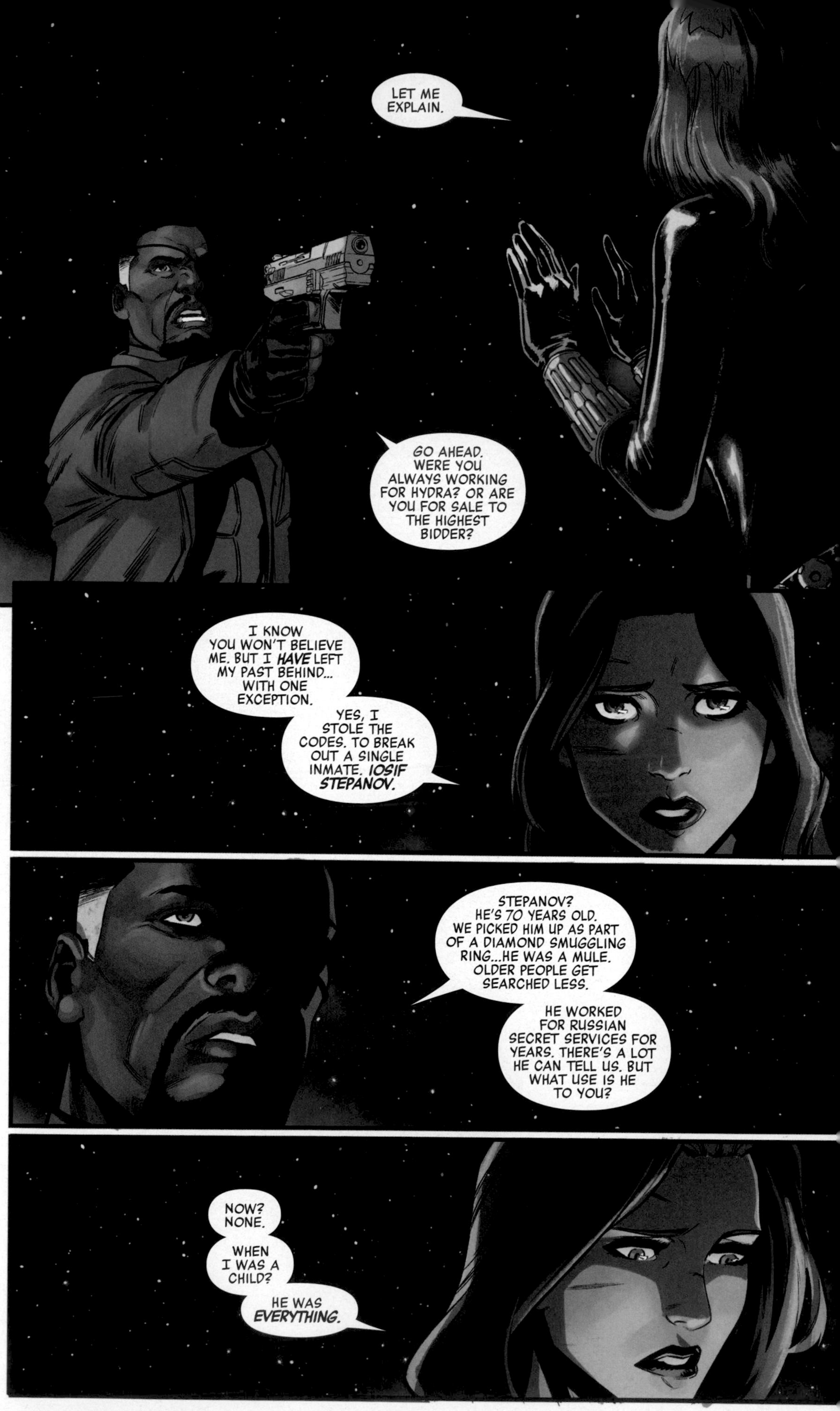

LET ME EXPLAIN.
GO AHEAD. WERE YOU ALWAYS WORKING FOR HYDRA? OR ARE YOU FOR SALE TO THE HIGHEST BIDDER?
I KNOW YOU WON'T BELIEVE ME. BUT I *HAVE* LEFT MY PAST BEHIND... WITH ONE EXCEPTION.
YES, I STOLE THE CODES. TO BREAK OUT A SINGLE INMATE. *IOSIF STEPANOV.*
STEPANOV? HE'S 70 YEARS OLD. WE PICKED HIM UP AS PART OF A DIAMOND SMUGGLING RING...HE WAS A MULE. OLDER PEOPLE GET SEARCHED LESS.
HE WORKED FOR RUSSIAN SECRET SERVICES FOR YEARS. THERE'S A LOT HE CAN TELL US. BUT WHAT USE IS HE TO YOU?
NOW? NONE.
WHEN I WAS A CHILD?
HE WAS *EVERYTHING.*

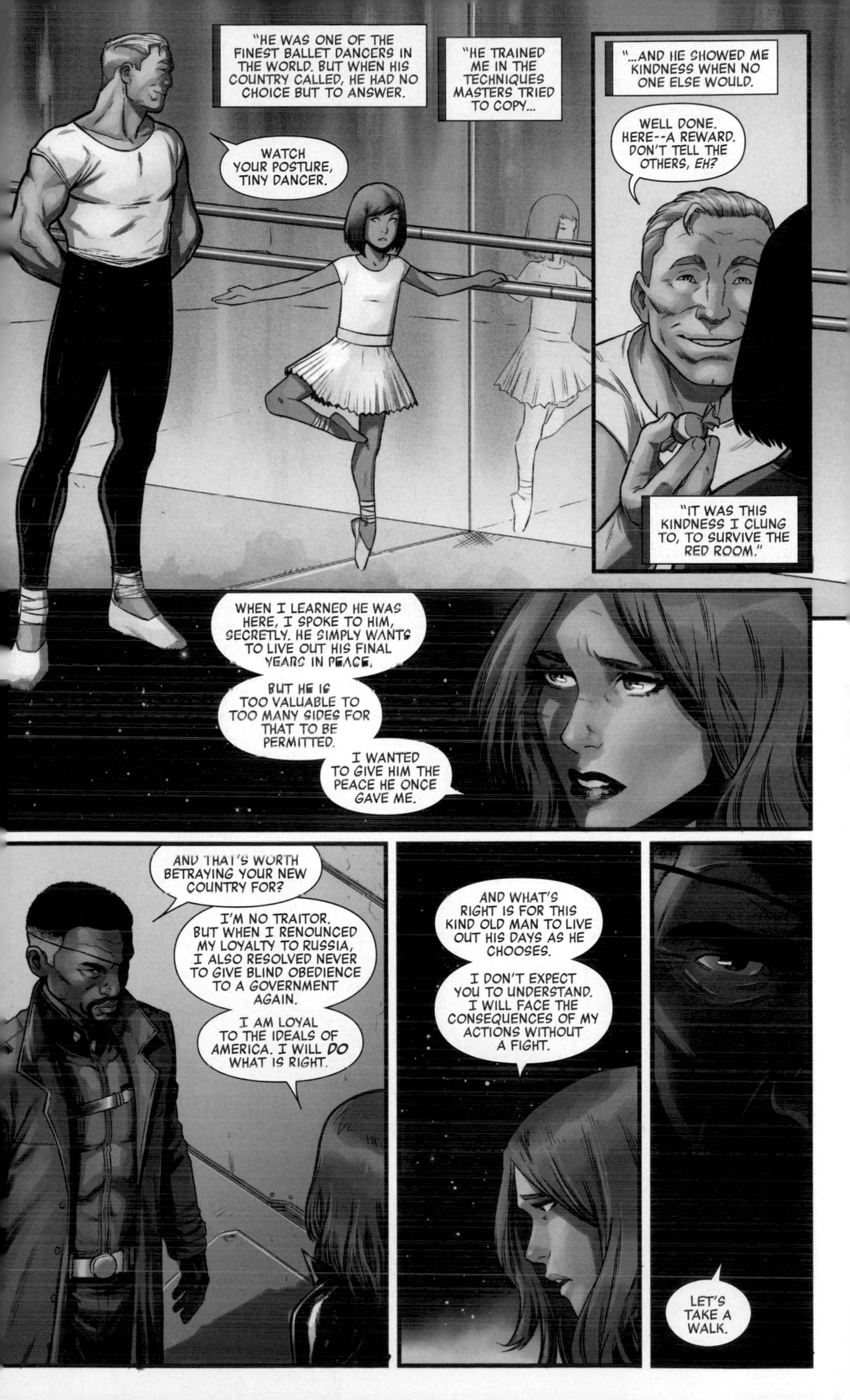
"HE WAS ONE OF THE FINEST BALLET DANCERS IN THE WORLD. BUT WHEN HIS COUNTRY CALLED, HE HAD NO CHOICE BUT TO ANSWER.
"HE TRAINED ME IN THE TECHNIQUES MASTERS TRIED TO COPY...
WATCH YOUR POSTURE, TINY DANCER.
"...AND HE SHOWED ME KINDNESS WHEN NO ONE ELSE WOULD.
WELL DONE. HERE--A REWARD. DON'T TELL THE OTHERS, EH?
"IT WAS THIS KINDNESS I CLUNG TO, TO SURVIVE THE RED ROOM."
WHEN I LEARNED HE WAS HERE, I SPOKE TO HIM, SECRETLY. HE SIMPLY WANTS TO LIVE OUT HIS FINAL YEARS IN PEACE.
BUT HE IS TOO VALUABLE TO TOO MANY SIDES FOR THAT TO BE PERMITTED.
I WANTED TO GIVE HIM THE PEACE HE ONCE GAVE ME.
AND THAT'S WORTH BETRAYING YOUR NEW COUNTRY FOR?
I'M NO TRAITOR. BUT WHEN I RENOUNCED MY LOYALTY TO RUSSIA, I ALSO RESOLVED NEVER TO GIVE BLIND OBEDIENCE TO A GOVERNMENT AGAIN.
I AM LOYAL TO THE IDEALS OF AMERICA. I WILL DO WHAT IS RIGHT.
AND WHAT'S RIGHT IS FOR THIS KIND OLD MAN TO LIVE OUT HIS DAYS AS HE CHOOSES.
I DON'T EXPECT YOU TO UNDERSTAND. I WILL FACE THE CONSEQUENCES OF MY ACTIONS WITHOUT A FIGHT.
LET'S TAKE A WALK.

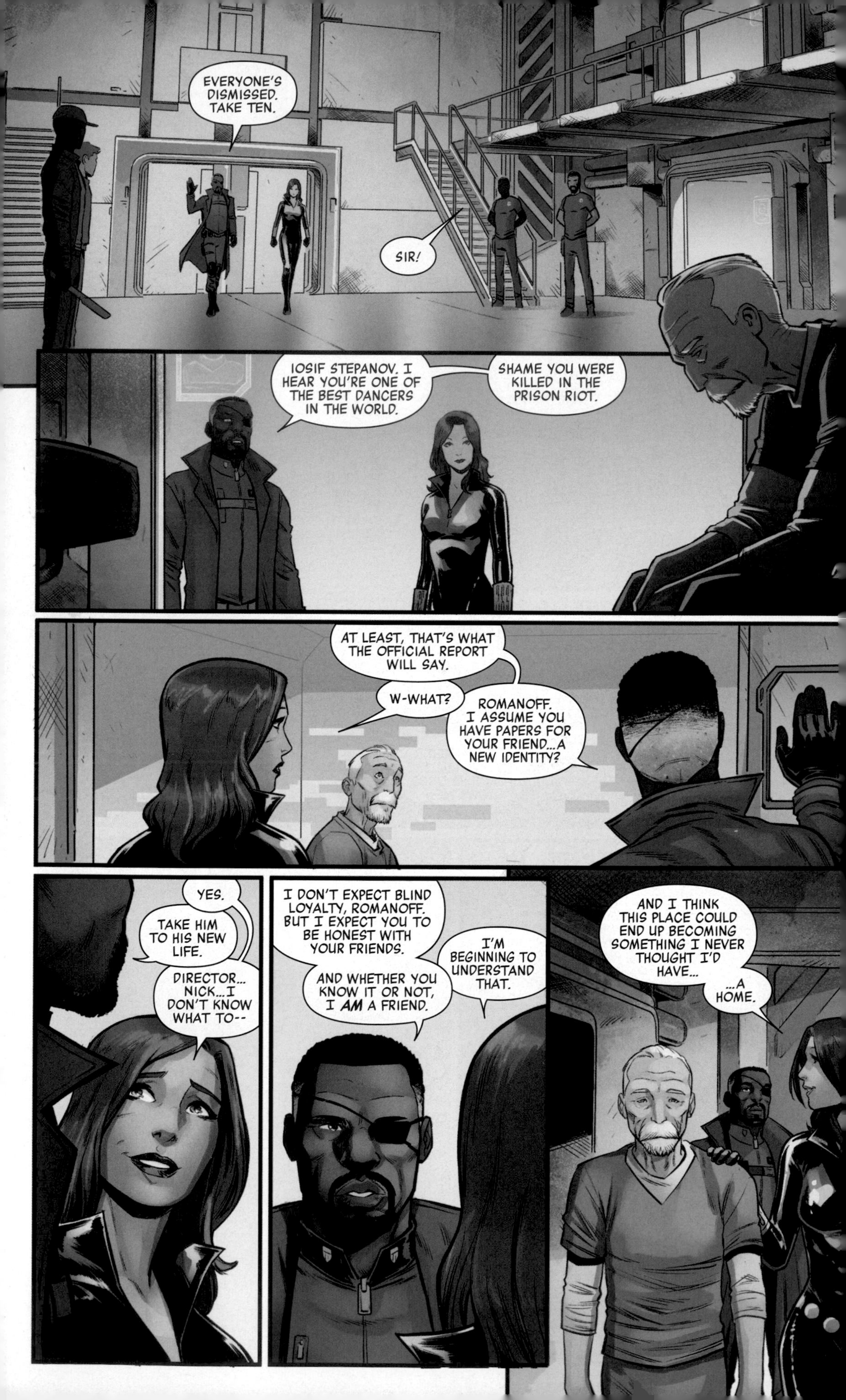

EVERYONE'S DISMISSED. TAKE TEN.
SIR!
IOSIF STEPANOV. I HEAR YOU'RE ONE OF THE BEST DANCERS IN THE WORLD.
SHAME YOU WERE KILLED IN THE PRISON RIOT.
AT LEAST, THAT'S WHAT THE OFFICIAL REPORT WILL SAY.
W-WHAT?
ROMANOFF. I ASSUME YOU HAVE PAPERS FOR YOUR FRIEND...A NEW IDENTITY?
YES.
TAKE HIM TO HIS NEW LIFE.
DIRECTOR... NICK...I DON'T KNOW WHAT TO--
I DON'T EXPECT BLIND LOYALTY, ROMANOFF. BUT I EXPECT YOU TO BE HONEST WITH YOUR FRIENDS.
AND WHETHER YOU KNOW IT OR NOT, I AM A FRIEND.
I'M BEGINNING TO UNDERSTAND THAT.
AND I THINK THIS PLACE COULD END UP BECOMING SOMETHING I NEVER THOUGHT I'D HAVE...
...A HOME.

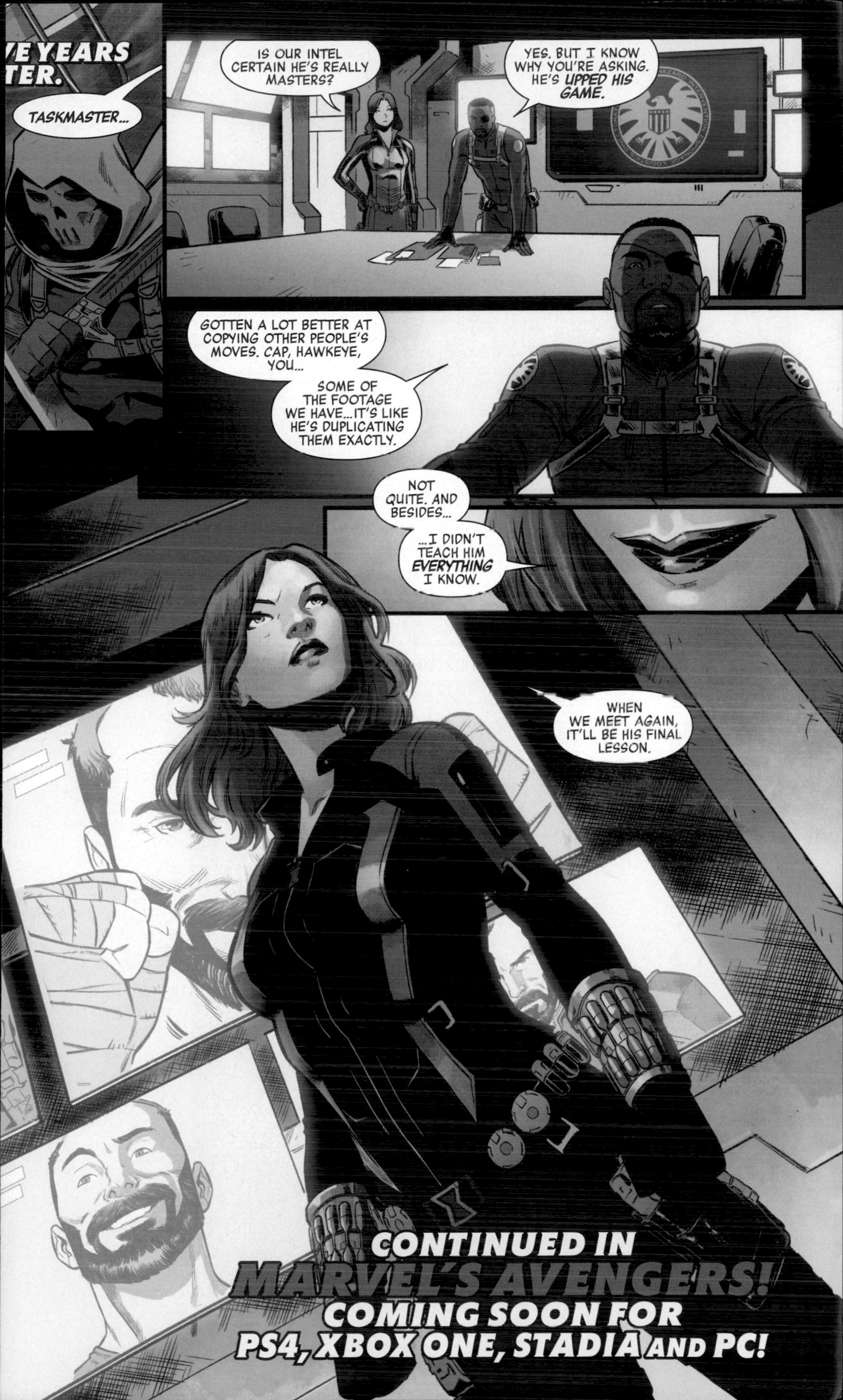
VE YEARS
TER.
TASKMASTER...
IS OUR INTEL CERTAIN HE'S REALLY MASTERS?
YES. BUT I KNOW WHY YOU'RE ASKING. HE'S UPPED HIS GAME.
GOTTEN A LOT BETTER AT COPYING OTHER PEOPLE'S MOVES. CAP, HAWKEYE, YOU...
SOME OF THE FOOTAGE WE HAVE...IT'S LIKE HE'S DUPLICATING THEM EXACTLY.
NOT QUITE. AND BESIDES...
...I DIDN'T TEACH HIM EVERYTHING I KNOW.
WHEN WE MEET AGAIN, IT'LL BE HIS FINAL LESSON.
CONTINUED IN
MARVEL'S AVENGERS!
COMING SOON FOR
PS4, XBOX ONE, STADIA AND PC!

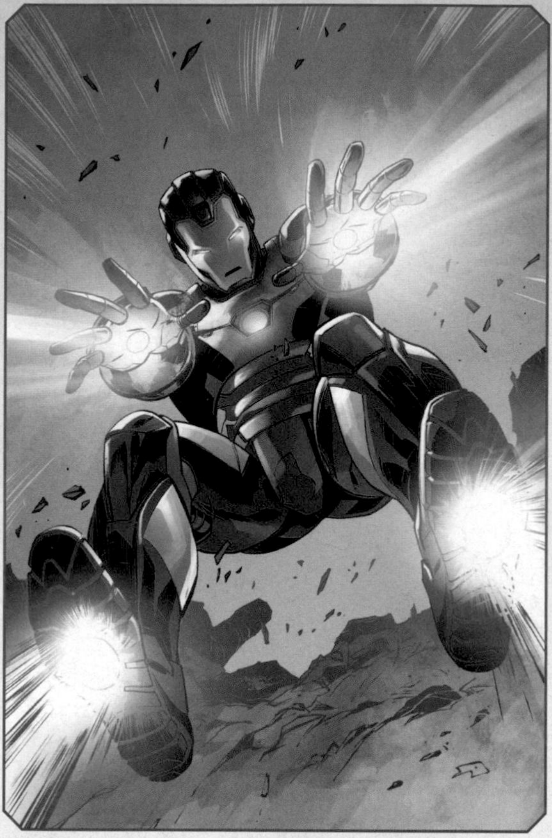

IRON MAN VARIANT BY **RYAN BENJAMIN** & **RAIN BEREDO**

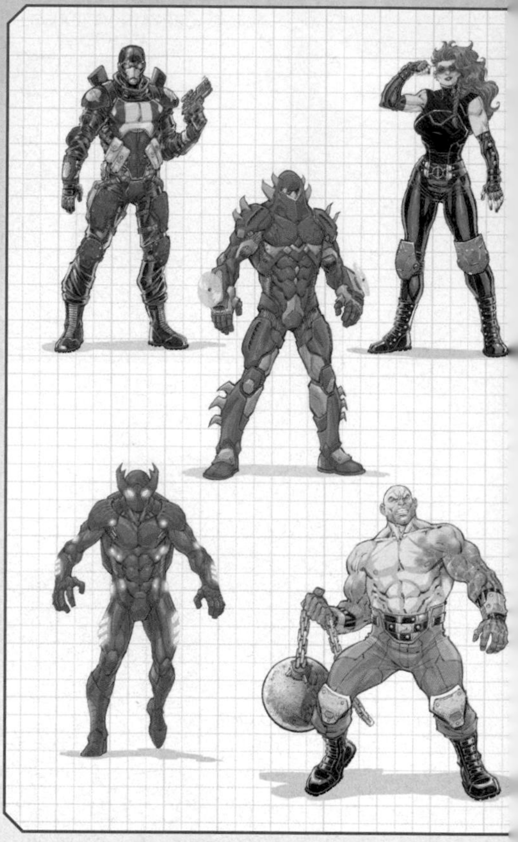

IRON MAN VILLAINS DESIGN VARIANT BY **TODD NAUCK**

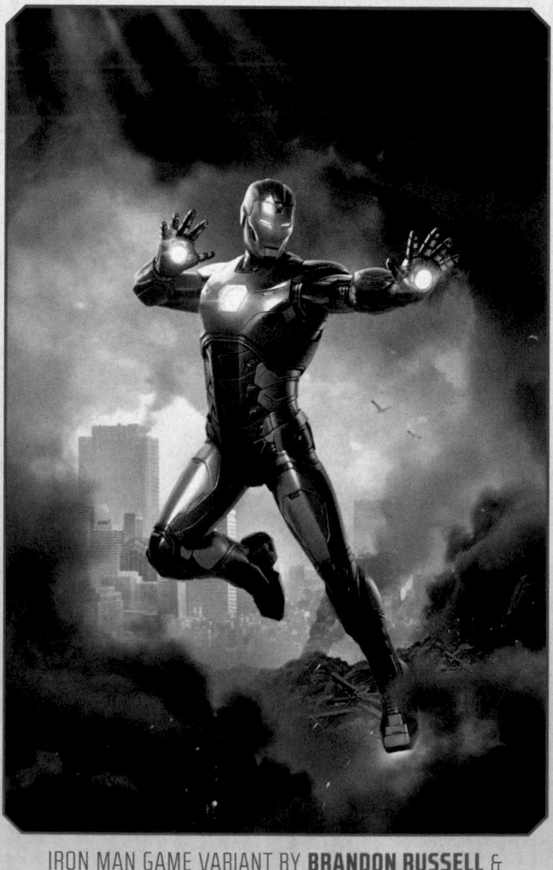

IRON MAN GAME VARIANT BY **BRANDON RUSSELL** & **CRYSTAL DYNAMICS**

THOR VARIANT BY **WOO-CHUL LEE**

HULK VARIANT BY **PYEONG-JUN PARK**

CAPTAIN AMERICA VARIANT BY
DALE KEOWN & **JESUS ABURTOV**

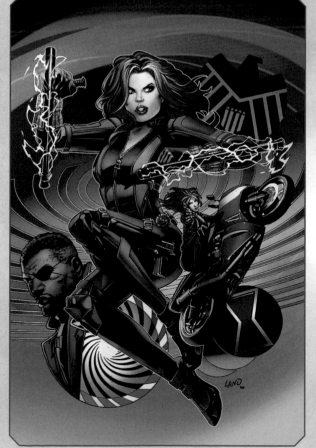

BLACK WIDOW VARIANT BY
GREG LAND & **FRANK D'ARMATA**